M000275606

DEAD, INSANE, OR IN JAIL: OVERWRITTEN

BOOK TWO IN THE SERIES

BY

ZACK BONNIE

Copyright © Zack Bonnie / Not With The Program 2018.
All rights reserved.
Not With The Program, Dyke, VA 22935
Printed in USA
ISBN 978-0-9963378-3-0
LCCN to come
All rights reserved. No part of this document may be reproduced or transmitted in any form or by any means, electronic, mechanical, photocopying, recording, or otherwise, without prior written permission of the publisher.

Book development, coaching, editing, and preproduction by
Anne M Carley of Chenille Books, who thanks Jane Friedman,
J.W. Stryder, Mary Sproles Martin, and Abigail Wiebe.
Thanks go, as well, to Ilyse Kazar, Noelle Beverley,
Jeanne Schlesinger, Rebecca Danis,
Richard J. Bonnie, Kathleen Ford, Barbara Danis,
and the other generous beta readers,
for their wonderfully constructive comments.

Art by Jonathan Weiner, who says:
Endless devotion and gratitude to my wife, for your support and love.
Thank you to Hyeyoon Song of Mission Grafica for your
instruction and guidance.
Thank you to the Mission Cultural Center for the Latino Arts for
providing the studio space, hours, and resources.
Thank you to SCRAP of San Francisco, for your beautiful, random,
circulating supply of raw materials and inspiration.
Thank you to Niku and Kiyomi, for your comforting weird.

*To advocates, and the program kids
whose numbers they wish to limit.*

*Dedicated also to my mother and father who created me,
and Anne M Carley and Jonathan Weiner
for helping me create this book.
It is another small miracle that Rebecca Danis,
almost without complaint, has for years allowed
the impossible schedule of this writing project.
Forever being, more delicate than in words, I love you.*

CONTENTS

COMING ATTRACTIONS

ILLUSTRATIONS

Artist Jonathan Weiner created eight drypoint prints to illustrate the book. He editioned the prints on BFK Rives paper. The prints were then scanned into the digital images used herein. For more information visit deadinsaneorinjail.com.

A DIJ PRIMER

Chronology of Key Events

Dead, Insane, or in Jail: A CEDU Memoir (Book 1)

- 11 July 1988 – Zack, age 14, is delivered to RMA for orientation. He joins Papoose family.
- July–August 1988 – Truth propheet (Staff = Tess Turnwell, Keith Rios, Prescott Freshwater; Student Support = Jasper Browning)
- September 1988 – Zack splits the RMA campus, calls parents from Spokane airport, is taken to foster care in Bonners Ferry, Idaho, then sent to a month of Survival in southern Idaho desert.
- October 1988 – Sheriff Darren Snipes and escort Albert Guerre return Zack to RMA.

Dead, Insane, or in Jail: Overwritten (Book 2)

- October 1988 – Zack's second RMA orientation
- November 1988 – Brothers Keeper propheet (Staff = George Daughtry, Tess Turnwell, Andrew Oswald; Student Support = Terrance Whittlemore)
- Zack joins Brave family.
- December 1988 – Parent visit to RMA campus
- Spring 1989 – Quest Expedition
- Spring 1989 – I Want To Live propheet (Staff = Nat Farmer, Darlayne Hammer, Kelly Grainger; Student Supports = Mariah Verdera, Tim Chalmers)
- Zack joins Warrior family.
- Summer 1989 – Zack's first home visit to Charlottesville, Virginia
- Late December 1989–January 1990 – Zack's second home visit
- Early spring, 1990 – Zack's full-time

Future Continuation of Dead, Insane, or in Jail

- Workshops
- December 1990 – Graduation

Glossary

Agreements – RMA's rules were disingenuously termed Agreements. The three major Agreements prohibited sex, drugs, and physical violence. Others required tucked-in shirts, showers lasting no more than five minutes, no unacceptable music, etc.

Bans – A student "on bans" from a person or group was forbidden to speak to, look at, or otherwise interact with them until the bans were lifted by a staff member.

Big Ben – A large tree around which RMA built the deck of the house.

Bonners Ferry, Idaho – Small town on the Kootenai River, near the border with the Canadian province of British Columbia. Closest town to RMA campus.

Bridge – Enclosed room in the house, next to the living room, with views of the kitchen and dining room. Students were prohibited from entering at most times. The phones for calls home to parents were here, as was a locked cabinet with prescription drugs for certain students. Music was controlled from here and some staff meetings took place in the Bridge.

CEDU – The CEDU schools are generally credited with establishing a new kind of boarding school for troubled teens. Drawing on Synanon's "encounter group" techniques and using interrogation practices to induce change in their teenaged charges, the two-and-a-half-year program included some academic subjects, and many labor assignments at the school's farm, woodlot, and buildings and grounds. The schools featured extended "raps" – highly confrontational encounter groups derived from Synanon's "the Game" – and "propheets" – overnight sessions of extreme stress, reputedly based on Khalil Gibran's *The Prophet*. CEDU's name, pronounced *see-doo*, suggests the educational method that ostensibly guided the for-profit schools. Although the schools explained the acronym as "See yourself as you are and do something about it," history indicates the initials first stood for Charles E. Dederich University, in honor of the founder of Synanon, who strongly influenced CEDU's founder, Mel Wasserman, a California businessman. The CEDU organization was founded in 1967 as CEDU Educational Services, Inc., and was acquired in 1998 by Brown Schools, Inc., under the name CEDU Education – Brown Schools, Inc. CEDU and Brown Schools closed and declared bankruptcy in 2005, thereby managing to sidestep financial settlements in lawsuits claiming student mistreatment, employee sexual abuse, and deceptive practices. Universal Health Services subsequently reopened some of these schools, as "behavioral health centers."

Challenge Expedition – Major outdoor expedition for upper-school RMA students. Also known as Wilderness Challenge.

Coeur d'Alene, Idaho – Resort and town where parents of RMA students attended workshops before visiting RMA campus.

DMTs – Confessional "deep meaningful talks" between students in evenings at the house.

Dooger – Name for everyone's inner child; interchangeable with "Me."

Educational consultants – A tiered network of individuals and small businesses formed the funnel that delivered students from troubled families into the CEDU system. The educational consultant field has grown and prospered, feeding students into the many programs that have proliferated.

Experientials – Physical fitness activities to train students for future wilderness expeditions; also included ropes courses, trust falls, and nature studies.

Families – Several peer groups of students belonged to a series of families, each with assigned staff members. To graduate, students needed to progress through all the families. [The RMA family sequence is abbreviated, and partially renamed, in the DIJ series.]

- Papoose
- Brave
- Warrior
- Summit

First light – Daily family meeting before work or classes.

a Full-time – Severe punishment for an unspecified number of days during which a student was limited to isolation at a booth in the dining room, except when performing Work Details, or attending raps.

Students on a full-time were given lengthy writing assignments to complete while at the booth, and were on bans from most students.

the House – The central building at RMA where last lights, Morning Meetings, and DMTs took place. The dining room, Bridge, and living room with hearth were all in the house.

Indict – A student or staff member indicted another student, from across the rap circle, often using confrontational, embarrassing, and often verbally abusive attack methods. Indictments could also express love, care, and concern.

Mr. Jade – Survival employee/consultant who corresponded with author's mother, and bonded with Zack during his time with SUWS.

Last light – Nightly school-wide meeting in the house.

LGAT – Abbreviation for Large Group Awareness Training, a phenomenon born out of the mid-twentieth-century encounter group model and favoring marathon group sessions purporting to give participants access to a nonreligious kind of personal rebirth.

Morning Meeting – Weekly school-wide Monday general meetings.

Needsy – The term for someone's motivations in raps or other encounters when they appeared to be helpful, but were really benefiting themselves, and/or trying to look good for staff.

Owyhee Desert – Barren area of southern Idaho where Survival program hiked and camped out.

PGs – Abbreviation for peer groups, usually ten to fifteen kids who arrived around the same time at RMA and continued through the family system together. RMA families were composed of several peer groups.

Propheets – Intense periodic overnight "emotional growth experiences." [The RMA propheet sequence is abbreviated in the DIJ series.]

- Truth
- Brothers Keeper (or Brothers)
- I Want To Live

The Prophet – Khalil Gibran's poetry collection, used as a sourcebook at RMA.

Purpose Brigade – RMA-approved group of upper-school students who were permitted to travel into Bonners Ferry on weekends.

Purpose Committees – Occasional project groups where students created handmade greeting cards, scrapbook pages, and assorted RMA memorabilia to support program milestones for other students.

Quest Expedition – Three-night group wilderness expedition for Brave family, involving canoeing, camping, rock climbing and rappelling, and a rap.

RMA (Rocky Mountain Academy) – The second school in the CEDU group of Troubled Teen facilities, it opened in 1982.

RMA Campus [Some RMA places are renamed in the DIJ series.]

- Denali
- the farm
- Garden house (dorm)
- the house
- Kootenai Lodge
- La Mancha (dorm)
- La Mancha Forest
- Quest trail (network of paths around RMA campus)
- Share Shack (dorm)
- Skinner (education building)
- Stellar Annex
- Walden (remote building for propheets)
- the wood corral

Rap – Key element of RMA's emotional curriculum, raps were confrontational group sessions held three afternoons each week, for three to four hours. Facilitated by staff. Based on Synanon's "the Game," raps included indictments, histrionic moments, and deep-seated introspection. When they became particularly intense they were called "hairball" raps.

Rock Bottom – The innocent little kid inside each RMA student. Interchangeable with "Me."

Santa's Workshop – Two-week period before Christmas when students created handmade gifts.

Smooshing – Chaste, clothed, physical affection, greatly encouraged among same-sex students.

Snot rippers – Zack's term for the special recorded songs played repeatedly during propheets and other emotionally charged events to elicit deep feelings.

Solo (at SUWS) – Four-day period at the end of Survival when kids are left to fend for themselves.

Splitting – Running away from RMA.

Spokane, Washington – Nearest major airport to Bonners Ferry, Idaho

Summit Workshop – Final multiple-day event consummating the RMA experience. Followed by graduation, and a six-month prohibition from revisiting the RMA campus.

SUWS – School of Urban and Wilderness Survival ("Survival" for short) was founded in southern Idaho in 1981 as a therapeutic wilderness program for youth aged fourteen to eighteen. A North Carolina program began in 2000. The SUWS programs became part of Aspen Education Group's portfolio of private teen facilities. Now owned by Bain Capital, Aspen has divested many of their schools and programs, including SUWS Idaho, citing reduced demand. After splitting RMA, and brief stays in two foster homes, Zack spent September of 1988 with two Survival groups, the first led by [Will Bender], the second by [Torque].

Synanon – Founded in Santa Monica, California in 1958 by Charles E. Dederich, Jr., as a behavior modification facility for addicts. Mel Wasserman was an early member. After he left Synanon, he founded CEDU. Initially, Synanon was a two-year treatment program, but over time its leaders changed the organization's mission, declaring that members could never leave the program, as addiction could never be completely cured or reversed. Forced to close in the United States in 1989 after problems with the IRS, the Synanon organization still exists in Germany.

Taking care of your feelings – Regular expressions of loud anger and deep pain and sadness which were expected in raps and other group settings.

Thinking – Discouraged, in favor of feeling, which comes from a truer self – the "Me."

Truth counseling sessions – Upper-school tool for scheduled introspective exercises including the two-chairs and two-partner outpourings of emotions known as "dyads."

WDs (abbreviation for Work Details) – Punishments in the form of manual labor, during which students were on bans from all other students.

Wilderness Challenge (WC) – Multiple-day outdoor excursion testing survival skills. Also known as Challenge Expedition.

Workshops – Multiple-day emotional growth experiences that occurred later in the **Dead, Insane, or in Jail** series and the CEDU program, and were even more intense than propheets.

- I and Me
- Summit

Writing Assignments – Staff assigned these to students for many reasons, requiring lists of their negative thinking, their "dirt" (bad acts, behavior out of agreement), etc.

As described in the Author's Statement, the **Dead, Insane, or in Jail** series makes simplifying adjustments to the actual number of propheets, renumbers and renames the RMA families, and rearranges buildings and other campus landmarks.

For more about CEDU and RMA terminology, visit https://wiki. fornits.com/index.php?title=CEDU_lingo

FOREWORD

In **Overwritten**, the second volume of his well-written memoir, Zack Bonnie explains some of the standard methods of mind control used to break down people's identities, to force them to dissociate, and to overwhelm them. Institutions like the one Zack endured, Rocky Mountain Academy, seem to behave the opposite of what a therapeutic environment should be. Such totalistic institutions use techniques of undue influence to build up a "cult-bot" identity that suppresses the real person's self. These schools also victimize the parents, who, to prove their dedication and love for their kids, then fund their institutional abuse. At the same time, the parents are made to feel guilty if they are not willing to spend the money, and selfish if they want to talk to or visit their kid.

By contrast, in a healing environment, a person is encouraged to feel safe, is encouraged to be in their body, and should be given tools to feel mastery over trauma from the past. In such a developmentally wholesome place, people are supported and encouraged to grow. They build up more insight, emotional intelligence, and social skills, in a climate of open information.

Meanwhile, the successful commercial "troubled teen" industry continues to be staffed by many people who appear not to be trained therapists and therefore do not have appropriate grounding in issues of ethical influence. Furthermore, there is no proper supervision from senior therapists. These institutions engage in methods that have been shown to be ineffective and potentially destructive. For example, the pillow–pounding exercise in Zack's book applies an out-of-date model for the human mind – that the mind is like a battery, and all you have to do to heal it is to discharge the battery. That's not a method to help someone become an integrated, functioning adult. In fact, research has shown that such exercises make you even angrier. By focusing more energy on anger – versus feeling calm, and feeling forgiveness – you create or exacerbate a problem.

However, healing from mind control can happen.

We need to have a healthy mind–body relationship. My life work with Freedom of Mind is based on the notion that one needs to be in one's body and in the here and now (not in the past or future). One needs to have the locus of one's life within oneself, not placed with some external authority figure. One needs to have control over one's thoughts, feelings, and behaviors in the context of a positive future orientation as opposed to dwelling in past trauma.

This is one reason why books like Zack's, and research like mine, can benefit so many people in need. When you read about what someone else has gone through in a different group, it can be easier to begin to process your own experience.

The people who have healed the most are the ones who haven't tried to put the experience in a closet, or tried to forget it, or say that they're fine. Healing happens for people who are willing to courageously and honestly look at what happened, and undertake reparative strategies and therapies with skilled and trained practitioners. I believe that having had these experiences ultimately makes us stronger as human beings.

Ex-members like Zack Bonnie and myself can function, on some level, like the immune system of the social body. We are in effect the white blood cells sensitized to the virus of mind control. So we have a strong reaction when we smell mind control tricks, tactics, and predatory narcissism from a person who claims to know everything, or lies, and then smiles and says, "I never said that."

For over forty years, I have dedicated my life to informing the public and supporting those who have been subjected to mind control programs. I am very appreciative of courageous people like Zack who are willing to share their stories. The importance of forming support systems for others who have also been in a cult or other high-control situation cannot be overstated. There's a role for former members like us to identify the imperative nature of freedom in light of dictators who want to deprive us of it. I applaud Zack Bonnie's bold, honest description of his journey through abuse. I commend him for wanting to understand it, dissect it, and digest it – and integrate it in a way that will help others.

Steven Hassan, Author, *Combating Cult Mind Control* and *Freedom of Mind: Helping Loved Ones Leave Controlling People, Cults and Beliefs*; Director, Freedom of Mind Resource Center, and Lead Investigator at Freedom from Undue Influence, a division of Dare Association, Inc. http://freedomfromundueinfluence.org

PREFACE

CEDU Educational Services – and its Rocky Mountain Academy – were in the business of psychological manipulation of kids, employees, and the parents to whom the programs catered. CEDU was in the business of customer satisfaction, and the parents were the customers. However, the program's extreme expectations of personal change were for us kids; the parents did not experience this directly, except through us, their children.

The stated and unstated demands upon me and other kids took place in an environment that was/is communal and isolated, dependent on the authority of its own doctrine, and totalistic in the expectation of conformity. We lived under a near-constant threat of assault to our autonomous identities.

Program life also provided the modicums of acceptance, approval, reinforcement of its own goodness, importance, and "love" that kept us present and growing. We affirmed by agreement, we said we were free. We acknowledged that we were saved from visceral harms by the program's existence.

Unlike the first book in this series, this sequel should give readers a snapshot into my life before Idaho, and what decisions led to my placement at RMA. To accurately continue to tell the story of treatment at CEDU, what we were supposed to do there, I had to look inward. To carry out the main reason for the series – chronicling "emotional growth" at RMA/CEDU – and do it justice, I had to provide my life as a template. Because of this necessity, and although the embedded emotional dealings with peers and friends are a very big part of any collective story, I don't know if every person ever sent to any program will be able to identify and find relevance here. I cannot tell anybody else's story.

For me to conform and mentally survive those years, I needed to prove to the program my changing beliefs. I needed to demonstrate so much undefined – but nevertheless expected – change, which was all enveloped in an atmosphere of mystery. The program-provided tools were not available to a child, and remained un-revealed until each milestone experience that the program also provided. Successive milestones were attained, then publicly celebrated and rewarded. The celebration and reward – you guessed it – were also artificially created. Longevity in the program was another unstated "tool" which had a strong influence on us kids.

Necessity demanded that I imitate staff, my peers, and all the older kids, in order to learn how to behave. (This leads to entire other realms of the research of human evolutionary psychology: why do we feel emotions, why and when do humans imitate one another? How did tribes deal with unruly teens before private residential facilities were invented?) I needed to relive the hows and whys of the unusual deep bonds that were forged, and why this occurred between kids there. This part of the story is difficult to tell.

Why and how a surrogate-parent situation develops between kids and the staff is also a deeply personalized experience for each individual experiencing this heightened temporary group love – artificial or not. Everyone acted a part within the already artificial environment. Hierarchy was itself a mid-range instrument at RMA by which the assimilation of program doctrine could be measured. At CEDU/RMA, this lent an even deeper significance and personal impact to the human attachment mechanism, the longevity of emotional manipulation, the constriction of information, and milieu control. These were just a few of the techniques that served to ensure the customer service that program parents were entitled to receive.

I hope my work highlights the variation of tactics that programs may use on "kids like me," in the modern era, and into the future. We will have to contend with institutionalized persuasion at many levels, wherever it is used to promote compliance through mental, psychological, and physical coercion.

The experience of CEDU is the group. But also the experience of psychological manipulation is invariably specific to each person. One chief thing to remember as you read is how individualized the CEDU program – or any other program where emotional growth is sold – will always be. You must know that institutionalized persuasion is practiced, on (or for) each child.

The community of students and scholars is growing. We are working toward better conditions for troubled families and their teens.

Zack Bonnie
Charlottesville, Virginia
2018

ACKNOWLEDGMENTS

A lot of people have been helpful. I want to recognize my early backers for contributing to the production of this volume, because you trusted me to follow through – and I resent you all for commanding a deadline! Thank you so much for your patience and support. It really means a lot.

Finally, thank you to my brother and sister; Greg O'Dell; Sandy and Daedalus Bookstore, Charlottesville; my county neighbors; K. Luthy, Diana P., Phil E., Sarah F., Matt P., Paul Y., Mostafiz, V.K., Dave, Sajid, Robin, Schweezle, Pickleman, Claudia, any other friends and family who still tolerate me, and you, who may read these books.

Zack Bonnie

PROLOGUE — ONE YEAR

What can happen in one year? A lot:

August 1987. My summer of international travel with my friend Chuck Driems and his mom. Freedom before failure. First love. The chasm and penetration and reflection of physical death. Training and airplaning alone! Art; my own, the drive to create it. Language, maturation in my recognition of class and privilege, reading, getting drunk, sneaking out, the gypsies whom I dreamt of joining in their caravans. Staying up, sleeping in, and doing it all at the same time.

September 1987. It made my parents' heads spin when I was thrown out of eighth grade at the prestigious Pennsylvania prep school so soon after I arrived. I went to local public schools for a few months. That did not end well, despite everyone telling me how easy it should be. Alternatively, it wasn't the schoolwork that bounced me outta there. I wasn't supposed to be at home that year, so I ran away a lot, and tried to be invisible.

January 1988. Around my fourteenth birthday, I was banned from the Charlottesville public school classrooms. I never completed middle school in Virginia.

Spring 1988. What would have been eighth grade for most kids was battle at home. I couldn't ever do anything right anymore. And life felt different than it ever had before. The only thing I wanted to do was listen to music alone in my room. I'd burn candles that were wedged in bottles, heating utensils like corkscrews and forks to sculpt the cooling wax in bulbous shapes around the base. The stolen wine bottles were mine, of course. And I smoked in the house a couple of times which sent my dad into hysterics. I mean he often went into hysterics, but now he'd grab me and shake the shit out of me or pump his fist or a shaking finger in my face a lot. Normally, when his skin turned the color of a plum, it was because of things I said. And we all agree that sometimes I'd say that stuff just to see him get purple. Then he'd say the things that the murderous part of me longed to hear. An expert at Johns Hopkins told my parents to keep me out of structured environments – like school – until my psychiatric problems had improved; to me, this was victory. I did not belong in school. What I didn't know

xiv

was that this meant a tradeoff; if I wasn't in school, I could not belong at home.

June 1988. I'd outgrown summer camp and wanted to see my girlfriend. I'd been addicted to girls for a long time. Impressing them with cuteness had evolved, the more I registered the difference between girls who wanted to hold hands and the girls who would go further. I resigned as a junior counselor at Camp Minnehaha and made my way home from West Virginia.

July 1988. I got home unassisted from Camp Minnehaha, after a couple of wild nights hitchhiking through sooty little coal towns. Mom and Dad and the camp people smeared the egg from their faces, and next thing I knew, in early July, Dad dumped me at RMA – Rocky Mountain Academy – in a wild place named Idaho.

July – August 1988. I lasted a little over a month on RMA's wooden campus. Forty-two days, to be exact, and I think for half of them I was in shock. I split RMA ("splitting" was the RMA term for running away) on my baby sister's third birthday in August, eventually making my way to a little airport in Spokane, Washington. From the airport payphone, I called my parents, to make arrangements to fly me home. But they sent Sheriff Snipes to catch up with me instead. He took me to stay in two foster homes. A week later, we flew down to Boise. Instead of handing me over to Mom and Dad as promised, Sheriff Snipes handed me over to Survival.

September 1988. In the month-long Survival program (School of Urban and Wilderness Survival or "SUWS"), counselors Will Bender and Leslie Starr led my small group of kids bumbling for more than a hundred miles around the vastness of a tan and boring desert in southern Idaho. Since my first counselor was a shithead, I was held back, and by the end had logged well over two hundred miles. Under the counselors' "tough love," we kids learned how to start primitive fires, ration our food and water, and cook our lentils, happy to snack on snakes and flour-cakes. At the end of Survival, the sheriff and Albert Guerre, an armed escort who reminded me of a totem-pole, brought my ass right back to RMA.

That was my year. You?

It would take a while to assimilate back to being inside, to having toilet paper and water faucets at my command.

A situation like this – stuck back at RMA for years – would have been unbelievable to me before Survival. Now lacking control to do anything I wanted to do, I'd accepted the one new chief principle that all the adults in my life did seem to agree on:

This Idaho place is for me, like it or not.

Therefore, this place's people are for me too.

Bottom line: I ran away from RMA to be able to see Mom and Dad. I needed a chance to convince them that I would change without completing my sentence in Idaho. But it was all an enormous backfire. I didn't get to see my parents, got tricked into foster care and then Survival, and now I came back – to this. A thirty-month sentence of it, to boot.

Back at RMA – the home of unacceptable thoughts, and daily labor, and structure. Now life will be my peer group, raps, the next propheet, and playing by all of RMA's weird unwritten rules.

Agreements, I mean.

†

Dear Doctor Denckla:

I thought it might be helpful to write to you before our visit to Baltimore in order to give a brief history of Zachary's problems and to convey our growing sense of desperation as to what we should do to improve our son's chances for a successful and happy life.

Zachary is fourteen and the second of our three children. His older brother ... graduated from high school after eleventh grade. He was a finalist in the National Merit Scholars Program and is now [attending a university]. [We have a] three-year-old daughter.

As a young boy [our older son] was considered "hyper-active" but we did not put him on medication and by age 12 he had been classified as "gifted" ...

When Zachary showed signs of "hyper-activity" we were prepared to follow the same non-intervention course, though we did move him after kindergarten from the local public school to a small private school, believing that he'd benefit from smaller classes and a "quieter" school environment. In fourth grade Zack returned to public school and that year we were told he was having trouble "behaving" in the classroom. We sought psychiatric help for Zack and were told he had A.D.D. In fifth grade, in the Spring, we put him on Ritalin for a trial period (the teacher was not informed) and the results were remarkable. He was made "Student of the Week" the week after taking Ritalin. In the summer he went off medication, and in the fall, we moved him back to the private school in hopes of avoiding the wild public intermediate school. Zack's school grades were average; tests indicated a great discrepancy between verbal skills (high) and visual-spatial abilities (poor).

In sixth grade, Zack continued on medication but began a slow slide into poor school performance by receiving mostly "C's" and "D's". In seventh grade he refused to take medication (claiming it wasn't helping him and he didn't need it) and the slide continued. Behaviorally he was becoming more and more diffi-cult – angry outbursts, inability to "attend" in class. He refused to allow us to help him. By now his "oppo-sitional" and defiant behavior had produced a home environment in which all of our interactions with Zack were negative. The situation had become, in a word, intolerable, and as a result we decided to try a board-ing school environment for eighth grade.

Zack went to the Hill School in Pottstown, Pennsylvania for just ten days during this academic year. They found his behavior (smoking, going off-grounds, disrespectful speech, disruption in class) impossible to deal with so we withdrew him and he returned home, entering the public school. This year has been filled with one disaster after another. Though Zack continues to see his therapist – once a week, as he has for several years, he has continued to refuse medication. He's been suspended from school three times, is receiving failing grades, does not do assignments, is verbally abusive and has on more than one occasion slammed his fist through walls. Lately, it's been a battle just to get him to go to school. Zack's psychiatrist says that in addition to A.D.D. Zack is depressed.

—From author's mother to specialist at Johns Hopkins, May, 1988

Author's Statement

A follow-up to **Dead, Insane, or in Jail: A CEDU Memoir**, the first book in the series, this book is also a memoir, meaning it is biased by and based on fact.

As in Book One of the series, I truncated events in a few instances to consolidate the narrative. I also made a few modifications to the details of the story, so that reading will be easier to manage than the realities of living it were. The spirit of my story remains undisturbed.

The materials from my personal archive included here are presented as is, with few very present-day asides or editing corrections. I have tried to keep them consecutive to assist the narrative. These quotations are taken *directly* from my journals or letters at that time.

In addition to constructing this sequel to envelop more time – almost two years, instead of the ten weeks in A CEDU Memoir – I condensed, for brevity and out of kindness to readers, the following: Instead of the RMA program's seven propheets, my series will only have four; instead of several expeditions, we'll have one major one in the next portion of the series. Instead of the several back-and-forth travel times in my second year and final months, here only three "home visits" occur.

I already squished together different program concepts, merging some of the so-called "propheets," and bypassing or only lightly referencing other physical exercises or program themes. You might remember that propheets were marathon LGAT sessions that lasted roughly 24 hours, occurred roughly every three months, and acted as milestones in the CEDU thirty-month timeline, which I completed in December of 1990.

All RMA student and staff characters in this book are composites, to protect confidentiality and to assist the narrative.

Here's a list of things that need mentioning:

1. The character of my grandmother is at once a metaphorical allegory and an archetype, a literary device not to be read as fact or evidence.

2. The Quest Expedition. I don't know that the canoeing memory took place during a proper expedition. But on the Quest, I did sleep in

a bivouac – tied into a mountain, which I had scaled.

3. The pit (hearth area in the house) also could be fitted with a wooden stage, where graduations happened. I omitted that detail here.

4. Some of the terminology I appropriated was used while I was at Rocky Mountain Academy/CEDU. However, I have no idea yet what "triangulation" might be in psychiatric or psychological jargon, nor have I researched the meaning or history of the terms "bio-energetic exercises," or "dyads." But clearly the system believed this integration of body-memory to be sacred.

5. Again, in my propheet descriptions, I took a few creative liberties. In the Brothers, two members of every peer group were chosen for ritualistic social exclusion. The second "outsider" in my own propheet was dropped two peer groups and did not rejoin us. In later stages, the program made sure to subject every student to similar exclusionary treatment. Combining physicalization, introspection, social isolation, and coerced confession, the program artificially created shame and a sense of separateness and manufactured hysteria for each student. Later installments of this narrative will deal in more detail with these factors, and their combined role in shaping the dynamics of the program.

6. An ornate grandfather clock did not appear in my I Want to Live Propheet.

7. A note on names: My editor and I have gone to terrific lengths to use invented names for the composite characters in this series, but one or two slipped through the cracks, and I didn't realize the coincidence until after publishing the first volume. This keeps me awake at night. Additionally, I have tried to make it easy for the reader by limiting myself to a few main characters, even though, at the time, each staff member and kid I knew meant something to me. All of which has led to this addendum: Any coincidence in names of people from any point in my life is exactly that. A co-incident. Please know that any use of names resembling those of people I've met, or will meet in the future, is inadvertent.

8. As in the first book, out of respect for my fellow students and their stories, I have tried to keep the focus on myself and not the emotional struggles of the people who were around me.

9. The same is true for physical alterations which I thought might shuffle and then flavor some of the staff characters. I've scrambled up their own physical identifiers, and also taken character traits from people not at RMA with me.

10. The llama was actually a horse.

11. Instead of thick blue cushions, the I Want To Live propheet actually took upholstered pillows from the facilitators' chairs. The metal zippers would sometimes cut hands and arms during the frenzy. Nothing would scare us more than seeing physical injuries on our older sisters and brothers when they came out of later propheets and workshops.

12. [Vera] sent her provocative letter soon after I left RMA, not while I was there. My full-time at RMA was based on another false accusation, which was not revealed to me for a time. These two incidents dominated my experience processing the final months of the program, as well as my graduation and transition into the real world.

13. Many of us remember boxes of potatoes from Washington State, so it could be misleading to say we ate Idaho potatoes at RMA.

—ZB

Whoever told you to be yourself
couldn't have given you worse advice.

—Unknown

No man, for any considerable period,
can wear one face to himself and
another to the multitude, without
finally getting bewildered
as to which may be the true.

—Nathaniel Hawthorne

To find yourself, think for yourself.

—Socrates

PART ONE

ONE

1 October 1988

So, I survived Survival. That wasn't a sure thing.

Yesterday morning, I finished my "Solo," the final fattening-up period that ended Survival.

I headed right back to Northern Idaho, to RMA. No going home to Virginia.

On Solo, I received my parents' letter outlining their decision points.

Dear Zack

[Visiting Idaho, we] spent several days learning about Rocky Mountain Academy and talking to the other parents and students. We spent time with [Paul, Crosby, and Evan]; and [Prescott and Walter] gave us a long tour when we visited the school. After spending so much time with these kids – your friends – we don't have any doubt that RMA is the right place for you. The school's most valuable asset is its students. They really care about each other, and about you. They have so much to offer you, if you will only let them.

You said that you don't like RMA because it's trying to "change" you. I don't see it that way. What they are trying to do is to help you be the kind of person you really are – sweet, affectionate, upbeat, and sensitive. What has happened over the last few years is that you have been so busy fighting your parents and teachers – making your statement about independence, I suppose – that you have forgotten who you really are and have lost sight of the kind of person you really want to be.

You could be a star at RMA – like [Paul] – if you will throw yourself into it, learning about yourself and being honest with yourself, and being a sensitive and understanding friend. The restrictions that you don't like will loosen up as time goes on. (I understand, for example that you'll have plenty of opportunities to go skiing this winter if you have a positive attitude.)

Well, that's enough of a pep talk. How are the lentils?

[....]We miss you and are anxious to hear about your experience when you get back to RMA. In the meantime, please know that I love you and that I am thinking about you.

Dad

—Letter from author's father dated 8 September 1988, received 27 September, at end of Survival

I'd reread the letter over my final campfire-cooked meal. As I waited for the lentils to boil in my carbon-crusted peach can, I reviewed:

The only way I'll ever see ol' Mom and Dad again is to return to RMA; the only way I'm going home again is to make my parents love me so much they don't ever want to have me so far away.

That's unlikely. I could be in Idaho forever.

Survival called its closing ceremony at the end of month-long ordeal, "Trail's End." Over a memorable hour at the Oxbow Truck Stop and Restaurant, we ate luxurious, greasy, diner food from plastic plates, and drank soda that I felt seep into my spongy teeth. I ate cooked food with abandon, followed by a shower in a dank stall. Clean clothes! One kid in our group tossed his cookies n' yogurt and got to shower twice.

Kids I'd never see again got to meet their parents and go home with them. Not me. I got into Sheriff Darren Snipe's cruiser for the long drive up along Idaho's spine, almost to Canada. Hardly anybody had spoken with me on Solo the last four days; come to think of it, I'd hardly spoken these last four weeks on Survival.

When we left Trail's End to begin the voyage north to my ill-re-garded destination, I got my first up-close glimpse at the sheriff's traveling companion, the infamous Albert Guerre. I'd seen him before, but I doubted he remembered. According to rumor, the former Army Green Beret – with a face so scarred it could have been etched by quartz, and a permanent grimace under eyes shiny like a crow – had made a full-time career out of nabbing kids in the middle of the night and taking them to places made for kids "like me." Sheriff Snipes, pasty-faced as ever, was still wearing the tan suit I'd first met him in.

Alternating driving duties, the two men kept the sheriff's cruiser in motion all night. I didn't sleep much due to the intestinal cramping and watery leakage of my active case of Survival-acquired giardiasis. Sheriff Snipes and the bounty hunter jabbered for hours about winter sports and hunting. When they talked to me, the conversation inevita-bly began, as so many would, with the question of what had nutrition-ally sustained me during the month-long forced march in the desert. At first, I felt like a hero talking about primitive fire-making, setting traps, and eating hand-caught fry and rattlesnake. But I quickly tired of my own anecdotes. I remembered why I was in the car – my certain captivity just hours away.

From the back seat I heard that my parents had made contingency plans. In case RMA had not permitted my reintegration, it appeared that Mom and Dad had also looked at sending me to CEDU – the California flagship of Sol Turnwell's business model, and sister school to RMA – among a host of other options to keep me away from Virginia.

Cold darkness and familiar stars greeted me when Sheriff Snipes and his companion released me from the car and delivered me to the door of my Rocky Mountain Academy dorm. My final moments under those stars didn't forebode anything, although they should have.

Albert Guerre followed me inside.

La Mancha, the dorm, had been named for a villa, which I thought of like a town park, not quite knowing the story of Don Quixote, although I had several times heard references in Idaho to Cervantes's epic. My dorm head, an older kid named Jasper Browning, flipped on a light and pointed up, just like on day one, back in July. I spotted a rolled-up comforter on an empty bunk space above his. Jasper's clock

3

told the awake people in the room that it was 3:30 AM. Guerre left us, saying "See you in the morning."

I'd spent the whole drive up here imagining the worst about coming back, in intestinal agony, wondering if I'd ever again see my little sister, my brother, or parents.

Or friends. I used to have friends, too.

I climbed up the bunk. The mattress under my body felt as foreign as my first French kiss.

Nothing in nature is this soft.

I sank into sleep.

Around 6 AM, thirty minutes before our regular time to rise, Jasper made the bed under me creak. Returning from the commode, he mixed a tremendous yawn with a disgruntled moan when he saw me nestled into the comforter above his bunk.

"Shit. That's right! Well, get up in five. Take a shit. I gotta take you up to the house so George can move you in. We'll get a shower after. Do they already know you're back? Dude! Your feet fuckin' reek!"

I shrugged from his eye level, knowing all that he suggested to be true. None of the other four dorm mates seemed to care that they were awakened thirty minutes early. One familiar face even smiled and waved. They'd all be heading for the house, too, in a little while, at breakfast time.

How different from yesterday will today be? I don't have to make a fire in order to eat? Wow! And, there will be breakfast and lunch!

Jasper ushered me to the house, RMA's central building. My armed escorts from Idaho's southern desert must have napped in the car before signing over my custodial paperwork. They both waved to-go coffee cups happily from the vehicle when they saw me with Jasper.

George Daughtry said good morning to Jasper, and then smiled eagerly at me. My return "interview" was gentle compared to the first time in July. That interview had been conducted by the oversized animal named Andrew Oswald, another RMA staffer, who'd also made me remove my clothes.

My hair had grown unacceptably long in the five weeks since I had split RMA. After mowing brown hair down with a crackling set of clippers in a cramped bathroom, George led us into the adjacent office.

Prescott Freshwater, the head of Brave Family, was waiting for us with a couple of paper grocery bags full of work jeans and flannels, and the other few belongings that I abandoned when I split.

Oh, shit! I see my journal. Did they read it?

Time to be strip searched. This wasn't because Prescott or George thought I had contraband; it was just CEDU policy to do this every time a kid left campus without permission. I wondered if the older kids that visit Bonners Ferry – the nearest town – were searched after every trip to the movies, every five-dollar-budgeted trip into a grocery for Mentos and Folger's instant coffee. Or if even the Warrior kids get searched after home visits?

This guy George who's searching me has got the juice to make those decisions.

For the fourth of four times this summer – and of all time – my strip search was unnecessary. Prescott and George, heads of Brave and Warrior families, respectively, wouldn't have allowed me into the dorm to sleep if there had been any doubt I had smuggled anything unacceptable onto campus.

This entire routine to get a kid started at RMA is called orientation, but it should be called "disorientation."

The smell of wood in my nostrils, George Daughtry's mangled face, the boxy, rugged work-jeans, T-shirt, and blue flannel I pulled on, all had undesired familiarity. George's cheek was sliced down one side, an injury sustained in an act of violence during his life before he worked for CEDU, but after he'd been a student. He wedged himself into a creaking wood seat. Prescott Freshwater and his puffy face lingered next to me while we watched George sign papers. Prescott's early-morning eyes were extremely red, the albino red of some of the ground-dwelling creatures I'd seen in the Owyhee Desert.

George squared the papers and put down his pen. From over the modest pine desk, he smiled with intensity, trying to make sparkles dance from his bright blue eyes into my bland browns. That one eyelid of his rested at only half-open because of a big scar down the side of his face. How was I supposed to look back at him without staring at his bulging, pale-blue orb?

5

I already know my way around campus. This interview is to make sure I'm remorseful for splitting.

"OK. Well firstly, welcome back. Bright and early. Your parents and I are hoping that you've got this out of your system, alright? Splitting didn't solve your problems, did it?"

"Hmm." I did not feel like answering George.

The running away from here, and the problem of being here for my problems were, in themselves, problems.

That August day when I split from here seems like a long time ago.

Oh, his question is not rhetorical.

"Um, no, I guess not. Sir." I was aware of my sunburned lips. They felt shriveled like dehydrated caterpillars on southern asphalt following a steamy rainstorm.

George Daughtry wet his shiny lips under a feeble mustache before continuing. I was anxious to get upstairs, but paid attention. I could smell toast and coffee, and hear kids banging around above us.

"You know, Bonnie, it doesn't have to be as bad as you think. There's no chains or locks here. We don't even lock the dorms. Remember? Choose to be here...to believe what this special place can offer you. It's your choice, you see."

The Warrior family head paused to see if I'd rebut this assertion. George's argument about the lack of locks on the RMA campus was void. The school surrounded itself with a no-man's land of impassible rivers and mountains.

I didn't take George's semantic word-bait about "choice," either. I knew that game well, from home, and here from raps.

Rocky Mountain Academy people play unfair word games.

We all knew I was acquainted with the upsized threats of worse places than this, with locks, fences, no food, and cells for dorms. And, worse than any military school, there were long-term deprivation scenarios like the Survival program – where I had just spent four weeks in the desert – that kept kids struggling against the elements outdoors, living in tipis, all year long, These places had also been mentioned between my parents, the educational consultant, and the parent communicator who worked in the basement of the new "academic building" here.

Choice? Not really.

Prescott's turn for my attention arrived. Insinuations of fruity break-fast oatmeal between his sentences flavored the air between words.

"So you probably understand a little more about consequences. About responsibility now, don't you? Taking responsibility for your own actions is one of the most important lessons a young man can learn. You're responsible for what you say, and do, and what you feel. Right? Like right this minute for example! Your parents don't make you feel angry, sad, happy, hurt, or whatever you're feeling; you choose to be angry as a consequence of your own actions. That's on you. Right? That'd be a choice to be angry or feel whatever you're feeling. In your gut, right now. You'll see. Consequence and awareness."

I detected slurs and a mild lisp in Prescott's voice. His breath made me hungry; I didn't know what he was talking about, either. That, along with my desire to get upstairs, was making me antsy.

Is he drunk?

It was early and they were still wearing comfortable sweatpants. Prescott hadn't made it into his customary suspenders – formal for night-time, and wide, red ones for the laborious forest-thinning occasions I would share with him in the months to come.

Prescott's last word bathed in the pine-and-food–incensed space between us. A nose whistle indicated more would be said:

"This place is expensive, Zack, and it cost you a lot splitting, didn't it? But it was worth it. Maybe you're the boy who's gone into the out-house and come back smelling like roses."

George signed another document.

"OK, let's get you moved back in. Er, Bonnie, we found your journal in your belongings. I'm returning it to you. Here. Be careful though – making a habit of thinking negative brings negativity, son. Can't you see that? It's the eternal struggle in the I Want To Live. Well, heh, hopefully we'll see you make it to Warrior, and I'm going to put in a special request that you be one of my kids when you get there? With me. Alright?"

"Oh, good."

George is talking about next summer!

A peer group goes into the I Want To Live propheet normally around the anniversary of starting here. George thinks I'll still be around in July or August of next year. I'll have to finish Papoose with Tess, and get through Brave with Prescott, before that.

Will I be here? Maybe so. What other option do I have but to perhaps plead my case at Christmas visits when I see Mom and Dad? Of course, that possibility is still three full months away – twice the amount of time I found unendurable here before.

TWO

Mandatory daily "first light" meetings were in the family's head-quarters. For me that meant the Papoose room. This was the largest of the three family rooms located in the second-biggest building on campus, called the Kootenai Lodge. I'd spent a month's worth of mornings in here already, before I split.

A dozen new Papoose kids' faces were crowded into the room. They had arrived during September, while I was away. A few other fading faces, Jon Garner's, for one, had disappeared from my peer group, joining that mysterious rank of kids that didn't stay through the whole program. But Cassandra Kinzeki, Kano, and Dylan were still there, representing the peer group above the one I was now trying to earn my way back into.

When gazing around the Papoose family headquarters, I realized I already had so much intimate knowledge about the familiar people. I had weeks of memories from before Survival to reintegrate. For example, when Dylan came into the room I remembered that his brother had killed himself. I knew the staff named Keith Rios's dirt about injecting needles into people's arms to deliver syringes full of heroin. I learned much of this secret info in my Truth propheet, during my first of many "disclosure circles." The rest had been brought up in raps, the encounter groups that glued the whole place together three afternoons every week. In fact, while I was out on Survival, being hiked into submission – er, before I had made the "choice" to be back at RMA – another month of raps, each lasting four hours or so, had occurred in this very space every Monday, Wednesday, and Friday.

Would I be allowed back in my former peer group with Bianca, the head of our PG, and Jamie Durant, who used to get his dog high, and conceited Micah from New York, and the lovely Ivy Larrabee sitting near me – one of a hundred kids here from San Francisco or Los Angeles? I could see Ernesto Quepa, my closest friend from my PG, and also Daphne, who everyone knew used to be a Grateful Deadhead, were lounging with familiarity in the family headquarters. Just saying "deadhead" would also be unacceptable since it's a crack in the music Agreement, I thought as my ears and eyes brought reminders to my

9

brain. Horatio Seguro sat in the corner, so still and quiet it was like he wanted to fade away.

I didn't know those new kids in the PG below mine yet. And anyway, it wouldn't be long before it would just stop fazing me as much when family members peeled off, got kicked out, pulled by parents, or split.

Tess Turnwell, daughter of the founder of our school, was still my Papoose family head. She was as skinny and bouncy as ever – Olive Oyl in the Northwest woods. I spied Darlayne Hammer, rocking in a plastic chair. Darlayne hadn't changed either. Buxom, blonde, and scary, when she made eye contact with me, she wore an expression that said she'd still like to see all of us boys in the room castrated.

I sat in a black plastic chair staring into the pattern of my blue checkered flannel. It felt like purgatory, not knowing which PG I would be in, or if I could hack it here. Tess quieted the room's buzz.

"People? Thank you. We're going to let Mr. Bonnie, Zack, have the option to earn his way back into his original peer group. So don't try to get him dirty and let's let him focus on the decisions he has to make, and do the work he'll need to do." Tess shot me a benign smile. "He wants to be in agreement here, right Zack? OK. Respect his bans. Let's go around the room and introduce any members of the family that Mr. Bonnie doesn't already know. Then we'll do 'new and goods'."

Tess was holding hands with Daphne O'Halloran and Wally Gold – both from my PG – which I found odd. Keith Rios and two of the other staff, nodding support for Tess, nuzzled up against the knees of a few dudes in our group, which was not odd.

Bans were lifted, but after these moments of introduction, every kid in that room would act like I wasn't even there. They weren't to even look in my direction – until Tess lifted "bans," the device by which they kept friends from talking and split/sex contracts from forming.

According to RMA, split/sex contracts happened when a boy and a girl ran away from the campus together, or even if they might have just floated the idea between the two of them. Darlayne Hammer called them "Split *for* sex" contracts, regardless of whether there was any "exchange of bodily fluids" as Mom would say. This included kissing.

As part of my welcome-back punishments, after this first light I'd be on bans from all Papooses and most girls. I was also getting all-day Work Details, which the place called "WDs." I wouldn't be yappin' it up with any girls or lower-school kids for months, since my presence in the room was a palpable reminder of the consequences of dissent. My return to this place – being here and having to be here – signaled my personal failures.

I wasn't sure about Micah, Bianca, or Craig Felder, either. They didn't seem so welcoming, or even fake happy, as I'd expected. More disappointingly, my buddy Ernesto had learned to contain himself better, so when his 'new and good' turn came he didn't talk like a robot, or express a love of unacceptable music. The furtive glances that I wanted to exchange with him were lacking.

After first light, when I exited the Papoose room's wide wooden doorway, my eyes confirmed that my magnification lens had lost its power. Originally, objects in Idaho – like trees, dogs, rooms, and kids – had seemed so much larger, but they didn't anymore. Mount 4032 now looked like a tall bump. The foothill-less mountains still slanted rigidly up toward Clifty Mountain's massive rock bowl adjacent to the campus.

My perspective has been re-set.

Unlike most of these kids and staff, I now know how to catch a fish with a rod, reel, line, and hook, all manufactured from plants! I can start a fire with rocks, and catch prey in hand-constructed, responsive wooden traps. I can shred a stick into points that might spear a fishy snack.

I could reflect on being young or being the fuckup that I was now, since everybody did that here. It was easy to live in, and in between, the different time zones in my brain because the program encouraged this. Life before. Life when I was a little kid. Life in Idaho.

A new life after Idaho, eventually, if ever a thing would exist for me, wouldn't come into focus for two years. The telescope that could let me see that far into the future I hadn't invented yet.

What would have happened if I'd died on Survival, or not come back here?

October would readjust my focus inward.

Zack Bonnie

THREE

Prescott Freshwater, the tubby, mustached Brave staff who liked to dress in suspenders, khaki Duck Head pants, "dirty bucks" for shoes, and tweedy sport jackets, the way Mom used to dress my brother and me for family photos, strode across the dining room with a parcel.

For me?

I was incredulous, but he headed right for me.

Tess said that Prescott wanted to be my next family head when I moved up to Brave from Papoose. George Daughtry would be in charge of me if I ever get to Warrior, and in some alternate universe where I was still here in two years, I'd be Nat Farmer's problem in Summit.

"Hey kiddo. Tess cleared this for you, and I want to tell you that I can't wait to get to know you. No doubt you're on your way to Brave, so I'll be waiting for you when you commit."

"Commit" was one of the CEDU terms they used for after you've already completed the thing; interchangeable with "graduate" or "complete." So, for example, if you completed the Wilderness Challenge, a two-week expedition in Warrior family, you had committed to the difficult assignment. I'd be committed to the Brave family around Thanksgiving time, if I kept following the Agreements and didn't self-sabotage – another word game used in raps.

The size of the package Prescott brought was to me extremely unusual, since neither of my parents ever believed in sending care packages. I remember one dinner party when my brother and I were in our first pairs of dirty bucks. We were starting sixth and third grades, respectively, so it must have been after my first year at summer camp. Mom announced to a dozen grown-ups sipping drinks and nibbling on peanuts, that there were two things she had always been sternly – maybe she used the word *austerely* – against: breast-feeding and care packages. I never did understand why that was funny. Her dinner guests laughed, though.

I ripped into the parcel, to discover acne medication, new work boots, and mountains of computer printout paper. A dossier contained copies of Mom's communications regarding me over the late August of foster care and the September of Survival. Then there were my parents' letters to me.

First the dossier. With dramatic flair, my mother thanked SUWS and CEDU for helping to arrange for the foster homes in Bonners Ferry where I stayed at the end of August. As to the month of September, well, basically, Survival had been a healthful speed bump in the road of her younger son's life. I had betrayed both Mom and Dad; I had scared them, but the right decisions had been made now. She was proud of my work on Survival, according to the letters she'd jotted last week to my old guidance counselor, a few hidden CEDU administrators like Hattie McCoy, and the sheriff. She thanked them for all they had done to me – er – for me – and especially for speaking on my behalf to RMA about what potential I had (to not be such a dipshit who was always in trouble) so that I could be granted permission to return.

Also included was a copy of Hedwig's letter in which she gave Mom permission to send this whole parcel to me. I worked my way down to the last layer of my parcel, to find my parents' letters to me.

"Decisions have had to be made for you your whole life. Now it's time to make these important decisions for yourself, and being a successful student at RMA is one of those steps." Dad's comments were included on purple sticky notes. They "don't want to give me mixed messages..." by giving me a chance to talk them into letting me come home. The program, and they, wouldn't risk any of my underhanded, deceitful self-sabotaging manipulations.

What Dad really meant was that I consumed too much thought and money. To me, it had been unbelievable that he had to bring me here in July, thousands of miles from home. To him, my time for questioning this reality "has reached an end." Embedded thickly in the subtext was the shameful drive home with Dad after they kicked me out of eighth grade at the Hill School in Pennsylvania.

To them, the whole fiasco of the summer had now passed. Stasis had been regained. It was not lost on me that my mother and father had signed my custody away to four different parties since June.

Like the RMA staff, my parents had this weird and unexplainable misconception that Survival was just an opportunity to "get something out of my system." The "something" was code for splitting, itself the RMA code for "running away from my problems." So they were

thrilled that I was back at RMA and considered it a big favor that
Rocky Mountain Academy had let me re-matriculate. All that I took
from the first "welcome back" letter.

Another letter to me from Mom, but signed by Dad, affirmed that
my folks were proud of what I must consider "accomplishments" in the
Owyhee Desert on Survival. It was justification to all who might ever
read it, why my parents – in addition to Dad's work schedule which
consisted of flying to Soviet Moscow to encourage mental hospitals to
become more humane in treating political dissidents and crazies – had
triangulated, or pointed responsibility for this important decision,
toward administrators from the CEDU and Survival programs. The
letters stated their regret that they had not participated at Trail's End
– that ritual of sprinting and eating and what was supposed to be cele-
brating with family on my final day in the desert – excused them from
material blame. It also negated any pride I could have displayed at the
end of my September march. Mom added, in a handwritten note, "Of
course, you're confused, but at least you're on the right trail now."

On my worst day on Survival it had occurred to me, not for the
first time, to just die and make everyone's day. I could have done it in
the middle of September, when hopes turned black and my knife was
sharp. Or I could have jabbed it into my field counselor Will Bender's
back.

I wished I hadn't ever dreamed my parents would be at Trail's End.
That wasn't part of their plan. My new-permanent removal from home
had not only strengthened my parents' position on sequestration, Mom
also relished the time it gave her for her writing again.

The plan is me in Idaho, at RMA.

It's confirmed by action as decisive as a double hernia operation.
Take it from a guy who knows: When I was in fourth grade, the anes-
thesiologist gave me an overdose that was very nearly tragic to Mom
and Dad. I later learned I might have lost a leg.

*There will never be the homecoming for which I'd longed. I already
know they don't want me home. But for the thirty-four-thousandth time
since fifth grade: Do they really hate me?*

If Mom and Dad had come to see me whip a fire out on my bow-
drill set in just a few minutes, set my traps and dead-falls like Tarzan
might, or seen the modicum of self-pride I felt in mastering these

timeless primitive skills, I thought, surely they'd have let me come home. I could survive without money or school, and I now had proof.

I don't know if I'll forgive them. I'm still mad at them for my existence.

†

January 7, 1974

The night before I leave the hospital after having a baby and already the wonder is fading. These moments of total glory are leaving faster than before. I am crying because I see the pattern of routine – the moment is gone forever – the responsibility staggers me under its weight.

Life and death – life and death the cycle – the peaks – the ultimate moments so soon one clutters life with the essential inessentials – and must try to find peaks there – artificial – no but only peaks – not the summit.

Goodbye glorious mountain – at least I have been there.

"and they fell back limp as a sack into the world of men."

KFB –

—Mother's journal entry from hospital, following author's birth (quoting Theodore Roethke)

FOUR

Back to sweating, back to cutting food and eating wood; just proving I'm sorry for running away. This is the administration's both implied and stated goal for me. Contrition.

I worked at my Work Detail sites meritoriously, or, as we said at RMA, with ethic. For this project, I gathered lengths of wood from the edge of the bustling wood corral and carried them to the back of the woodshed. I then sawed the firewood, filled up the wheelbarrow with two-foot lengths, and wheeled them to the house. Here I deposited the firewood behind the kitchen and in the storage bays that flanked the big fireplace, called the pit, in the main house. Then, returning to the wood corral, I cleaned up any debris I had left on the paths.

The kitchen stove was fueled by wood that Papooses had cut to size, schlepped, and neatly stacked there. Several other buildings were also wholly or partially fueled by wood or wood pellets supplied by us, and dragged by groups of us in large primitive carts. Seeing the kids rip the saws back and forth, mawling, and sledge-and-wedging, by the smoldering fire pit, was like looking at a frontier logging operation from a hundred years before.

During WDs, I'm on bans from all of the other kids around the campus anyway, so I don't fuck around. I must convince my parents, the staff, older kids, and my peer group of my sincerity so I don't get dropped a peer group. Joining kids just arriving here now would mean an extension of my total time in Idaho. I can't let that happen.

I took a "tool" I had learned on Survival.

Zack, Just Do It.

They said it here also.

Don't just stare at this pile of logs.

Cut it. Stack it.

"Plumb and square," I repeated to myself in rhythm – words I'd never used before Keith Rios, the Papoose staff, had used them.

Keith Rios watched me from his kitchen window behind the wood corral. Knowing that he reported to Tess, I sawed all morning. Some staff were on campus 24 hours; Keith lived above the kids in his own separate unit over some dorm rooms. My dorm didn't have any adult living in it, which made it more susceptible to random walk-throughs by staff and armed night watchmen.

Removed from my new family behind the hangar-sized wood bay during the Papoose family's morning labors, I saw the flower boxes, the paths, and fence posts that Brave kids created. I saw more of them carrying piles of rocks in wheelbarrows, and arranging them just so, according to Hedwig's instructions. I sawed and watched Warrior kids walk toward the farm for chores, and Summit kids in little splotches of affectionate arm-spreading and hand-holding groups amble to Skinner, our academic building.

The WD should last about two weeks. During WDs, I'm not allowed to talk to or look at other kids. The bans from talking to lower school kids could last months, though. As long as someone is on bans, he isn't allowed to sit near, eat near, or even walk near anyone they are on bans from. You could be on bans from one person, or, like I currently am, from half of the school. No idea for how long.

I thought about the older kids we were supposed to call "big brothers" here. Summit Pioneers and look-good older kids made such public displays of their emotional turmoil that there were times I entered the main house, saw an older kid bawling, and needed several long moments to realize they weren't just laughing hard.

I'll never be able to do that kind of screaming or sobbing breakdown the right way. I don't have that depth of emotion and anguish to express, do I?

One thought stayed with me during the first week of raps as I hauled and sawed RMA's wood: The growing conflict inside of me, which still justified RMA keeping me here, was a proxy war for the longer-lived conflict between my parents and me. They wanted me to do something impossible – like stay here for years. By surrendering, accepting that I was staying, even if I didn't yet believe I needed to be here, I joined the herd. We – all of us kids at RMA, and even the ol' parents at home – had entered a trap.

This place is an emotional petri dish. We are the hive.

Our campus environment that was becoming home, was at once a web, cage, and a metaphor for traps. The only way to escape was to turn eighteen, lose one's mental faculties, or maybe die. In my understanding of Darwin's theory, this bolstered RMA's claim that kids here were deformed. We had to be here, and could only be aided in evolving into a higher form if we committed to the program, all the way through the final Summit Workshop.

The trap was as simple as a Chinese finger trap, and at the same time complex, like the movement of wave energy. The more we struggled to learn and succeed in the web, the more enmeshed our lives became with the perceptions of staff and other kids, and the more adapted we became. While sequestered from society, we could reinterpret, replace, and be handed a new code with new language.

Mom and Dad didn't want me before, so maybe they'll like a CEDU-adapted, better version. This is what they're so invested in. I'd better perform if I want to keep living and eventually get a driver's license — the ultimate runaway tool.

The headmaster, Nat, had recently said during last light:

"The goal is to overcome all subconscious thinking with over-conscientious thinking."

See, the goal is also the trap.

FIVE

Your most recent milestone in the program meant everything – both to how you were viewed, and how you did the viewing. It was the unspoken "respect," of having been through a certain wilderness experience or a propheet that others hadn't yet, that kept the program's mystique alive.

The staff, too, chose to stay and learn it all. Like every kid here, the staff were required to go through the program's propheets and work-shops in consecutive order. Thus staff weren't proper "power staff," and weren't even allowed to facilitate raps, or co-run propheets, until they completed the entire propheet series with a student peer group, and completed a Summit Workshop. Wastoids like me and the rest of the lower school wouldn't even get an overnight away from the campus at the hotel in the small town of Sandpoint (we called it "Sandpit") until we'd been there almost a year. Sandpit was about half-way between RMA and Coeur d'Alene, which was on the way to Spokane – where my independent adventure had ended in August. We wouldn't go home for a visit until after the I Want To Live propheet – an eternal year after arriving as Papooses.

Since younger kids knew nothing about the details of propheets, the longer I was here the more words like "friend," "truth," or "choice" took on special identities. In general, but especially in raps, the coding among those of us who'd been in those propheet rooms was a library of inside jokes – commonalities that held peer groups and families together the way individual units comprised army battalions in tank warfare.

"Don't you want to know what Tim Chalmers knows? See how Jennifer Oyama is using the tools here? Can't you see the sparkle in Hedwig, and how much she loves the campus? You'll know more after the Brothers! Ari just glows after he runs his shit, doesn't he? I'm so proud of you letting yourselves trust this process, let yourselves slow down and tap into that feeling. Did you really listen, not just hear, what they shared? Serious shit they've worked through with their time here. I can't wait for you little doogers to get through your Summit! Don't you respect our Summit Graduates? I do. Well, I'm not going to take tools out of the experience, but I can say we're saving the best for last! Right, Tess? I'm still getting mine, digesting it every day! I love my Summit. We'd never ask you to do something we wouldn't do, or haven't done ourselves. The tools you are learning here are the most important thing in your world today. Everything else is a distraction."

Power staffers like George Daughtry, Prescott Freshwater, and Tess Turnwell said things like this all the time, all of it intended to get us to look up to the older kids and staff, keep our minds off home, and credit the program. They encouraged us to be curious about the special knowledge, secret words like *struggle*, *Thinking*, and those skills like the bizarre pidgin English that only the staff and more senior kids had decrypted over time, with gradually acquired propheet tools.

†

When you've been subject to brainwashing you still have freedom of choice. But your choices are based upon what you believe ... and your beliefs have been changed. Your allegiances have been changed. Your family has been changed. And therefore you will choose based upon your new family, your new values, your new allegiance and your new beliefs.

How do they do that? The first thing they do is the encounter group.

[...] What Mao learned through trial and error was then used in the prisons but it was initially used in the university in China and you had people – being told that they were sick and they needed help, needed to be part of the new society – who came voluntarily ... In that setting, brainwashing success was far greater than it was in prisons.

The trick isn't so much the leader ... somebody who's working on one person – the trick is ... the person who is most influential is the person who's most like you, has maybe been there a year and a half...

"I was kinda like you...I gotta tell you, man, it worked for me...."

It's the guy who's further along in the program who draws you in.

—Paul Morantz, Esq., author of *Escape: My Life Long War Against Cults*, "Cults, Confession and Mind Control," interviewed by Liam Scheff. Transcribed from http://www.paulmorantz.com

†

You couldn't skip a propheet like skipping a grade; if you hadn't been all the way through the Summit, you couldn't yet be confident or content. Only here and at the CEDU campus in California were these benedictions offered.

What bothered me was the sense of urgency – the pressure to adapt into the new design. We needed to know, to *want* to know, what the staff wanted to teach us, when they wanted to teach it. Then we had to verbalize the lessons as they were learned, usually in raps, so that staff could monitor our progress. We weren't allowed bad days where we didn't want to work or go to raps.

Non-rap-running junior staff were on rented soil, too, we learned. These often-younger-aged staff would show up for a few weeks or months and leave, to be replaced by another adult almost as fast as Papoose headquarters emptied and filled up with new kids for the wood corral. Like Dorothy in Oz: "People come and go so frequently here."

Woolly balaclavas ("It's Klingon for hat," I'd tell the Papooses the next year). Telemark skiing. Time for sealing my boots with mink oil, and learning – in case I ever needed to know – how to make snow-shoes. Here, late October meant winter, and winter was a whole new ballgame in the panhandle of Northern Idaho.

I was still in Papoose, earning my way back into the PG fold. By the time the upcoming Brothers Keeper propheet arrived around Thanksgiving time, I'd be moved up to Brave, to join the rest of my PG. Then, two more years before graduation.

Never. I'll never make it.

We had a school-wide Morning Meeting every Monday. Prescott Freshwater, the Brave family head, or George Daughtry, from Warrior, were normally the lead characters, causing me to continue to think of them as united in some way – like Laurel and Hardy, Ponch and Baker, or The Blues Brothers. The weekly Morning Meetings, which we knew also went on at our sister school in California, were an orchestrated part of Sol Turnwell's master plan.

One of the all-self-important mating pair of Nat and Hedwig Farmer was always present. It is ever unclear what Hedwig's job titles were beyond grounds Kommandant, but I knew they were both pioneers, and chummy with Sol, who was Tess's father and the owner and founder of this place. And I knew that Nat was at once the headmaster, president, and Summit family head.

Who made which decisions at RMA, like letting George lead today? I have to keep an eye on him, and impress him. He already warned me at orientation, my first day back, that he'd be watching me, and would be my senior counselor when I got to Warrior. If I really have to stay here, I need to understand the hierarchy, to know who'll be in charge of me.

Only by listening and keying into dynamics among the numerous staff could we kids gather tidbits about them. What were their lives like before working here? Did they have a dog? Walter Nemecek, or Darlayne Hammer, or Hedwig Farmer might share something in a rap, or in a propheet. If they were original "pioneer" staff like Hedwig or Nat, or had gone to CEDU as kids themselves – especially the rap-facilitator power staff like Darlayne and Keith – they usually were the hardest to impress. I wanted to know more of their secrets.

This week Hedwig and Nat sat together behind George. Hedwig, famous for being born in Scandinavia, was in charge of beautifying the two growing campuses with laborious assignments which she relished mandating and overseeing. Each staff represented a character or archetype, and Hedwig was known to have empathic abilities, especially for girls and adopted kids. Hedwig, with her tiny white sneakers and long gray ponytail, had made an appearance as an owl in my Truth propheet, back before I split RMA and went on Survival. It all seemed like a long time ago.

I sat in a chair at the perimeter. Tess insisted on having her back propped against my legs so I couldn't cross them. Jennifer Oyama, a big-boned girl freshly anointed as a Warrior, smooshed between Tess's legs, so we took in the morning's monologue together.

Zack, the biological sample, the active culture, sits there with them, contemplating the discussion.

The topic du jour was allowing ourselves to admit what lowlifes we were before arriving here. The most important thing I could do was absorb any embedded special lesson and start applying it to daily life, so I could demonstrate it in raps that week. I'd already done most of that, having no idea that this need to prove my belief in the tenets of the program would remain a constant. Like a neutron star feeding off its own energy, it wouldn't be long before I felt that every snarky, sarcastic thought that popped into my head was causing an infernal reaction that could eventually end with my total destruction.

George's recitals continued: There was greater potential here with CEDU/RMA to permanently impact our future lives than at any other program or normal school in the world for kids and people. We should forgive parents, ourselves, and anyone that ever hurt us. The world mistreats everyone, and that's why our parents are victims. In order to avoid the pratfalls of society, we must bust one another on the abandonment and trust issues that we all have. We must all save our friends from Thinking.

It sounded confusing, but it wouldn't be after we spent enough time meditating on it.

We must commit to work the program to this end – the way the most senior kids here now demonstrated. And, eventually, we'd learn to tell everyone in the world how wonderful it is to be enlightened with the uncommon knowledge bestowed on us in northern Idaho. Right now, I was supposed to learn why I didn't trust the love of my older brothers and sisters.

The contrast between the complicated, fragmented muddle of the unbeliever's life and the pure simplicity of true belief is often emphasized by ideologues who understand the power of uncertainty to frighten and unnerve people who may already feel that their lives are out of control.

—Kathleen Taylor, PhD, "Thought Crime," *The Guardian*, 7 Oct 2005

Spreading the gospel of what we'd learn in the Summit was intended for the Summit Pioneers – they were next to hatch like immaculate butterflies from the dung caterpillars that they used to be; after this metamorphosis, the Summit Pioneers'd be ready to soar from the isolated campus to take on the whole world.

In some ways, I was curious what they knew and why they acted so strange after their final workshop, standing and talking weirder than usual, some even changing their names, and sharing frequently with one another in coded pidgin talk. The staff also treated them like equals after the Summit Workshop. They could occasionally change the music in the Bridge, use the phone at their own discretion, and could hitch a ride to and from campus with one of the staff when they took us to doctor's appointments in town.

Soon the new graduates'd be all gussied up and staring blankly into the camera, like the rows of blushing or unnaturally pale-skinned graduates populating a dozen photographs down in Warrior headquarters, in the old Kootenai Lodge. Paul Renssalaer, one of the guys who gave me my tour the first day, was immortalized among the photo faces in frame, looking as opaque and vacant as ever. I looked over to the red-headed rich kid, Crosby Rohrback; his PG's picture was scheduled to go on the wall before Christmas.

Summit Pioneers were to spread the gospel of Sol and CEDU/RMA and to use this specialized knowledge to effect global conversion. That was their chief mission, I gathered.

There was a dark side to the beaming rainbows and butterflies fluttering in the little doogers who dwelt inside us. The evil of Stinking Thinking would haunt and grow in there too. Like jungle snakes, our Thinking would constrict our abundant hearts as they beat in our chests, eventually killing us. We could be saved only if we discovered – and learned to master and confront – that Thinking with CEDU/RMA's specialized weapons.

Otherwise, unnatural deaths would inevitably befall each of us. They were preventable, if we could learn practical use of the metaphorical tools so mysteriously referred to in the series of propheets, capped by the final Summit Workshop. I pictured Mr. Spock mind-melding on *Star Trek*. Once I got to the Summit, though, I learned that it wasn't like that at all.

These gradual improvements also promised positive relationships with our families, supplying whatever it was that we had lacked before.

The program would repair our families' perceptions of us, too, to neutral, or better.

> Emotional control is essentially making a person
> feel special and chosen – they are going to help save
> the world, on the one hand, ... but the rest is guilt and
> fear and manipulation.
>
> —Steve Hassan, "Undue Influence: Brainwashing,
> Mind Control, and How It All Works," remarks
> delivered at For Justice, London, UK, 22 May 2015.
> Transcribed from https://www.youtube.com/
> watch?v=OiIxbBKvrp8

Nat let George lead the weekly ceremony with phony verve. Upperschool girls loved George Daughtry and had crushes on him. An overconfident and arrogant worm, George Daughtry often wept extravagantly. The one eye rested at half-shut, which made the remaining bright blue one shine even brighter after he got emotional.

Prospective parents and other adults were present for George's performance. Hedwig, the headmaster's wife, huddled with the small group of women we heard called "educational consultants." With the cluster was the parent communicator assigned to me, Hattie McCoy. I suspected she was the reason I was even back in this huge wooden structure we called the house. Hattie's letters were in one of the dossiers in Mom's box, convincing my parents that a lock-up in Utah would be the place to send me after Survival – in the event RMA and CEDU wouldn't have me back. I always acted extra grown up and happy when Hattie was around.

George prattled on, I tried to look studious. "You know, guys, even these Agreements that you think of as small, like the ups n' downs, the music Agreements, and things like side conversations in raps, bad-rapping everybody – well, they're here for a reason. They're all important. We're not here to play it safe, but to make it safe! We're here to go for broke! What are we here for?"

"To go for broke!" Everybody responded with questionable authenticity.

"I can't hear you? What are we here for?" George Daughtry made a big show of cupping his hand around his ear like Hulk Hogan, to influence us to produce more exuberance.

"TO GO FOR BROKE." Louder, with enthusiasm – especially from the middle school families of Brave and Warrior. The Papoose family members mostly still seethed at the weekly farce.

"Alright. The Agreements keep the place, and us, safe while we work with and for ourselves, right everybody? Right. One more time: Everybody?"

"RIGHT!"

"This is a special place. We take real ownership and pride here. OK?"

George Daughtry, reveling in the moment, stroked his chin before wrenching his arm back to his side. All staff were also required to attend these weekly pep talks, thus advertising the lie of unanimous love for our campus life. George lapped up the attention in the room like a lost dog reunited with its owner, pointing to anyone he caught making eye contact with him.

All you ever wanted was the best for your child... happiness, comfort, hope, success, and a future filled with opportunities. You've always known that a good education and emotional maturity were the keys to achieving that dream. So you looked for a place where that could happen. And now, you've found it. It's a place where your child will be safe – and part of another loving family – for a while.

—Transcribed from CEDU Schools promotional video, 1995, https://www.youtube.com/watch?v=TouE-6GIoDFk&feature=youtu.be

"...We don't even believe in drugs here, except for specific, real medical concerns. A lot of you were labeled before joining us here. Right? Yeah, Ari. OK, Griffin, good. Crosby, where are you? That's right.

Maybe as depressed? What else?" The crowd murmured responses. I hated how George called people out like that. Soon, though, I would come to like having staff attentions bestowed on me in this way. "A runaway? Dropout, right, Zack?..."

What the fuck do you know?

But of course, it only stings and makes me defensive because it must be true. I may not like it, but I can accept the reduction that he has made of me. It is "true" especially from my parents' point of view: I am a fuckup.

George was only getting warmed up. "…as manic depressive, crazy, maybe as something else? All sorts of labels. What about as hyperactive or ADD or some sh — uh, other label before you got sent here, I know a lot of you have heard that, and accepted those labels in the past. What good did that do? Did you like wearing that uniform? NO! I didn't think so. Where's Cassandra? Some of you have actually learned that those actions that caused that problem or learning disability were your own doing. And now we know how we've sought to control it, right Dylan? Keep an eye on him, Tim! Yo! Yeah, you're going to do great out there, don't worry." George directed asides whether a kid was falling asleep or taking careful notes.

"Well, what we understand here is that awareness, that self-under-standing, is the key. We learn the skills here. Sometimes it's just about being calm. Self-identifying the underlying causes of our labels and negative traits that make it hard to learn. To behave correctly in a toxic classroom environment or with all the negativity going on at home? Nobody can learn there. The parents don't learn, you won't learn. Growth gets stunted and failures start to take over. Right? Patterns became established. SO, we're going to slow it down and yeah, it takes years. But sometimes it's slowing down. Just being present in the moment. . . . Just breathing. This will give us the intention to tap into all that we become aware of here. A chance to use our contracts in all encounters, where we lacked those tools before. So being aware to be deliberate in the moment."

George paused, turning his face up to the ceiling standing for a full minute with his hands by his sides in a weird posture that I would learn meant he was "open." At the end, he lowered his face and opened his eyes very purposefully and whispered the words, "Thank you."

The cuddle comprised of Tess and Jennifer Oyama shifted near my feet. George Daughtry's pitch seemed to lull us, the longer his voice warbled up and down. Watching everyone draped on the wooden furniture, four to a couch, seated in front of the couches, or nestled in each other's shoulders and crotches on the smoosh pillows, I felt a twinge of regret or jealousy. I wanted touch, someone to rub my neck or hair during the meetings and at night during house time, even to be tucked in and asked if I wanted water, as when I was young. Of course I hadn't realized that, and never would have, without what I was already learning in this loony bin.

George Daughtry made it sound like each one of us would have become a prostitute, a drug addict, a victim of murder or suicide, or have been banished to crushing loneliness with people who don't even know what real friendship is – we'd be lonely, and eke out unlivable, wasted lives. I didn't believe that – not yet.

Without George's Monday lessons, would I be dead?

> Members are programmed either overtly or subtly... to believe that if they ever leave, they will die of some horrible disease, be hit by a car, be killed in a plane crash, or perhaps even cause the death of loved ones. ... Yet cult-induced phobias are so cleverly created and implanted that people often don't even know they exist.
>
> —Steven Hassan, *Combating Cult Mind Control*, Freedom of Mind Press, 2015 (25th anniversary edition), p 97

"Those people that exist in that state of being out of sync with the cornucopia of life – I call them 'perambulating corpses'."

It wasn't the first time I had heard George and other staff use that phrase. George's hands pumped the syllables like gospel. Bart Lennerton, a kid from Memphis who was in the PG behind mine, laughed out loud. Ari Korta, from Terrance's PG, who was two full-sized couches away, publicly snapped at Bart.

"Hey! Get your fucking feet off of our couch and pay attention, DUDE!"

Ari had been in a world of shit and on a full-time when I first arrived at RMA. He had changed. Instead of commanding shame, he now commanded respect.

I'll have to remember to keep myself on bans from Bart — if I ever get off the bans I'm already on.

It'll be a lingering reminder of what a shit I am.

Prescott Freshwater and even Nat Farmer himself both shot Bart nasty looks.

George Daughtry yanked his hand from his chin again, in a show of self-regulation, before regaining his concentration. I looked to the visiting parents who would soon be taken on the tour of the school. These occasional visitor's tours seemed to be timed to avoid both the shivering or sweating morning work crews, and the bizarre, obscene, and unique alchemy that each rap room manifested during that afternoon's raps. Later, being one of these student liaisons and tour guides for parents became a task at which I excelled. It was something else I did to make Nat, the bearded elder, know my name.

While the first few months I resented being part of the CEDU propaganda, dazzling the occasional outsiders with our submissive will, and impressing staff with the requisite interest, eventually I would buy into almost all of it, to the point of emotional bankruptcy. I successfully led those tours, and became the big brother to the new kids their parents left there because of my convincing tour.

George was a natural look-good and walking attention game. I could see occasional eye-rolls subtly telegraphed between Darlayne and Keith.

George still wasn't done. "And uh, filling the absence of the very real hurt in our lives. When we're done doing that work, the other stuff comes naturally. That very important work of focusing on our inner hurt and filling those voids. We can repair the esteem issues, stay clean obviously, and focus eventually, in our later stages like upper school, and get back to a classroom setting. But for now, let's head to work crews and earn our lunch! Let me see ten — OK, twenty hands that will spend a few extra minutes making sure the house is tightened up like a duck butt?"

Morning Meeting was over. Hattie, Hedwig, and the cluster of visiting consultants and parents filed out.

George Daughtry mandated the volunteers to re-order the couches and pillows, just the right way. Putting furniture and smoosh pillows back were tokens of low dominance in the pecking order. Then we went to assigned family chores — wood science for Papoose, forest thinning for Brave, and studies in animal husbandry for Warrior.

Animal husbandry?

✝

Academics was an area I did not have as much time for in this trip as I would have liked. However, teachers are free to draw on the children's thinking, experiences, and feelings in conducting their lessons. This helps the students see things in new ways, which is what education should be all about. An exercise in an English class I sat in on demonstrated to me how the whole child concept is brought into their classrooms. The teacher played several selections of music, and after each, had the students write what the selection made them think of. Comparing reactions at the end of the class, it was striking how similar each student's independent reactions were to each selection. The lesson I learned from the exercise was how it demonstrated how music is a language that clearly communicates nonverbal images.

—Lon Woodbury, "Schools, Programs, & Visit Reports," *Woodbury Reports,* June, 1991 (reviewing his April 1991 visit to RMA's sister school, CEDU, in Running Springs, California)

Six

After lunch, every Monday, Wednesday, and Friday, the rap sheets were read out to us. This second daily school-wide headcount also told everyone which room to go to, and who would be the rap facilitators for the day. Today's rap was no longer much of a surprise since I knew that almost every time we'd reassemble in one of the family headquarters inside the Kootenai Lodge, the only building standing on campus when Sol, Nat, and Hedwig, and the original pioneers first came from CEDU in California.

With a dozen or so kids, I ambled across pine boards to my rap with Mariah and Terrance. The new Papoose, Bart Lennerton, followed along with Jasper and Ari from my dorm. Just for a moment, I felt mature and accepted, to be seen with older, not-suspected-of-being-dirty, kids. I knew their names and they knew mine.

Some kids peeled off and went into the Papoose room. Through the open door, I glimpsed the wall of the familiar room's array of photographs in eight-by-twelve-inch homemade frames that I'd stared at for the first time in July. Smudges of glue and tiny tacks could be spied holding the little slats of pine together. We would use similar wooden slats and fasteners to assemble our own frames during Santa's Workshop in two months' time.

One black and white photo bordered by beige pine focused crisply on a big black dude, clearly older than eighteen, sitting in a rap circle. A guy I assume was Sol Turnwell is cuddling the big bear dude with one hand, while pointing an indictment at someone out of frame in the foreground. The image telegraphs the personal issues of the sobbing man, and presents Sol on his quest to confront the next victim, blurry in the foreground. The weeping black guy's indictments have ended, and a new one is just beginning, for someone else. You can tell from the quality of photo print that some years have passed since the picture was snapped. Sol's face is thin, and he is motionless, his pointer extended crookedly in accusation.

Having been in a bunch of raps in that room, I'd seen those faces time and again, always frozen in solemn contemplation, some contorted by outpourings of expressions that I only ever witnessed here in northern Idaho.

Our CEDU villa, RMA, had its roots in gatherings that Sol hosted for adults and runaway kids at his home back in California. The ancestry of our raps and his invention of the propheets all started in his living room, so those photos could date back to early days before my PG was even born!

Sol owns this whole place. He taught the RMA staff everything they know.

Will raps be photographed in my future too?

Our rap would be with Prescott in Brave HQ, the room with neighboring walls to both Papoose and Warrior HQs. Pretty soon, when I moved up to Brave this would be the room I'd go to, instead of Papoose headquarters, every morning for daily first light with my family.

As I plopped down in a black plastic chair in the Brave headquarters, the only real distractions were photos of loggers and sawyers, plus, on the wall ahead of me, a big map of the world. A lot of rooms had maps. This one was my favorite. Three-dimensional ripples crushed against Central Asia where the words *Gobi Desert* spread onto flat land – a relief map.

We were about to begin. I'd spaced out for some of the mini ice breaker that loosened us up for introspection. Mariah and Griffin's rap voices made me tear my eyes from the map. I didn't want to be indicted for making the room "unsafe" by staring at the map and shifting my focus out of the room.

This rap's razzing process had pleasantly continued for nearly an hour, lulling me, but there was a price to pay. I had come to notice this as an internal superstition that shouldn't be named: if the casual ice breaking that started the rap lasted unusually long, the intensity of the remainder of the rap increased. I think this was because we wanted to show appreciation to the counselors for first lightening the burden of the four-hour afternoon slog. Today's rap was showing those signs.

I muscled my eyeballs from the logger photos and the map on the wall, back to the rap, which was easy since the ice breaker had turned to Griffin, from Mariah's PG.

Walter Nemecek, the Brave staff who sent my PG off to our Truth propheet, sat forward in his chair and cleared his throat.

"We also have Griffin Petersen. How's it going? What's new and good with you?"

There was something wrong with Walter's leg, so he didn't go on expeditions. Instead, he seemed to focus on honing his teacher-advisor skills.

Griffin, like Mariah, could've won a boot-and-lumberjack-attire beauty contest any day. If such a thing existed. Griffin had always been nice to me, and I'd heard some things about her life in other raps, narrated in her sing-songy voice.

"I've got a lot going on. I feel like I always do. Mostly I'm good. Still working with the tools from my program and tying it to academics. I did get a 'B' on a paper that was buggin' me out."

"OK, so you've got some work to do in here today?" Prescott's off-time bassoon voice.

"I guess. Yeah."

"OK. I'm going to hold you to that. Moving on. Don't need to be reminded of ol' Terrance's last name. Hi."

"Hi." Terrance Whittlemore wasn't saying anything else if he could help it. I knew some of his story and he'd been through a hell of a lot more than most of us.

Walter spent a moment with Prescott, mocking Terrance's manner, " 'Hi.' "

"Hi."

"No, no, wait. I got it... 'Hi.' "

"Ohboyoyboy. I wonder if today you're going to impress me? Let's razz you up and start the rap. Do you not want Zack to get moved up to Brave, Terrance." Commented Prescott, without a question.

But Tess interjected in a staccato tone: "Aren't you still hanging around with Papooses a little much? I think – and I did when you were in my family – that you slide by. You two sort of slide by a lot around here. Well – don't you?" Tess's neck had snapped to me at the end.

"And I bet they hear this in every fucking rap."

Tess or Walter would be there every step of the way for Prescott during the rap. Just as they had been ready to pick on, or joke about, each of us during the opening ceremony of reading off the rap list, they'd support the direction Prescott wanted to take a kid's indictment.

"Terrance, it's true I see you and Zack spending a lot of time together. Are you supporting the positive in him?"

"What do you think? Anybody?" Tess was right on Prescott's heels.

The rap seemed to get started and then stopped, like a cassette tape being eaten. It was difficult to "stay in the moment" in raps with intermittent razzing like this.

"Zack, this is going be an important time when you start to listen to the feedback from other people, such as your older brothers and sisters. You guys are a lot alike." Tess quipped, so Terrance and I both knew we'd be hearing more presently.

"OK." Terrance and I nodded at each other.

"You think you're ready to move up to Brave?" Prescott just had to say that, to get me verbal, test our growing "relationship," give Tess the option to gauge my response, and expose me to everyone in the rap too.

I have to answer him.

Make sure to be self-deprecating, or humble. That much I've learned. Always admit self-ignorance, and don't blame anyone or anything else.

"Well, I think I am. I've been working bustin' butt, and I wrote that letter to my folks. I copped out to all my dirt. Working with the Truth. You know, tools. I feel...I want to be with my peer group, you know, instead of the babies. Terrance is positive, you know a good support. He shows me plenty of stuff. I try to let my defenses down around him."

I had sneaked in a double-entendre, based on my hours of chess talk with Terrance. Since I wasn't allowed to ask or talk about friends from home, my daily concerns now were about my peers, and dramas among my older RMA brothers, staff, and me.

I had to talk. It was drivel, I knew, but I had to say stuff to keep the rap in motion. It was true that I worked hard "busting ass" or "with ethic" on morning crews Monday thru Saturday, whether the day's task was cleaning buildings, splitting wood, or tending to chores at the farm on Saturday crews.

Out of program love, Mariah Verdera did not let the rap's attention shift away from me. To love me was to stretch me, to make me uncomfortable – which would make me grow. Months before, the night of my Truth propheet, Mariah had told me all about her story, a version of pre-RMA life, and I, too, disclosed all my juicy secrets and confessions to her. By all standard protocols, Mariah was a big sister, and a friend to me now. But she wasn't presently in a space to see how what she'd started had spilled on to me. Part of me couldn't help but blame her for how the rap had zoomed in on the most personal issues of my life and my most intimate thought processes.

But I did know that Tess approved of the relationship with Mariah because she had pointed out, "You've got to try to let yourself trust someone here. I know Mariah is a great kid who's been through the wringer lately, so try to let her in. It'll be worth it, I promise. Let yourself feel, let yourself trust Mariah."

Mariah began. "Tess told you that I was going to be on you like paint on a house. So the first thing we've got to talk about is how much time I see you spending playing sports all the time, and your overtime with Papooses. And I know you don't talk to any girls yet really, but still – you ought to know how much the new guys need support. Also, I know you're struggling with feeling on the outside and I just want to hear you talk about that?"

I cleared my throat. "Well, yeah I guess I've sort of been struggling with healthy thoughts, you know, I'm not going to split, and I'm not corrupting any Papooses, I'm only allowed to talk to the ones that I do. I'm here in agreement, but it's hard to be here – "

"What's hard?" Tess interrupted.

"Not being as free, not being able to get away with shit and being pulled up all the time. Having to stay here sucks, but I understand my parents' need for change. You know, that I need to be a better person. But, like even here, it seems I can't do anything right. I still feel like maybe I'm not getting it."

"No, Zack, you're really right where you need to be." Prescott wanted attention. "We'll come back to you in a minute."

"SO! Mariah. Let's talk about your feelings for Zack. You really want him to succeed here, don't you?" Walter chimed in. Not surprising since he had worked with Mariah, Terrance, and Griffin when they were in Brave. Mariah looked me in the eye.

"Yeah, I know what it is to be on the outside, and not have the support you need around here. Not to feel you do anyway, and I just want you to know that I've been learning so much. So much that I wish I could share with you. If you would let me in."

Prescott added, "Go ahead, Mariah, let that come up."

I didn't yet understand this language, but something told me Prescott was setting several things in motion here when he gave Mariah permission to "let that come up." Mariah's face changed, as if she was brooding on Prescott's statement, even while letting me have it.

"Zack, sometimes it feels like when we spend time together, like at our appointment last night, for example, that you're not even there. Or half-there. It's like you'll only let people in just that one inch and anything more than that would go straight to your heart."

"It would just HURT TOO MUCH, right?"

"Choose to be vulnerable! Let your fucking defenses down."

"Choose to trust me. Choose to let us in. Why can't Spider-man let people in to play?"

Tess pulled from my Truth propheet toolbox with that Spider-man comment.

The statements came to me, or between Mariah and me, in rapid succession, interspersed with commentary from around the room. In order to indict me from across the circle, people next to me moved to other seats; I too would move around several times in the next two hours, as the sequence of indictments played out. A good part of the rap would be spent bouncing back to Mariah but the first volley included me since we evidently cared for each other.

"You put on such a good show! Great tough guy routine!"

"So good at pushing people away! I wonder when you're going to start letting people in around here!"

"It ain't working for you, Honey."

"Exactly. You're so afraid of letting us in, man. What's up with that? What would happen if you let yourself trust someone here?"

"Yeah, you pretend that you are getting to know me, but seriously, if you're not sharing yourself with me, THEN WHAT ARE YOU SPENDING TIME WITH ME FOR!"

"RRRRRRIGHT, and what's THAT THOUGHT right there now, sweetie?" Tess coaxed Mariah.

Mariah was almost talking to herself. "I – just thinks Zack is spending time with me and Me's sharing all this with him and Me doesn't FEEL LOVED! I THINKS ME CAN'T HAVE LOVE! WHAT THE FUCK?"

The rap had a few minutes taken off the clock while Mariah kept muttering. In this moment I felt gratitude for Mariah because by being a vehicle for her to do introspective work, I was showing the dozen other kids and staff in the room that she trusted me, that she liked me, that I was special. I felt myself cheering her on deeper, listening so I could know her better.

It is sort of sad to see her upset. Maybe she's stuck in her head.

I kept my focus on her even though it would have been easier to look away, to not let myself care for Mariah, the words, the energy that she put into displaying her care for me.

"That's RIGHT! Tell him how that FEELS! What's coming up – LET IT GO?"

"LET'S HEAR THAT STRUGGLE! What does that struggle sound like?"

"YOU DON'T LOVE ME, NOBODY CAN LOVE ME, I CAN'T...FUUUUUUUCK....."

"You've got to start getting out of your head, too, Zack. Be here for people! God, you hold back! You hold back so much! You have so much potential, Zack. You're not going anywhere! Why can't you put some effort in around here?"

I hadn't known how Mariah, or those other Summit kids I'd seen before, could know when to turn any one of us into objects of memory the way staff always did. It had to be an upper-school tool that allowed them to care so much for us; just as I was being used to assist bringing her cathartic emotions to bear.

Then I started to see. I was a tool, a way for her to shake loose her own issues to lay bare for the rap. Of course, it opened the window to indictments for me, and gave me the opportunity to get wound up.

Jasper, my dorm head and a champion snorer, had long since moved across the circle: "Don't you feel lonely when you walk around here?"

"Totally. You are, Zack. He is. He looks like you, Jasper, how he slinks around the campus! COME ON Jasper, that's a projection! I EXPECT YOU TO PARTICIPATE FULLY TODAY! NO MORE SLIDING BY!" Prescott also evidently had a hard-on today for my dorm head, and these asides were standard.

"...how he has to be around other people all the time? You're like that, only the way you reflect that is to stay alone? You see?"

"Still trying to figure it all out!"

"Exactly, you're still so in your head around here, and you give some good comments in raps sometimes, but it's shallow. You're afraid of not being accepted, of not fitting in!"

"Don't skirt too close to the fire – gotta figure it out first! Who's going to like me?"

"THAT'S WHY I CAN'T TRUST! Right, Zack?"

Prescott held out a hand. "Tranquillo. Hold up, I want to give Zacko a chance to talk. Zaco the Taco, maybe I'll call ya. So. Let's hear what Mariah and the rest of these people, that obviously care for you, are bringing up."

"Why don't you tell us a little more about what's going on with you?" Tess rounded out now that Prescott had made space for me to demonstrate my program knowledge.

My instantaneous thought was automatic.

No, not yet.

But instead I said, "It's true, I guess I do feel kind of like I'm not fitting in here. Ever since Survival, and I know I've only been through the Truth, I feel just kind of sad. And like I'm always going to disappoint them."

"Them?" Tess coaxed knowing fully well that my "them" was operative not just for my PG, and impressing the staff, too, but also for my parents. This entire ritual was code for questioning my own act, my traditional self and learned reactions – looking like I was becoming content here, crossing over from acting into the reality of the senses. It went deeper even than the senses. The chemistry in these rooms, the

importance of exploring what was wrong with my world, our world –
it usually went back to being young.

"Like I'm always going to disappoint who exactly?" Prescott got
into it now.

"Mom and Dad. Like in the program. I know they want me gone."

"Let's talk more about THAT, yes?"

"What's that feel like – knowing that your parents don't want you?"
Tess knew the answer.

"Just like shit. Like I'm trapped in what they think of me. I'm
always going to be."

"Be trapped."

"Yeah."

"And I bet you always felt that way?"

"True."

Obvious, I know, but the reality was that my bottom lip suddenly
had a Mexican jumping bean in it, and pictures of first my brother,
then Dad and Mom, and finally my little sister flashed through my
imagination. But not in a good way – it was them hating me, them
yelling. Wishing I was away. Or not theirs. Walking in the rain, after
dark, wishing there was somewhere better than a bomb shelter to go.
Not wanting to go home, where I was so unwanted. So much regret
for everything. Guilt. It'd been better if I'd died. I'd never "share" those
thoughts here, I thought with conscious malice.

"How does it feel?"

"Yeah, we're beyond having to pull this out of you, right?"

"You're going to get so much from the Brothers. I can't wait to have
you experience that."

"I don't think you've got any idea of the pain you're really in, kid.
Or the way you're reacting to the pain in your life."

"I wonder who did such a number on you, kid."

Pause.

Are we done now?

Sometimes the indictment branched off to someone else, but this
time, it stuck around like a stomach ache.

"What did you do to get sent here? I mean, I know some of it, but you're really evasive, and guarded about it." Terrance talking.

"Um. I ran away. Failed at school. Bad fighting at home. Started using a little, you know." I felt responsible for my wording and was practicing at what the program calls being accountable with my words, but it wasn't enough.

People jumped right back in, breaking the feelings I was going for.

"You're not even looking!"

"Totally disconnected from your emotions right now!"

"Total denial. That's a choice. You don't even know what you are, do you?"

"...thinks his shit doesn't stink."

"Who's Zack really, anyway? Without the reactions and insecurities! Without your defense mechanisms." Tess waved her skinny wrist with annoyance, at having to point out the obvious.

"Or without the games!"

Then Prescott's conspicuous counselor concern filled the briefest of pauses: "What's coming up right now? YES! THAT FEELING! That's the one. Oooh! Look at that look. Think you can intimidate people with looks like that?"

Prescott's interpretations of my face and flip-flop of emotions took me off kilter.

"I'm not trying to look like that! I'm just looking back."

I felt like perhaps I was missing the boat. My mind searched for a way to make people see how hard I was trying to look open, and honest. Being honest meant identifying my feelings, and reducing my emotions down to anger, sadness, hurt; feeling alone, trapped, or loved. Hoping to impress the group with emotional content that was deeper than I could presently communicate, I wanted to go below the surface of my reactions to my emotions, the way respected older kids did.

Mariah got louder. "How much time are you going to waste? I gotta tell you, I went through my Brothers dirty – I'm not saying you are dirty, but you probably are. The feeling that I had sabotaged myself is exactly what I think – I KNOW – YOU ARE DOING. DON'T SABOTAGE THIS EXPERIENCE FOR YOURSELF."

"Yeah. Like even today! Dude, I know what you're dealing with. I know the feeling that you can't trust anyone yet, you want to, but you don't have the understanding of what you do to push people away. The Brothers will be great for you."

Prescott jumped in. "So right on, what Griffin's saying! And listen to everyone here. These people, even if you can't believe it yet, they fucking care about you! Especially Mariah! But you can't even feel that!"

"It's no wonder you've become so isolated and that you're getting that kind of feedback."

Terrance wound up analytically with, "Yeah dude. I mean, I know we're kind of friends, but you do play the outside a lot, so my question for you is, 'How many friends do you even have here?'"

"Great question, Terry!" Prescott actually clapped three times to show his approval.

That was a hard question to answer. Had they asked me at another moment of time, I could have answered differently, naming Ernesto and acquaintances from Papoose, or some of the very people now asking me the question. Just hours before, I felt generous to myself in this very regard, on my way into the rap room. Here on the spot, and after these indictments from people I was sure were my friends, I couldn't name a single person.

"Nobody, I guess," I declared humbly.

This got me a rub on the back from Tess, but I was back to thinking about home. Home when I was young, how much I loved, how empty I felt in the house, the world where Mom's typewriter begged to snap and spit ink, the world where I waited for Dad to finish work.

"That's the sad fucking truth, isn't it? Let's let you sit in that a while."

Prescott's decision to let me stew had a new and strange impact on me – I wanted to impress him even more than Tess now, and would for a good portion of the next year work to deliver to him whatever I thought he wanted of me.

The room began its bustle again, leaving me in emotional purgatory. Walter had moved next to me for the sole purpose of bringing the spotlight back to Mariah.

Verbal warfare in the Papoose room down the hall of the Kootenai Lodge jutted into my thoughts during the time in between indictments, or during pauses when someone started to emote. Part of me struggled still to believe that raps were good.

Watching, hearing kids relive molestations and beatings, makes me privy to people's most intimate thoughts. Especially about themselves. This knowledge is beneficial, so pay attention.

Staring into my own secret issues and turning them into words for the program is a process I should trust.

But I can't yet, and I'm not sure I believe in it either.

Darlayne's voice traveled from Papoose and made the pine walls in our room shudder. Sol's photo was probably rattling against the wall next door. And, from Warrior headquarters on the other side, my left ear could detect the familiar voices of two girls in Hedwig's rap, weeping and shrieking.

A rap room sandwich.

In our Brave room, the substance of my sandwich, only a few moments had rolled by, but something was happening with Mariah, and it was happening fast, too fast to make sense of it. Seated next to me, Tess took aim at Mariah on her boxy black chair across the circle.

"Who's not using their struggle? Who is going to be that girl with the *reputation* for the rest of your life? No? Well, GIVE IT A VOICE! What's your Thinking saying, RIGHT NOW? Just surrender and give it a fucking voice, Mariah!"

Her second round of indictments began. Mariah's demeanor, coming into the room, had first been passive and welcoming, but now she appeared frantic and desperate.

Through tears, Mariah began to rock in her chair as if choking, the way her cheeks and eyes were puffing out. "I know. I KNOW! I know. I know. I guess I don't know what else you want me to do. I mean I've been talking the whole fucking rap!"

"And everybody in here can see that you're about to FUCKING BURST! Right everybody? Look at that NIGHTMARE! Who's been USED? Who's BEEN LEFT? WHO'S BEEN HURT BY EVERY-ONE?...Look at that 'GIRL WITH THE REPUTATION!'"

Walter, the Brave staff, got up and limped across the circle, to exchange seats with me so he could sit next to my big sister. In a way that could happen only in raps and propheets at CEDU schools, they were including me in Mariah's work.

43

"Come on Mariah, point your finger at him, Honey. He's right here. You know what to do."

Walter began pointing at me from across the circle. Following his example, Mariah lifted a shaking finger halfheartedly as Walter kept pressing.

"You know what I'm talking about. Let me hear it! Put him in this room and just FUCKING TELL HIM! I was with you in the I Want To Live and I know what you worked with! How HARD YOU CAN FIGHT! I'm not going to WIPE YOUR ASS in here! You want to be A DOORMAT the rest of your life? YEAH? And who's RUNNING THE SHOW RIGHT NOW? THAT'S THE GIRL WITH THE REPUTATION? He's sitting right across from you! Now you CHOOSE. What are you going to choose, Mariah? LIFE? TO FIGHT? Or…? That's it."

Mariah had twisted up into herself, wrapped her legs around those of the black chair, and disappeared into her sweatshirt. Walter switched chairs with Prescott, who took a turn counseling Mariah. "You know what I think? I think you're at the brink, but you aren't using your values. Where's that FUCKING COURAGE? You're there but you won't WORK FOR IT WHEN IT COUNTS! LIKE RIGHT NOW! FIGHT FOR IT?! WHY DOESN'T MARIAH FIGHT FOR HER FUCKING LIFE?"

Prescott went silent. The frenzy and volume in the room ebbed as the last indictments trailed off.

"…TRUE WHEN YOU'RE only going half way into those feelings!"

"…happened when you were young and had to do that to feel loved. But NOT HERE, Honey."

There had been little mercy for my feelings when the rap moved on so suddenly, and now there was even less quarter being shown to Mariah. By physicalizing this retraction into her sweatshirt, she was hiding from her work. By leading the rap in a different direction than Prescott wanted it, she'd disappointed us.

For being friends with a loner little druggie like me.

I prayed for an asteroid to smash into the rap circle. In the beginning, I didn't believe everything the group said to Mariah, but if the staff and people who knew her better insisted for an hour that she wasn't using her program tools to alleviate the massive tension that stunk up the room, the negative feedback must have merit. That is, we should feel ashamed of her. It hadn't been taught to me yet how to be ashamed *for her – and with her.* Because of the manufactured pressure though, I acted out of instinct.

"Please." I offered, the word slipping out almost without my permission.

Prescott Freshwater, the bowtie-wearing Brave family head, was becoming a patriarch figure to me and my PG. His sinister expression, over that stupid handlebar mustache, had been giving me the eyeball around campus ever since my move-in after splitting and Survival.

"You don't want to see Mariah in pain, Bonnie? Is that right?" Prescott's voice noodled me for a response.

How does he know that I dislike being called by my last name?

I nodded. We locked eyes. He kept talking to me as if his words in this rap were the most important things said in galactic history. I weighed them for truth.

"She always brings this on herself, if you CARED ABOUT HER PAIN! Mariah has SOLD OUT TO HER PAIN, she's sucked cock for cocaine…What'dya think about that?"

"If you say so."

"Well, she has."

"OK, I'd say 'we heard that already.'"

"You're probably just like the fucking scumbag that made her do it? Well, you'll learn that the work Mariah here is doing is important, but I suppose a little shit-bag druggie like you wouldn't know that. You like cocaine, son?"

I wasn't sure how I'd gotten sucked into this exchange. It was my intent to get Prescott to like me, not to be seen as standing up to him in any way. Had I successfully suspended the continuation of Mariah's pain by my plea for mercy, or was the rap flipping on me again?

Right. I'm negative here even though I'm doing the "right" thing.

Even though I'd not been introduced to the tools that explained how or why negative tapes, or Thinking, were playing in my head, I was already struggling to counter them.

45

Am I good or bad? Instead of answering the question for myself, as I may ordinarily have done from time to time in life before Idaho, from now on I was dependent on what the people in the world I lived in thought of me.

Just like at home, but the wrong here is right.

I watched Prescott's focus switch between Mariah and me. This moment wasn't about me; it was about Mariah. Prescott and Tess made sure I knew that. After a look from Prescott, Walter started up again. I was still sitting across from Mariah.

"Who're you fighting for? Don't just project on him, Mariah, MAKE IT REAL! Make it count for something. You can trust Zack to be here for you...LET HIM KNOW!"

Mariah lifted her face out of her lap. No longer the pretty face that I'd gotten to know over the weeks, it was the face of anguish. The imperial pain imprinted on Mariah's face reminded me of a mask from an ancient Greek tragedy. Her eyes had become black, the orbits sunk inside unnatural wrinkles. Eruption of some variety was clearly imminent. The rest of the kids were locked into place in their black stackable chairs.

Mariah locked a quivering finger directly at me! When her head rose up from muttering at the floor, Mariah's face exploded in salty tears and mucus as she screamed an unintelligible, rising, crescendo of a shriek in my direction that lasted fifteen seconds. Tears squirted from her reddening cheeks and she stabbed and grabbed the air between us with shaky hands.

"YOU MADE ME SUCK YOUR COCK! I HATE YOU, DUMB COKEHEAD MOTHER FUCKERRRRRRRRR! WHYYYY! I TRUSTED YOU, I NEEDED YOU."

Fresh tears drew her head back down. She yanked the scrunchie out of her hair, which piled up in a puddle of snot and tears at her feet.

"Who are you talking to?" Prescott asked, as a concerned doctor would.

"I don't know. I guess – Alan. FUCKING ALAN."

"Right. Tell the rap who's Alan?"

"He was my boyfriend before I came here."

"Yeah. What's going on? Where are you, now?"

"In his car. I want to be sick FUCK FUUUUUUCK!" Mariah seemed to retch and fight the impulse to vomit. She had to pause to swallow several times, but only got a moment to breathe.

"What are you going to do? Are you gonna let your struggle consume you? You're going to FIGHT. TELL HIM UNTIL HE LISTENS. THAT'S IT!"

"I fucking HATE YOU! STOP TOUCHING ME, YOU DON'T LOVE ME, YOU'RE NOT HERE FOR ME. YOU DON'T EVEN FUCKING WAAAAAAANT MEEEEE!" Mariah thrashed in her chair and her voice trailed off into a long shaky whimpering sob of finality.

"You're still struggling with being wanted, aren't you? Yeah. Being loved? Yeah. Who'd that little girl really want those nights in the car?"

"My Daddy."

"That's right!" *Pause.* "How's it make you feel?"

"Broken."

"Are you broken?"

"NO!"

"That's right! Say that again!"

"I'm NOT FUCKING BROKEN. I'm not believing it as I FUCKING SAY IT! I AM BROKEN! I AM A WORTHLESS FUCKING DO-OOOOORRRRMAAAAAT!" Mariah crumbled almost onto the floor. Her nose dropped snot.

The impassioned part of me faded away. I looked less for reasons to question the methods. The treatment specialists, our rap facilitators, had tools and ways to talk to us that no shrinks, parents, or any other authority at home would ever use. Nobody had ever bothered to make us open up the way propheets and raps could. Prescott and Tess were pros.

"That's because you're not ready to say goodbye yet! Mariah, you gotta fucking FIGHT YOUR THINKING! When are you just going to surrender to being alone? You know who this is really about!"

Walter and Tess had been active and Walter seemed to have become a different entity than the junior staff I had pegged him for. He layered more and more personal issues on my big sister.

47

"You have the fucking tools to get through what you are feeling right now! What's that say about YOU? And yet you're choosing to be THE FUCKING DOORMAT! IT'S FUCKING DISGUSTING! You disgust me."

Walter rounded out his finale with cruelty. I could feel my mind spilling over – all my attention was shot. I tried to blot out the voices in the building, and turn them into mumbles like the adults in *Charlie Brown*. Part of my focus left the room when my eyes landed again on the relief map on the wall. My brain finally floated off into China or Madagascar; any distraction became a salvation. Zack's mind's sanctuary.

†

The extreme toughness of love also presents another major problem: its ideology is essentially antisocial. The message presented by every tough love program in this book is that hurting others "helps" them, and that empathy and sympathy are weaknesses.

—Maia Szalavitz, *Help at Any Cost: How the Troubled Teen Industry Cons Parents and Hurts Kids*, Riverhead Books, 2006, p 255

†

PTSD is not a normal consequence of adolescent misbehavior. it does not occur in the absence of trauma, and few middle-class kids ever experience anything as likely to cause sustained trauma (aside from child abuse) as these programs are, even in the course of genuine addiction. The atmosphere in the programs – in which emotional attacks are unrelenting, privacy is nonexistent, sleep and food deprivation are common, and the person has little if any control over his environment – is exactly the type that research has found most likely to produce PTSD.

[T]he more researchers learn, in fact, the greater the evidence becomes that being put in any kind of situation of total powerlessness for a significant

48

length of time has the capacity to produce lasting damage to the brain's stress system, especially when it happens to a young person.

—Maia Szalavitz, *Help at Any Cost: How the Troubled Teen Industry Cons Parents and Hurts Kids*, Riverhead Books, 2006, p 249

✝

When my brain again shifted back into the goings on in our rap circle, Mariah still hadn't found the tools Walter and Prescott had wanted her to use, and she hadn't regained her composure. She was still covering her face and shaking her head, hiding her internal thoughts from the room. She must be lost in her Thinking, I concluded.

Prescott and Tess would leave her this way at the end of the afternoon.

Why would they do that? Is she going to stay this freaked out for her last six months here? Or are they setting her up for a successful Summit? Whatever that means.

Noise from other rap rooms filled in the pauses in ours.

"Well, we've got some more time left. Oh, yeah, I remember. Zack, didn't you also want to say something to Jasper? He's your dorm support, isn't that right?"

I cleared my throat. "Dorm head."

"Wait a minute!" Tess's voice went up a notch. "Jasper. Look at me. You're a dorm head? When did that happen? Well, if I didn't know you know better, I'd bet it's the messiest dorm on the campus. This explains why you're still in Friday raps with Mariah, though, doesn't it? Dorm head – OK...How's that going?"

"OK, I guess."

"I'm going to check with George and tell him to make positive your dorm is tight, so don't bullshit me. You know I'll find out."

Tess decided to bring me back into the indictment, turning to me with a wide genuine smile.

"Zack, do you like living with Jasper?"

Mariah still sobbed alone while Prescott watched the room like a tennis judge. He absorbed information about each of us while his rap went the final hour.

"He's OK. I mean after Andre got kicked out, he was being kind of a dick."

"That was your dorm? I FUCKING TRUSTED YOU!" Tess roared. "You're supposed to be looking out for my Papooses and instead they're sleeping where a fucking sex contract is taking place! That's your fucking fault, kiddo. That fucking PISSES ME OFF! There's no way I'm letting George keep you in charge down there with Zack. Zack, come sit over here. That's it. I want to hear everything that goes on in La Mancha. That's why I gave you your ups and downs. Did you know about Andre and Geordi? Did you know about the things that were going on down in La Mancha that made it okay for them to do that?" She was referring to a secret homosexual liaison that had been uncovered a few months before, but had had lasting implications for all of us.

A blank-faced boy from Brave piped in. "Yeah. That was fucked up. There were definitely things that made that OK in La Mancha."

"I want to hear more about that dorm! Zack, you have the forum. Really tell Jasper something, get it off your chest, because it's there, I can see it."

"Yeah. I guess. Well, OK. I mean he pissed me off when we were walking up the other day, and made me tuck in my shirt even though we weren't even inside."

"Well, don't tell me about it, that's why we're in the fucking rap! Right? We're in this room to do this. Don't waste our time today; Jasper won't hate you. 'The harder the truth to tell, the truer the friend to tell it'...And words can't hurt, remember? We've got to use the Truth propheet every day we walk around here. So TELL HIM!"

"Alright, dude..." I started.

Tess jumped on it. "Who are you talking to? Be accountable. Use his name. This is for you."

"Jasper. Jasper, we weren't even up the porch yet, dude. What the fuck? Why'd you pull me up, asshole? Are you really that insecure about your status as an older student, or whatever, that you need to act like it matters? You're not Siddhartha, OK! That was a needsy pull-up."

I could tell I had the support of the rap, because people were moving into the seats on my side of the circle. Tess and Prescott sicced the rap on my dorm head and it was evident that Tess wanted action from me before the end of the day. During my asides with Tess, other voices filled in gaps that kept Jasper on the hot seat. It was always like that in raps. Whoever got loudest usually took the floor.

"Uh-hunh," said Tess. "And how did that make you feel?"

"It was needsy. I already have my fucking ups and downs privilege anyway. I was just keeping you company because you said you were reaching out to me, that you'd been feeling lonesome or whatever – so, I don't fucking care."

"Now THAT'S RIGHT!" Walter boomed at me.

"And HOW does it make you feel to get pulled up by a needsy older student, Mister Bonnie? Be a friend to Jasper and let him know how you really feel around him."

To my knowledge I was the only student Tess called "Mister." Tess used the term affectionately between us. I felt encouraged at the pace of the rap, the din from voices in this room and others down the hall, and of course, the hope to please Tess enough to end my girl-bans and WDs.

"Um, pissed. I guess."

"Well then, BE pissed, Zack, TELL him. It's OK to get this out. Come on, don't make me and Prescott wipe your ass, here. He's a big boy, and words can only hurt if he makes that choice to let them." That was, of course, total bullshit. Some words could hurt like hell. But I knew what was what, and even though I hate to admit it, I let Jasper have it a notch higher on my fire.

"It pissed me off, dude, I hate living with him. He's a dickhead! Living with you sort of sucks because you're always, like, right fucking there telling me to space the closets, telling me to get out of the shower, or scrub the garbage can again. Well!? I did it, didn't I? So don't keep fucking with me!"

He started to retort, "But you didn't...You're fucking...like all hiding behind the violence Agreement! I'm not that bad, I just want you all to LIKE ME! AND I'M STRUGGLING BEING ACCOUNTABLE...," but nobody was paying attention to him. All eyes were on the exchange between Tess and me, getting with the program.

I was slowly learning here that not only could I channel my angry feelings – at being here, at Mom and Dad for sending me here and creating the situation that was Survival, and the mixed-up feelings I felt about myself – but I was supposed to make an important mental connection. I was supposed to learn another thing that didn't exist in "the real world" – that what I *feel* is more important than what I *say*. This is another thing that Tess and other staff meant when they said that words can't hurt.

"Sorry, I didn't mean to hide behind the Agreement before or whatever you said, ASSHOLE! But you shouldn't be SO FUCKING NEEDSY, JUST BECAUSE YOU'RE LONELY! TELLING ME TO TUCK IN MY FUCKING SHIRT, you are a NEEDSY ASSHOLE!"

My voice boomed into the room at level six of a possible ten. The only time I ever had reached an enraged "ten" was yelling with my parents before I first came to this loony bin. The voices of Mariah, Terrance, and the rest of the kids supporting me told me, even though I felt weird, that I was doing "it" right – I was leading an indictment and tapping into my personal anger, the way they wanted.

This is what my parents are paying for; these are the lessons I'm going to be exploring in the upcoming Brothers Keeper propheet.

Even though I wasn't really angry with Jasper – I didn't feel one way or the other about the guy – the simple fact that I had nothing of substance to say to him, itself, became a factor! It was his fault he felt lonesome, and because of my bans, I could relate personally to that struggle. It started making me angry just looking at him. Since Tess kept going, "Yeah," or, "That's right, tell him, good! Is he listening to you? Nope, he isn't listening to you! Go on!" I continued until a surge of anger rattled in my stomach and I felt tears well up in my eyes. I stopped then.

I felt sick. I was shaking a saber for no real reason. If I let go I could totally flip out. I had only ever displayed that anger at home after fights with Mom and Dad. I wasn't going to punch a wall here, or leap out of my seat, with violence, onto Jasper's face. But that's why I went silent. It didn't feel good. Approaching the degree of anger at Jasper that Tess wanted me to charge into reminded me of when I was eight or nine, and skirted too close to a bonfire and was burned at Camp Minnehaha, or fist-fights with my brother growing up. Now I was supposed to tap into and sustain that rage on command.

"See what it is you're feeling right now? It doesn't FEEL GOOD, DOES IT? That's what YOU WALK AROUND WITH EVERY DAY, MISTER! DON'T FUCKING LAUGH BECAUSE IT'S TRUE ISN'T IT, KIDDO? AND ONE OF THESE DAYS YOU'RE GOING TO HAVE TO TAKE A GOOD LOOK AT THAT FUCKING ANGER INSIDE OF YOU! NOW, THAT'S THE GODDAMN WORK! TAKE A GOOD LOOK."

Tess had teared up, showing me how easy it was to let it out. Tess could scream it out, I didn't yet know how to purge like that.

Tess wanted me to obey that little inclination. She wanted me to have a complete unadulterated explosion.

So far, being brought to the brink of my own fury in Idaho – once when I stood up to Darlayne before splitting, and once with Will Bender on Survival – had almost gotten me starved to death, so I wasn't exactly sure yet what Tess was playing at. I wanted to trust her, to trust the process here, to believe she could counsel or facilitate that anger out of me forever, but I couldn't even trust myself when the anger started to come up.

I already knew that anger was a powerful thing, and if I believed the program, my anger had to be addressed at Rocky Mountain Academy in Idaho – the only place equipped to handle it. Even if they did help manufacture it, Prescott, Tess, and the rest of the staff knew how we felt, and how to focus our anger at being in Idaho was a key lesson in our CEDU development.

Physical escape ceased to be worth pondering long ago, so I was half in Zaire on the relief map, and half stuck with the choice to submerge in the volcanic muck inside of me. Tone, words, and volume of raps had stopped bothering me so much. The silences between loud shrieks of indictments became comfortable, perhaps even predictable, while we followed staff suggestions to investigate our behavior, or our reactions, and say or do what we thought would impress them. Within the therapy of raps, the indictments all became deserved and the staff had the power and oversight of predetermination.

As the group finished taking Jasper apart, and Tess stopped nipping into my psyche, I tried to put it together. Those feelings of anger I'd brought forth indicting Jasper – that state of getting frenzied up inside – how that was beneficial to me? Perhaps I was beginning to understand now how making rap indictments between us all kept the campus "safer," in the program.

I wasn't feeling safer and kept wondering if Tess or Prescott would tell me how to stop feeling this rage. I tried to hide my shaking hands – they were still upset. A feeling like having an angry wasp trapped in my stomach was still there. A strange thought occurred to me.

I wish there'd been a little more time. Tess was right. I'm a wuss.

I should have looked at why I felt like this now. It was inevitable that I'd express this anger eventually.

I should have looked closer at this issue today. I'm a coward for dreading and not wanting to do more introspection.

In the three or four years before RMA, fights at my house were commonplace. Seldom physical, but vengefully verbal, these everyday fights were the talk of the other parents in my neighborhood, and all of my school tutors, and anyone else who witnessed it happening between Mom and Dad and me. Nothing could stop these fights from happening. Dad's morning rants at me finally ceased only when he brought me here, and my leave of absence from home had remedied all.

I was the anger.

At some point when I was younger, it seemed like Dad stopped being my only remaining ally at home.

I tried to resist feeling what came out of my brain and mouth in the rap that day, like I'd done the rest of my days, but it wasn't possible; each of us here had stuffed a primal anger deep down, and we were expected to uncage, unharness, and let it surge at RMA. I had to protect parts of my brain that couldn't compute this: now it was time for those parts to retire or die.

We all knew the rap was finishing up when Tess began the cooling-off period. She said, gently, "Zack, the suit's too big for you now, but you're going to grow into it nicely."

In other words, fake it till you make it; look as though you're a good, pro-program kid.

Tess closed out the rap with a quiet word to Mariah. "I know it doesn't feel like it now, Mariah, but this is exactly how you're supposed to be feeling, going into your final workshop. The Summit is going to reveal the opposite of whatever you're feeling now. You know that, don't you, honey? It's important for you to feel like there's no way out. We have to explore the dis-eases in us before we can create the win-win within us."

While I was spacing out, Jasper had taken up the last few minutes of the rap to talk about how he was struggling to balance his responsibilities. Like me, he hated school, but, unlike me, he had full-time classes these days. He was fearful about leaving and rejoining the real world because of how much he hated and struggled with academics. He didn't go into any hysterics, just a couple of tissues at the end to blow out some loose drips. The last minutes were subdued, allowing the anger inside of me to dissipate. It was a total surprise, when to end the main theater of that rap, Jasper addressed me:

"Well, Zack thanks for letting me know how you felt, seriously. And Tess, I know the dorm isn't perfect, it's just really hard for me to be doing full-time classes again. My flags are flying, and I'm going to work with my feelings. Would it be OK to make an appointment for a DMT? Zack, I just really appreciate you opening up to me with your feedback, and I know you don't really think I'm an asshole."

DMT, short for Deep Meaningful Talk, was a private confessional between two people. After dinner in the house, DMTs were what kids did together. Everybody smooshed around the pit by the huge stone fireplace, and shared stories from their past – all the bad things they had done, the family problems, school problems, run-ins with the law, tribulations of being here – all that. Jasper's requesting an appointment for a DMT with me was not exactly what I would have expected to hear from him, but that was the game here; we were supposed to be closer now that I'd cleared up the typical-seeming dorm grievances.

Prescott spoke for me. "That's a great idea. Jasper, take Zack under your wing, share your story with him, OK? Let's close the raps with some hugs. Who's going to be in charge of making things tight in here?"

"Thank you, Jasper. Zack, you help him out? You really are right where you need to be going into the Brothers and Brave." Tess closed in for a back-rubby, swaying hug. "I'm impressed, Mr. Bonnie. This has been a good rap for you. Get together with Griff and Terrance this weekend too."

You are? It has? I will.

That rap outlasted the daylight. It made sense that they got us used to waking up so early since it got dark at 4 PM this time of year. Jasper, more dejectedly than he'd let on at the end of the rap, walked with me to the dorm to wash and change for dinner.

"By Santa's Workshop it will be dark at three. Shit, it will stay dark until first light too. You'll see. That sucks. But sometimes you can see the northern lights, which is fresh!"

For Friday night, the biweekly schedule mandated Idaho State potatoes, loaded with scallions, tomatoes, luxurious pre-grated cheese, and bacon bits. At smoosh time with Jasper, we skipped around parts of our stories for each other. Neither of us said much about that day's rap. We both seemed to be patching up our wounds during the last light. Our hugs when it was over felt almost ordinary.

Another night at RMA – clumping atop the tundra to the dorm, slamming the snow and ice off boots before removing them and the rest of my clothes, slipping under the comforter in my bunk bed.

Each kid on the campus indeed has a role to play. Much of our destinies were already etched out, and had been since Papoose family. Probably before.

After that Friday rap, my attraction or desire for Mariah was gone.

I'd been in enough raps to know that all Mariah needed to do was go just a little deeper into her anguish. How had she missed a cue? Like me realizing that Tess was showing me something important about my anger, Mariah must have known what Prescott was asking of her. Even though I didn't know what that "something" was that Mariah should have done, I hated her for not getting there today – and for making me witness her mistreatment and be part of the indictments that had affected her.

I hadn't yet experienced for myself Mariah's embodied self-flagellation. I didn't yet understand the extremes the program would go to, to impress on us the importance of the tools. It would be more than a year later, on my full-time, when I came to understand the program's need to manipulate everything – my feelings and even my thoughts.

SEVEN

They didn't just automatically move you up to Brave. As the rest of my PG had already done, I wrote up an application folder, a retrospective of our time in Papoose, to demonstrate my program absorption rate. I was prepared for the next step in my ascent through the RMA / CEDU system.

My application to the Brave Family was a ploy on my part to continue to look good. Although I didn't yet understand this, it also signaled my potential to get with the program – eventually. Though still a runt, I wasn't part of the lowest caste anymore. There were five months' worth of new kids. I carefully completed every prescribed section before they let me into Prescott Freshwater's Brave family. My thesis on Papoose follows:

✝

In the Brothers Keeper propheet I learned about how I hurt people and what I do when I get hurt. I now know how I push people away especially when I need them the most.

The most important thing I learned in there was how I put myself on the outside. And then when I find myself on the inside I sabotage it or dislike it and put myself on the opposite side.

I turn my back on people all the time and I wish I knew a long time ago how much I need friends. I also realize now that it is hard but it's okay to trust a friend.

—Author, [Brave] application, from "the Brothers Propheet" page

✝

Something in raps that has changed 100% is my righteousness. I used to fight and bitch and moan, argue and disagree to everything. I have learned to listen and absorb everything that is in touch.

Raps help me to slow down and look at myself which is something I've never done. Raps enabled me to help others while I helped myself. I had many chances to take care of my feelings but I chose not to until recently.

The hardest thing in raps for me was listening to what people had to say without getting righteous. Another thing that was hard for me was letting people know who I am and opening up. In raps, I could share with people safely. How I felt about them. My biggest goal with raps was learning to use them. It's good when friends get honest with each other, even if it hurts, because it builds an honest relationship. Most of my relationships were built in raps. I realize I'm not nearly as numb to my feelings as I was at first. I know I have a long way to go but I'm willing to do the work.

—Author, [Brave] application, from the "Raps" page

Mortensen Math for me was not easy. I had a tough time telling myself to get back to work. A reason for this is when I didn't understand something right off the bat I gave up and said there was no point to it. I do feel very stupid in math and as an excuse I say it is because the last grade I completed was the seventh. But all in all I didn't like it very much.

I was, at times, a pain in class, but more often I was good and got a lot of work done.

I started with the attitude that it would be easy and I could mess around. I leave with the attitude that I had better get myself in gear.

—Author, [Brave] application, from the "Math" page

60

I liked writing class a whole lot. I liked going into
class sitting down and writing in almost complete
silence where I can write about my past present,
future, stories, and songs. I liked that I could, if I was
stuck, simply write funny little mindstorming and
it might give us an idea. My mother is a writer and
one of my dreams is to be a poet so I will ask to be
exposed to some techniques. Another thing I like is it
is the only time I get to write.

—Author, [Brave] application, from the "Writing
Class" page

✝

Also, I had to compose an approved (meaning monitored and
censored) letter to my mom, which Prescott made me rewrite a few
times, plus a mandatory writing assignment on what I had learned in
the Truth propheet.

"But Prescott, I did write about the Truth. I just didn't remember
it so well because of Survival, which intervened." My explanation was
sound. This unknowingly set me up for two things.

"Well, I did notice that you didn't put your dooger card in there.
Didn't that experience mean anything to you? How about you make a
separate evaluation of what you learned on Survival that can contribute
to supporting both the work, and your family here? And the warm-up
for the Truth propheet is Friday. You've been teaching chess to that kid
from Memphis, right? Get him ready? What's his name?"

"Bart. Yeah, I'll spend time with him."

Really, Prescott's assignment was a feebly disguised attempt to
check if I was still apologetic for splitting; to investigate whether I still
thought about escaping the program, and to see whether I could now
be seen as some kind of leader or eventual role model to the PGs below
mine. He was setting me up to contribute to being a big brother to
Bart.

✝

Wilderness Survival was by far the hardest thing
I've ever done in my life. [...] The reason I went back

61

to a different group was because I was not accepting nearly as much responsibility for myself as I should have been. When I found out I was on my way to [S]olo I was more proud of myself than I ever have been in my life. Solo for me was wonderful. I learned that if I put my mind to doing something I can do anything. Coming back to the school I realized how much I had changed for the better. I would love to do survival again under different conditions. I feel much better knowing I did it by myself.

—Author, [Brave] application, from the "Survival" page

†

In Brave, under Prescott's family leadership, we'd be cutting down trees and doing daily maintenance, shoveling snow off the campus's various parking areas, then salting the paths between buildings, as needed. I could expect to maintain the campus with Brave for about six months, until I moved up to work at the farm with Warrior.

Being part of a team in charge of thinning the forest and bringing wood to the Papoose wood corral gave us all a feeling of accomplishment. In the dead of winter, I'd be allowed to walk around the main campus alone, even though the Brothers taught me that I oughtn't, or oughtn't want to.

†

Dear Mom and Dad,

[...] After raps. For the very first time I took care of my Feelings. I'm so proud of myself. I'm really looking forward to visits. I really don't know what to write about....

—Letter from author to parents, Nov 1988

PART ONE RESOURCES

Today's Sunday and I still have to finish telling
[Bart Lennerton & Tim Chalmers] my story. I might
not make sense because I just got out of bed. [...]
I hate my dorm head so much his name is [Jasper
Browning]. He pisses me off so fucking much ASS
HOLE FUCKER. [...] I am a different person than when
I last wrote in sept. and august. I am much more will-
ing to try new things.

—Author journal entry

Dear Zack, I'm sorry if I don't sound excited when I
answer the phone. I'm just so surprised I don't know
what to say. I love you and I'm sorry if I haven't been a
very good brother. When you get home I want for us
to be closer. After all, you are the only brother I'll ever
have.

I don't know whether you can write me back, or
even if you can read this! Tell me what your day is
like.... - your brother

—Letter from author's brother, 10 December 1988

Dear Zack

[Your brother] wrote you a letter, but I don't know
if you can receive it. Will you find out? I think [he] feels
bad that you two didn't get to talk when you called.
He feels bad because he called us to the phone right
away and he worries that YOU MIGHT THINK that he
didn't want to talk to you, BUT HE DID WANT TO TALK
TO YOU, and later he felt terrible. Daddy and I might
have impressed the RMA rules on [him] too forcefully,

63

and he was concerned that he'd be doing something which was against the rules. The fact is, following the rules is probably one of the most important things a person will ever learn. I'm sorry it's been hard for you, but everyone who loves you (your brother included) wants you to learn this!!!!!!

—Letter from author's mother, 10 December 1988

†

Charles E. Dederich...was the recovered alcoholic who founded the legendary drug program Synanon, where junkies rehabbed on the California beach; for a time, Mel Wasserman was associated with Synanon in a sponsorship capacity.

[...] Mel Wasserman replies that, in addition to Synanon techniques, he also used his own experiences in conventional therapy to mold his program. He also says that he was not a fan of Dederich, whose sessions could get brutal and assaultive. He was aiming for something warmer: "There was a lot of conflict between me and some of the people I hired from Synanon. They wanted to redo Synanon. I didn't want a place where we had so much power that people would pee in their pants when you walked by. Synanon was fear-based. Our work was feeling-based."

—Nina Burleigh, "Death of a Salesman," *Details* magazine, 1 Oct 2000, interviewing Mel Wasserman (founder of CEDU)
http://www.ninaburleigh.com/journalism/death-of-a-salesman.html

†

[...] Mel was an imposing figure and the imprint of his ideas and philosophy of education was in evidence everywhere in the cultural environment of CEDU. The story of Mel and his wife Brigitte having started CEDU in their home in Palm Springs, California in 1967 was already a legend in the school's history.

[...] Long before the world would become familiar with the phrase "the child within", Mel was creating an education whose core was dedicated to, in his words, "the liberation of the child within" all of us. Three decades before the term "Emotional Quotient" would appear acknowledging the importance of emotions, Mel was pioneering the creation of an educational approach that would address equally the development of the individual's emotional knowledge, as well as one's intellectual capacity, civic participation, and personal responsibility.

[...] The contributions [Mel] and Brigitte made to the hundreds of faculty, staff, and thousands of students, parents, families, and schools cannot be spelled out in these few, wanting, words of tribute.

[...] The impact of Mel Wasserman's revolutionary contribution to education lives on in the lives of the individuals and the schools that bear his imprint. If there was ever a book worthy of writing, it would be "A Golden Age – Mel Wasserman's CEDU Education".

—Dan Earle, "Tribute to Mel Wasserman," *Woodbury Reports News & Views*, May, 2002 Issue #93 (shortly after the death of Wasserman, who founded CEDU and RMA)

†

Organized in 1967, CEDU School is ... continuing to evolve to meet the changing needs of its student population, and to utilize the increasing body of knowledge of how to work with dysfunctional children and families.

What caught my attention most was the explanation of her job by Liz Holmes, the head of CEDU's parent communications. What she told me was, "Parents are not a problem. When parents enroll their child, they have needs only the school can meet."

[...] CEDU is incorporating the latest knowledge of how to work with children with behavioral problems. This attitude starts with the assumption that

65

the parent is not necessarily bad, but needs the help
the school can provide. It is my hope that legislatures
and Health and Welfare Departments will adopt this
philosophy and get themselves out of the philosophy
of the seventies that starts with the assumption that
the parent is the enemy.

—Lon Woodbury, "Schools, Programs, & Visit
Reports," *Woodbury Reports*, June, 1991, (reviewing
his April 1991 visit to RMA's sister school, CEDU, in
Running Springs, California)

✝

Largely because of a quirk of brain development,
adolescents, on average, experience more anxiety
and fear and have a harder time learning how not to
be afraid than either children or adults.

[...] It turns out that the brain circuit for processing
fear — the amygdala — is precocious and develops
way ahead of the prefrontal cortex, the seat of
reasoning and executive control. This means that adolescents have a brain that is wired with an enhanced
capacity for fear and anxiety, but is relatively under-
developed when it comes to calm reasoning.

[...T]he brain's reward center, just like its fear
circuit, matures earlier than the prefrontal cortex.
That reward center drives much of teenagers' risky
behavior. This behavioral paradox also helps explain
why adolescents are particularly prone to injury and
trauma. The top three killers of teenagers are accidents, homicide and suicide.

[...O]nce previously threatening cues or situations
become safe, we have to be able to re-evaluate them
and suppress our learned fear associations. People
with anxiety disorders have trouble doing this and
experience persistent fear in the absence of threat —
better known as anxiety.

—Richard A Friedman, "Why Teenagers Act Crazy,"
New York Times, 29 June 2014 http://www.nytimes.
com/2014/06/29/opinion/sunday/why-teenagers-act-
crazy.html

†

The implications of research on adolescent brain plasticity are intriguing, as they suggest a mechanism that shapes the very health and evolution of societies through time. If the environment can literally shape the way the brain processes social and emotional stimuli, it offers an explanation of why environmental influences during adolescence have a persistent effect on the later life of the individual. The fact that plasticity is heightened during adolescence also suggests that attention to environmental factors during the adolescent years deserves particular attention and investment. This research has potential implications for a human rights perspective. For example, sustained human rights abuses of adolescents, such as verbal, sexual, or physical abuse, might result in detrimental changes in their brain structures (Andersen et al. 2008; Teicher et al. 2004).

—Jacqueline Bhabha, editor, *Human Rights and Adolescence*, University of Pennsylvania Press, 2014 pp 108–109

†

Dear Mom and Dad,

I am listening to Simon and Garfunkel. I have almost forgotten how to write so bear with me.

I went through my Brothers profeet so I couldn't write for a while. The Brothers was the best. It was like I learned how much I wish I were [my sister's] age. … I have been thinking about home a lot and it makes me sad.

I hope we can have a nice dinner [when you visit] or something.

—Letter from author to parents, Nov 1988

Zack Bonnie

PART TWO

Zack Bonnie

EIGHT

The Brothers propheet took place after Thanksgiving. Four weeks later, on the days immediately following Christmas, our parent visits would happen and older kids would be permitted to leave campus for short home visits. Those home visits were scheduled, I learned, to make sure that the kids'd be under parental supervision over New Year's Eve, or July Fourth, depending on their graduation cycle.

†

Dear Parents:

Just a brief note to inform you that your child has recently moved into the [Brave] Family. [Brave] represents a significant stage of development in your child's emotional growth. During the next five to six months, they will be involved in the following experiences.

Work at the farm, centering around the care of our animals. This involves daily chores, feeding and a variety of work projects including fence and corral building, shelter construction and maintenance, gardening and/or specialized animal projects. We emphasize good hard work, careful planning and doing the job right the first time. [...]

Participation in three group sessions per week and the [I Want To Live] ...propheet...

A five to seven day wilderness experience...which implements a variety of outdoor skills....

An academic program that is carefully coordinated with a child's emotional growth. Many of these youngsters have experienced failure in an academic setting. Thus, the focus at this time is exploring perceived limitations and enhancing one's confidence. [...]

71

[Brave] is a time of intently examining old behaviors and "trying on" new ones as your child continues to work towards a healthy identity and self-acceptance. Your child will be presented with the following opportunities during the next few months: [...]

- Writing to people outside the immediate family who have been approved. These people would be aunts, uncles, grandparents and siblings if not previously approved.
- Dorm support positions
- An overnight visit with parent(s) and siblings, based on your child's development and with previous approval. [...]

Your professional Parent Communicator will be calling you by telephone at least once each month to help keep you informed of your child's growth.

We all look forward to working with you and your child. No dream is impossible if we build strong foundations under them.

Best Regards,

[Prescott Freshwater]

Family Head [Brave] Family

—Letter from [Brave] family head to author's parents

The Brothers Keeper propheet snared me in its trap. Its lessons were too intense, twisting everything I thought I knew before Idaho. The web of lessons and the gradual revelations of the sacred tools that night flashed back to me for months – just as they were designed to do.

The impact of moving up after the Brothers into Brave was immediate and undeniable: I'd earned the right to see my parents. They'd be coming to RMA at Christmastime.

Everyone at RMA got to see when I moved up to Brave. We were all in the house for the warm-up before the next Truth propheet. A little like reunions that we'd later have for reviewing each propheet, these warm-up refreshers gave older kids the chance to revisit some of the propheet music and principles, all ciphered enough not to give away any of the surprises that were in store for them that night. I remembered how uncertain-feeling the Truth propheet had been for me, back in the summer before I split. Just hearing the opening strains of Kenny Rogers's *Tell It All* was enough to get my feelings going again.

During the warm-up for Bart's Truth, my PG made cards for our friends, and for all the Papooses getting ready to go into their first propheet. I was assigned to make a card for Bart. This got me thinking about my latest propheet – as intended.

I knew my parents were never going to understand what really happened in the Brothers. I only had short, monitored, phone calls with them until they arrived for their visit in another month at Christmas. I had to sort this out for myself and it was going to take time.

Prescott and George volunteered me and Bart Lennerton, a Papoose from the PG below mine, to stand in the pit.

George warbled with bravado, "Tonight, there's two young men here that deserve a little recognition. First, everyone welcome Zack to the pit! Man, I gotta tell you how much I've seen you growing since you've come back to the campus. He's been bustin' it to get to finally be off of bans and moved to Brave. So, come up here, and bring that knucklehead you're with!"

Making sure my shirt was acceptably tucked, I dragged Bart to George Daughtry in the pit. My job was to look worthy of ascent to Brave. Bart's job was to demonstrate that I had started bonding with a younger brother, and be supported by me and his bigger brothers. This meant we'd make him cards and reserve the next night with him after his Truth, even though we knew he'd be exhausted. Concerned that George thought well of me now, I was thinking ahead to Warrior.

"Yeah. Hi everyone. I'm so glad to share with you all that I'm off of WDs and all bans. I never thought that would happen! Or that I'd be getting to this point. Glad I got to know Tess so well. I wish she was here to see me commit...um, I'm glad I'll get to know Prescott though. He's cool. And George. Oh! No more wood corral! So long, Keith! Finally going to get a chance to work with the maintenance crew. So I'll have the chance to prove my ethic. Is that enough?"

Reclining on a bovine-skinned pillow in the pit, George prompted, "What about vulnerabilities?"

"Yeah, I forgot. So, I need to ask Tim, where are you, Rooster?" Tim reacted to his dooger nickname with a signature bird-caw noise across the house, and stood from his outcropping of bodies. "Tim, when I first got back a few weeks ago I was really glad that you like, still accepted me or whatever. I'm not saying I'm going to be like 'here forever' or anything, not to be sarcastic, but if it weren't for you, I know I wouldn't be standing here now; I thank you for your support, bro. And where's Terrance! Yo, dude! Thanks for your patience and perseverance in teaching me chess. I'm glad I'm getting to know you. Thanks for sticking by me and my bullshit so far. I'm representing to be able to go on a day hike with you tomorrow? You can? Sweet, 12:30 by Big Ben? I'll be there!"

Now I had turned to Bart, and realized that the moment we were having was equally, or even more uncomfortable for him, but there was no stopping now. Since I was a feature of tonight's warm-up and last light, I was sucking up attention from George and Hedwig, the two senior staff on floor duty that night.

"Finally, I am glad that I'm getting to know you, too, Bart. I know you're still making the decision to be here, but like – and I know how hard it is, believe me – I don't love it here yet or anything and I'm not trying to look good. The Truth *is* in you, and you're going to get a lot from tonight. I'll be here when you get out tomorrow, young buck. Oh, and the Truth is: Don't Drink the Water!" I had to say that, in the great RMA tradition.

"Knucklehead." George released his arms from around the two Warrior girls he was with and good-naturedly shoved Bart and me off the sunken stone stage. Since I officially was off of bans with everyone, my PG clapped me on the back, and Crosby Rohrback scruffed my head when I went back to sit down. It was cool to get moved up, seen by George, be off of bans, and I felt all proud and warm and touchy.

Bart became my first little brother, although, like I imagine happens in any big family, the older he got in the program, the less the six months between our PGs felt significant. Bart, whose Truth propheet was going in, was the kid I would have gotten dirty with, the way I had been before. But now I felt I had to help keep Bart at RMA, prevent him from splitting, and pull him up for breaking the petty

Agreements. This way we'd inoculate him against committing the bigger mistakes that could get him kicked out of the program.

When the warm-up ended, and the Papooses were led away to their Truth, the rest of us were weeping and smooshing, sprawled out in a clothed orgy of platonic love. We were awake later than usual, which made the night even more special. Like when the Summit Workshops got out, warm-ups like this one – bizarre hug-fests that I first looked on so judgmentally – had become special events that I welcomed.

A wall of fallen snow greeted us as we approached the house. It was the beginning of December, and a cramped-up sky dumped the white crap down on us. The boys in my PG sometimes skipped breakfast to rid the porches and pathways of the thickening ice-dust, so it wouldn't be there when staff came to work. In the morning darkness, we huffed and pushed snow with our shovels, salting the woodwork behind us.

This could only mean one thing: We'd lose electricity! We'd have days of Sunday sleepy schedules playing board games, or card games like Crazy 8s and Spades. We wouldn't be working for long in this shit!

I was dead wrong. Things went on normally. We acclimated to dark, sub-zero temperatures. We became nonplussed by tundra-like conditions, and layers of specialized clothes meant to protect us from frostbite. Wherever there were work crews, one of the nearby firepits would be smoldering and stinking of wet wool. I loved trampling and burrowing through the incredible endless white heft. It was amusing the way snow caked on my wool sweaters but remained dry. After parent visits, like any good logger, I would have more than one union suit!

My PG had stopped shedding members. Maybe we were the ship-wreck survivors who had made it to the Brave family shore. Along with our new tasks in the day-to-day world, we also pledged to monitor one another's progress now, especially regarding the most recent work of our Brothers Keeper propheet.

My unawareness keeps me alone and unlovable.

†

> Let me tell you about my brothers keeper prophet.
> In it my whole peer group made a circle and I was "on
> the outside" and had to get in any way I could. I got
> really banged up. Then we got with partners and we
> literally pushed each other away and simultaneously
> repeated I don't need you. Then we turned our backs
> on each other. These exercises were really sad. I
> learned a lot about my shit. Gotta go.
>
> —Author journal after Brothers propheet

†

During the long night-day-night of the Brothers, every kid had gotten their own special "lug" – short for luggage. Lugs were a secret tool from the propheet, so only Brave kids and above knew about the issues they figuratively schlepped around.

My "lug" from the Brothers, and memories on why and how I received it, accompanied me everywhere:

My unawareness keeps me alone and unlovable.

I still felt rejected and lonely, which meant I appeared standoffish, distrusting, closed-off, or worse. The bans, though lifted when I moved up, had done their job. Being prevented from speaking or interacting with anyone had reinforced the perception that my pre-ordained personality had to be compensated for with new propheet tools.

I was still reeling from how space and time were intermingling in my brain, and still trying to make sense of my lug. In some ways, like the mind-numbing disclosure circle and the hairball rap, the Brothers resembled the Truth. But the ways in which it differed were notable. After the Brothers, every rap I'd ever have in Idaho would remind me of that night.

Meanwhile, I couldn't shut down my distrust of the program. My shame was my currency. If I spent it right, someday I might be lovable, forgiven, and understood. The program code of conduct said so.

[It's] what Freud called the herd instinct.... We adapt to our environment...but at the same time, there are additional pressures....The key is confession. We all have guilt. We all have things we wish we hadn't done. We all think we hurt our mom, or our brother, or Dad did something wrong to me. So two things that go on:

First is, have the person build a confession. In Mao's world, ... the confessions were never good enough. It was, "Go back, and write more. You haven't confessed enough."

[Then] the message is implied that Dad and Mom were never very good anyway. Denounce your dad, denounce your mom – we're your mom and dad now – and separate from your family. This is your new family.

—Paul Morantz, Esq., author of *Escape: My Life Long War Against Cults*, "Cults, Confession and Mind Control," interviewed by Liam Scheff. Transcribed from http://www.paulmorantz.com

My unawareness keeps me alone and unlovable.

NINE

It was all because of the Brothers.

After things got physical for the first time, on the morning after the long night during the Brothers Keeper propheet, any innocence or bystander feeling I had about the program vanished. Once my body played a part, I felt the importance of the program's messages in a powerful new way. Just as it had taken almost half a year of raps for me to believe in their intrinsic value, at the same pace I now began to see the program as a metaphor for every aspect of life. It was just the way power staff kept insisting: Every friendship, and every family or social relationship I ever had deserved to come under program scrutiny. I thought about that a lot when I saw my Mom and Dad when they visited those two days after Christmas.

I could not stop remembering because I live in my body and brain. I knew the individual Rock Bottom inside each kid, and the lug that had caused it harm. Everyone Brave and up had a lug that they worked with, and everything they said and did was in reaction to their luggage. Now I did too.

†

The morning's sun spilled through cracks in the covered windows. Up until this point, both propheets had been filled with segments, like an ice breaker, followed by thematic discussion of the very visual words of Kahlil Gibran, which led to our disclosure circles, the nightmare rap, and liturgical exercises that had been, so far, practiced from dreaded standing positions that seemed to last forever. Now, that pattern was broken. The Brothers turned a different brand of personal.

Dylan Vandy, my partner for this new experience, sat down cross-legged in front of me, so closely that my knees were against his. My legs enjoyed the prospect of sitting on the floor. As directed, along with everyone else, I stared into my partner's eyes. The music came up louder. Through the gaps in the lyrics Louis Armstrong was singing, I could hear grunting. That was a new noise. In my periphery, pairs of kids leaned awkwardly and yelled. George moved over to Dylan and me.

"Yeah, think of how you push each other away all the time. Think of how you push everyone away and PUSH Zack! That's it, good. How does it feel? It hurts, doesn't it? Go on! Really push, Zack, show him that you don't want to be his friend."

Imitating what was going on with the rest of the twosomes, I shoved at Dylan's shoulders. George's warbling voice coincided with rising music and I felt the moments etch with finality into my brain.

This much physical exertion should have had louder, harder music than What a Wonderful World.

Dylan's face morphed into one, first of confusion, and then appreciation, as he recognized the emotional content of the exercise. Our looks both turned to emotional pain as we thrashed. Evidently, mirroring each other's facial expressions further, Dylan's eyes squished shut as he called more memories to bear. Dylan's brother had died in a suicide a few years before. I pushed harder into Dylan's shoulder, yelling at my mother that I didn't need her, either.

We did not pull away from the shoves. We lurched into the force and offered counter resistance in order to be more present to our partner's work.

The three staff – Andrew, Tess, and George – wandered around among us and urged us to vocalize and put words to what we were thinking and doing. While we paused to breathe, we took in everyone else sitting and shoving and grunting. It was in these pauses that I couldn't not forever memorize the songs. I couldn't not make metaphors in them that apply to life. To my life.

Yells, crying, and the panting sounds people make when breathing hard, marinated the room with the exertion of movement. Nobody was sleepy now. The girls shrieked loudest.

"I don't need you! I don't trust you! You're just going to LEAVE ME!"

"Why do you push me away? Why did you push me away, MOMMY?"

"You made me FEEL SO FUCKING ALONE WHEN YOU LEFT ME!"

"Every day I push my friends away. My big brothers, my dad. I push away people who reach out to me all the time! Ernie, I push him away!"

79

"You push me away when you use me. My pervert uncle. GET AWAY!"

"He used to come home DRUNK AND BEAT MY MOTHER. WHY DID YOU ALWAYS PUSH US ALL AWAY?"

"I just wanted to BE CLOSE TO YOU!"

"I hate pushing people away I HATE MYSELF, WHY DO I MAKE IT SO HARD FOR MYSELF?"

"I PUSH YOU AWAY, I DO WANT TO BE YOUR FRIEND! WHY DON'T I LET MYSELF TRUST? WHY CAN'T PEOPLE LOVE ME?"

"I PUSH AWAY THE PEOPLE THAT TRY HARDEST TO LOVE ME."

Every few minutes the staff would have to remind us gently to return to the knee-against-knee position, because the shoves had separated us from our partner. Tess and especially Andrew Oswald were particularly conscientious at keeping us in the close, knee-to-knee position.

For close to an hour this went on. Whenever the room would start to seem too quiet, the music and words provided a mesh net that swirled, catching every private thought and lonesome feeling. Sweating and shaky. Mind sweats – body shakes.

At some points during the propheet, I couldn't help but sometimes see myself as a different self. Zack would rather have performed the ritual longer than to have to watch the other half of the room. Zack was very thirsty. Fracturing inside reminded me of all sorts of things, including my first day in Idaho when Dad left me to Andrew and this.

George took a position near my pairing. Like a referee watching a wrestling match, George's hands were clasped behind his back and he bowed deeply so that his mangled cheek, in front of my left eye, was between Dylan and me. I noticed guitar-pick sized clumps of dandruff in George's hair.

He's right up in our business.

"That's RIGHT. Look how we push and we QUIT on our FRIEND EVERY DAY. Keep going, you do it every day! How it was hard work to push people away!"

Though my voice was shot and my arms seemed heavy as cannon, I went on. Another part of the propheet was coming up soon, I continually reminded myself.

This was the most physical we had been with each other yet. Even though we were only sitting, it was aerobic and immediate. This wasn't hugging and smooshing; it felt like a cross between sumo wrestling and water polo. We continued yelling and shoving through several volume-enhanced replays of the old song about what a wonderful world it is.

George finally shut down the music and Tess dimmed the lights. We got a water break, and I took a piss. My hands shook while yellow urine spiraled into the toilet.

After we re-congregated on the floor of Walden, my PG scooted around to new partners the staff designated. Once we all were in place, Louis Armstrong's song came up loudly again and the staff came around to us and showed us what to do.

"Zack, let Andrew tell you he wants you to be his friend." I hadn't wanted to be Andrew Oswald's partner, and I didn't want to be Andrew's friend, nor did I want to hear his round, nasally voice tell me he wanted a deeper relationship with me, but I went along with the ruse, not deviating from the course that Tess or George had planned. Why go against the wishes of two staff, my new lug, and the group as a whole? I didn't want to think about what could happen if I *didn't* follow the prescriptions and use the tools I was learning about *real* friendship.

Andrew Oswald (Partner A): "Zack, I take your friendship and put it in my heart."

"Zack, turn your back on Andrew."

An easy directive to follow. I wouldn't have to stare up at hulking old Lemur-Face.

Zack Bonnie (Partner B): "I don't want you, I don't need you. Leave me alone."

Zack turned his back on Andrew Oswald.

Then Zack told Andrew Oswald that he wanted to be friends with him. Andrew turned his back on Zack.

The metaphor of back turning was not lost on me, but it intermixed with memories of my parents. Having started the back-turning exercise with Andrew – the man who strip-searched me when Dad left me here, perversely incorporating a search of my asshole as part of his duty at the time – overcame any innocent intent by RMA that I ought to be appreciative of my chance to now forgive it. I could not shake the haunting memory of that betrayal, and how it felt when I bent over that day and showed my asshole to Andrew. This memory lingered with me as we changed to different partners for more shoving and back turning.

While the exercise went on, and my PG switched partners around at staff behest, I came to see that it was much easier to have people turn their backs on me than it was for me to leave, hurt, betray, abandon, and trust, forgive, or love them.

I guess this sort of thing can change with time, now that I know about it.

Noting that some of my peers were affected deeply – either by this exercise, or by the overall continuation of our collective evening – I felt a stronger bond with them. Especially the friends in my group who were adopted, or whose parents were divorced or dead. Unfortunately, the staff in the room had a plan for doubting this bond I was starting to feel for my peers, my friends, in the propheet room in Walden.

George pulled our fatigued bodies into a standing group, close in, to make a snug circle of feet.

In the huddle, the smells of morning breath and body odors misted collectively. Our elbows hooked on to those of the persons next to us. From the outside, George pushed on our backs and the circle tightened in with impenetrable, cramped familiarity.

Then George pulled me out of the peer-group circle. My neighbors let me out and re-closed their ranks. I could hear the other staff addressing the remaining circle while George took me to the corner of the room and whispered in my ear:

"You never get to be a part of the group. It takes a lot of your energy to keep yourself on the outside, doesn't it?"

I nodded.

"Always on the outside, being put on the outside. Putting yourself outside of groups? Yeah. It takes a lot of work to remain like that, Zack. No man is an island. Now, go join the group."

George switched the tape to Simon and Garfunkel's *I Am a Rock,* a song I knew from home. Now it would take on significance and new meaning.

I approached the backs of my peer group in their locked circle.

George returned and shoved me. "Well, go on! Join in again."

"Excuse me. Can I get back in?"

I tried to wedge into my original position. My peers didn't budge. Then, suddenly and even more strangely, the entire circle bucked, sending me unexpectedly onto my ass.

"What's the matter? Aren't these more people that are supposed to love you, but DON'T? Don't you want to be with everybody else? Isn't this the group you WORKED SO HARD TO BE A PART OF?"

George yelled at me across the room over crescendoing music, while Tess stayed with the group. I could hear her voice rising into the huddle like a quarterback before the rest of the faculty voices inter-twined:

"That's what you do every day, isn't it? 'He's not good enough for me,' RIGHT, BIANCA? He's not good looking enough. He's not going to be part of OUR GROUP! HE'S ON THE OUTSIDE! SHOW HOW YOU OSTRACIZE PEOPLE EVERY DAY! JUDGMENTS IN PLACE, THAT'S RIGHT! GET THOSE FUCKING WALLS UP! LET'S HEAR SOME MORE! I DON'T WANT TO BE YOUR FRIEND! COME ON. THIS IS WHAT YOU DO TO EACH OTHER EVERY DAY! EVERY FUCKING DAY!"

Thrusting elbows and hips greeted me as I tried to penetrate the cluster of my peer group's backs. From the music station, George yelled for me to keep attempting integration. This time having spied an open-ing between legs set akimbo, I wriggled in between the legs and was rising to my feet in the center, when Tess demonstrated to the group how to "kick" me out of the circle.

She opened the human fence linkage between Ernesto and Yu-Yu and I was "let out" of it – urged out verbally, while being pushed by a dozen rough hands.

Then we did it again – the song, the staff voices, George grabbing at me, Andrew and Tess repeating the orchestra of rejections the whole time. In a short time, I succeeded in breaking into the circle again. Shoeless feet, padding blows from feet, and then their words:

83

"Get out!"

"You are unwanted here!"

"STAY ON THE OUTSIDE!"

"You ARE NOT ONE of US!" declared Ernesto with surprising sincerity, so that I had to wonder if he meant it.

Maybe I deserve this?

I leaped over the shoulders of Yu-Yu, landing at the feet of my PG. This time my peer group had to yell over the music, as they pushed and kicked me out of the circle. It all became intensely more personal.

"Get BACK on the OUTSIDE!"

"Yeah, because WE DON'T EVEN KNOW YOU!"

"YOU'RE UNLOVABLE!"

"NOBODY WANTS YOU! SEE! GET OUT!"

"THIS IS HOW YOU WANT IT! THIS IS HOW YOU SET IT ALL UP EVERY DAY!"

"YOU'RE THE LONER. YOU WANT TO BE ON THE OUTSIDE! IT MAKES US FEEL POWERFUL. ELITE! RIGHT? LET'S HEAR IT PEOPLE!"

Tess egged my peer group on until they were shouting and repeating whatever else was yelled.

"BECAUSE YOU SPLIT!"

"You make THE ENVIRONMENT UNSAFE."

"BECAUSE YOU KEEP ME DIRTY!"

Horatio blurted, "BECAUSE YOU'RE FAT." Insults don't have to be in touch.

"BECAUSE YOU DON'T FIT IN!"

"Yeah, you're a SQUARE PEG."

That one I had never heard before Idaho, but it stays with me.

At some point, I became aware that I was not the guinea pig for this process. Sometimes it seemed I was often the first asked to share, or do some exercise or displays for the PG. But in this propheet exercise I was not the first of many; nobody else ever played the role of the person on the outside in our Brothers Keeper propheet. No, it was not through the laws of randomness that I was selected to act this role.

My unawareness keeps me alone and unlovable.

The snot-ripper song branded into my ears. *"And a rock feels no pain, and an island never cries."* I would never afterward be able to listen to those words without finding myself returned to Walden's interior, where I was repeatedly excluded from a circle of my peers.

With the understanding that I was to be alone in this ordeal came the knowledge that I deserved it. Zack always had. At home as a little boy. At school, too, the teachers had washed my mouth out. One time, when I was nine, the teacher locked me in the broom closet and forgot I was there. The custodian let me out that evening after school.

A few years later, in eighth grade, for several weeks, I sat alone in a little office during the entire school day! It was only partially under the guise of "refusing schoolwork." I was not permitted to eat lunch with other kids, not allowed in homeroom, banned from gym class, and excluded from field trips. My parents' worst fears realized, I had become both unteachable and uncontrollable.

My need to be isolated from the kids in my public school had seemed a triumph at times, only briefly punctuated by feelings I didn't know needed addressing before Idaho and the Brothers. Now I paid that price. Now, my soul nagged me: George and Tess were ensuring that I would never again feel a part of any group.

I am the loner. I am the pariah – and this fact was as plain as the sun's rays that squeaked past the cardboard sun-blocks into the room. It was the middle of the tomorrow I'd been longing for last night, and I had learned so much more about what people thought of people, since yesterday. But I felt worse by a magnitude of twenty. The metaphor of being on the outside weighed on me, and left me feeling in stark contrast to the rest of the members of my PG.

My unawareness keeps me alone and unlovable.

I was going to be processing what happened in the Brothers, and my lug, forever.

TEN

Raps were not every day; on Tuesday and Thursday afternoons, instead of raps, we gathered for writing and reading class, art, or "Experientials," designed to train middle-schoolers like me for future wilderness expeditions. Physical fitness activities like jogging, hiking, and skiing would increase in intensity until we could carry heavy packs on specialized snow gear in unreasonably inclement conditions.

Compared to raps and propheets, Experientials were like going to a carnival, even though they were also apt to be terrifically boring at first. As time passed, I looked forward to them. And by the time the sun started to warm us in early spring, I came to enjoy the puzzles, trust falls, knot practicing, pushups, jogging, and occasional games of manhunt – a super-sized version of hide and seek – that let us explore thickening woods. The staff who taught these specialized outdoor skills – like how to pack backpacks, solve puzzles, or use maps – would come up with all sorts of exercises for my peer group to practice and pass the afternoon hours.

We congregated after lunch one Thursday at the Quest trail, which meandered around the campus. Chet Lively, a short, bearded staff that I used to bad-rap by calling a "shit midget," didn't usually address us, but this was his element. No longer Papooses, we were beyond rolling our eyes, and paid Chet enhanced respect.

"OK crew! Bans between each of you for the afternoon! Ivy, come stand here. You're the team leader for this afternoon. You are the ONLY one that may speak. One at a time, I want all of you to get over this rope. But how? Without using tools, or things like logs and rocks, and without touching the rope in any way whatsoever, using your bodies and these two trees, your mission is to get the entire group over the rope. One at a time. The objective is to get over the rope as a team, not for us to have to set a broken leg. That's an exercise for a later time."

With that, Chet stopped talking. He just watched us all closely after that, and took notes.

It took us what felt like about an hour of pantomiming ideas for Ivy. After a few failed attempts, Micah took a shortcut to using a stick to draw a quick blueprint on the ground: A body pyramid was the way to go. Six of us formed a three-layer tower of kids, against the tree at one end of the rope. When Yu-Yu scrambled up the tower, and made her way over without touching the rope, we knew it worked. She had an awkward descent, though, and fell hard on the forest floor. Why wasn't someone there to break her fall? We needed to rethink.

Ivy seemed to get a brainstorm. She called us around, and explained, "Nobody said we had to stay on only one side of the rope. Micah, go over there to the other side of the tree, and Ernesto, climb up on his shoulders. Jamie, go up top there, so you're almost as high as the rope."

"I wish," Jamie retorted, under his breath.

"Bans, you fucking stoner!" I threw back.

With the rest of us using only gestures and occasional grunts for project-related attention, we re-formed our tower of six bodies so it extended under the rope. Now, after crossing over the rope, a kid would have a kid-ladder to climb down until it was safe to jump the rest of the distance to the ground. Fantastic.

Ivy grew more animated and we had a few good laughs as we planned: two more girls climbed up the pyramid and over the rope, crawling gently onto Jamie's broad back. Ernie's feet, on Micah's shoulders, were six feet off the ground. After my turn, Ivy pulled me over to act as a structural support since Micah and Ernie were struggling to hold the tower together. Our pyramid was becoming more of a pile. I leaned against the tree and two sets of feet stood on my shoulders. Half of my PG succeeded in getting over the rope.

We had to get the other half of the group over the rope. We reformed the body pyramid two more times, and, at the end, added more kids to prop it up, to get Yu-Yu – our lightest, final PG member – over the top of the rope, and watch her scurry safely down to the thawing ground.

We whooped as she jumped up, bans lifted, nobody ignoring the multiple layers of flirting, the personalities that continued being unmasked during the non-verbal Experiential that day. I reflected on the leadership role that Micah had taken, and how Ivy was applying her newfound courage. The goal of the Experiential could have been achieved earlier, it's true. I'd had the same idea as Micah had, I just hadn't had the idea to use a stick to try and explain it to everyone. I didn't want to pay Ivy attention in front of the group. I was afraid that people would see attraction and misconstrue it the way that Darlayne did so forcefully before I split. Also, things had been strained between Ivy and me since the intensity of the Brothers.

I couldn't tell what the kids in my peer group really thought of me. I was sure I could have gotten us all over that rope faster, but because of the last propheet, and perhaps the time I'd missed on Survival, I was already the pariah.

Stupid manufactured group dynamics.

It was clear that staff were interested in watching the reactions of my peer group as we interacted. I felt like the data accumulated was for something more important than just future rap and propheet content.

We got to know the different staff members the more we appeared in the raps they facilitated or supported in. Hedwig or Nat Farmer usually got the Summit kids. In this way, just as Tess had done when we were Papooses, every staff would get months to connect with me and my peer group. Even before we moved up to Brave family, Prescott had seemed to be around my PG more often; now George was doing the same thing, lurking about and having us in his raps. He was going to get us next when we moved up to Warrior family. Well, if we moved up. Almost all of us would. Kids still left, but it seemed like if a kid was here a year, he could expect to be here the other eighteen months.

I marveled at all the intelligence that had been gathered. They knew our disclosures! The staff members spent inordinate amounts of time getting to know us: where we were from, what brand of "mommy or daddy issues" we had, who had had an abortion, who'd lied or split, who'd been molested, or had a school rep as a look-good or a jock who wanted to impress people with physical prowess like Micah. The staff paid a lot of attention to us, they knew us individually, they knew much more about me than my parents – and likewise they included me in the details of their lives.

We kids knew things about the staff: which staff had kids, who didn't have a mother or father, who had committed break-ins, done serious drugs, screwed animals, or liked it up the ass, which staff had had previous lives in the military, and even which were more financially insecure. Nat and Hedwig had pulled the absolutely toxic, and almost unbelievable disclosure from another staff right in front of my eyes. When one staff admitted he'd rather jerk off to girl students than fuck his wife, I found a new level of appreciation for growing up. It took me time to get there though; I was a bit judgmental when I first heard it.

It was only natural because they hadn't been here as kids and had had more time to accrue their disclosed secrets – their own negative internal voices – and to puppet what their Thinking said. So to me this partially explained why these people were working here.

Like us kids, they were special because they were choosing to be here too.

As though she was a shrink or priest, Tess certainly knew more about me than any family, or former friends at home had known me ... in some ways. In other ways, Tess, Keith, George, Prescott, and the rest of the staff were only getting a façade of who I am, I thought. They were getting a sedate, secretive, scared copy – the me I thought they wanted – plus some new identities that I tried on through trial and error.

Another me – not yet asserted at RMA – had the personal, hidden agenda of keeping my individual thoughts to myself. An iota of the self-reality that had made me stand up to Darlayne Hammer when I split still remained inside me. It knew the injustice of sequestration, and continued to exist in a parallel dimension. It couldn't stamp out my sexual instinct, couldn't stop questioning CEDU's intent to enlighten me; and it didn't want my mom to get a conformed, boarding-school kid with short hair, and whatever else she was paying this program to mold me into.

The only important things I'd learned so far, were to keep my truest thoughts and feelings inside my red binder – the secret stash spot in the back of my brain – and to make sure to have other feelings, not so close to the heart, available to hang out for public consumption and rap interrogations.

ELEVEN

Thanksgiving (whole roasted turkeys!) and the Brothers Keeper propheet (untoasted white-bread mustard and cheese sandwiches) had come and gone. Santa's Workshop happened soon after, and was admittedly one of the coolest things to yet occur. From the second week of December until Christmas and parent visits on December 26th, life was golden and easy. Students didn't have work crews. Instead, every kid on campus (who wasn't on a full-time) had Santa's Workshop. If they were being punished with a full-time, they sat in a booth, speaking to no one, just like any other time of year.

This two-week period was a magical time, in which we were fattened up like good little elves – all jolly and extra child-like, going from building to building – woodworking, and stamping leather goods with special scrapers, hooks, and mallets. There were specialized cutting wheels for slicing shards of stained glass, that squeaked during the process. We learned how to slip the minimized shards of glass into the lead binding, and to solder the colorful bits together. Endless hours of card making, since everyone had to make at least 25 cards for other students and staff. Girls and boys alike, even Wally and Micah, spent hours crocheting and knitting.

Plus there were rituals: a certain way to set up the house, deck the tree, or set the order in which my PG could open the presents from home. The whole campus now talked about home and being young. On the nights during Santa's Workshop, every moment was special, every rap meaningful. I could glimpse a past where I could embrace my best, most loved early memories; where I felt fulfilled.

First, Kenny G, Barry Manilow, and Cat Stevens became familiar. Now we met Vivaldi and Beethoven. If the speakers weren't dispensing classical music, it was bound to be James Taylor, Steely Dan, or an occasional early Beatles song, so there were new words to listen to. It depended on the speed of the house, and especially whether there had been a rap or a propheet going in or getting out that determined the auditory stimulation *de la nuit*.

John Lennon's *Imagine* really *meant something*, and we surmised that the former Beatle must have something to do with the upper-school workshops, because of the reactions older kids had to the lyrics, which they clearly already knew.

> [Large Group Awareness Trainings] like to use pop-ular music as part of their indoctrination. ... It creates a strong association in the individual's unconscious, which without proper counseling can take months, sometimes years, to overcome. Music is used by many cults for indoctrination, because it forms a strong anchor for emotional states via memory.
>
> —Steven Hassan, *Combating Cult Mind Control*, Freedom of Mind Press, 2015 (25th anniversary edition), p 279

†

A healthy ten-foot blue spruce tree (see my wood science!) appeared in the corner of the main house in a large cement-filled tub, shored up with sacks of pellets so it wouldn't lean. At every last light until parent visits we had a little ritual where students would place different ornaments on the harvested conifer. Wrapped gifts accumulated on the festive green fabric that skirted the tub. Cards to friends, photographs of RMA kids as children, or other knickknacks grew the tree shaggy with paper, tinsel, photos, wooden trinkets, and the occasional hanging Hot Wheels matchbox car. On the last night, colorful gift-wrapped presents for 150 kids stretched deep into our usual smoosh area, push-ing us closer together.

Since there was no money in this place, everything we gave one another was handmade, which made the gifts – and the acts of cre-ating, giving, and receiving them – priceless. We had access to many materials with which to make gifts for family and friends. I worked leather, antler, wood, wax, glass, and I took organic items from the forest. I made a Native-American style dream-catcher from birch bark for my mother, and a junior-sized one for Ivy. I made a lamp that said "I love you" out of red-stained Tamarack wood for the mantel at home. I also knitted my sister a scarf, and scrimshawed a bone paperweight with his name for my brother. That took me almost an entire hand-cramping week of stippling – basically tattooing the bone. Finally, I learned to crochet with the off-time, and so made a ridiculous looking potholder for my grandmother. It read "Sparkle Special" in glued-on sequins. I sandwiched the woven square between two pieces of glass so the thing wouldn't melt the first time Grandma used it. I had to consult Kelly when I couldn't remember if "sparkle" had a Christian connotation to it, since we weren't supposed to get too religious. I didn't have any other grandparents left.

Mother's mother wasn't just stiff. She was one of the people I'd conjured up in the Truth propheet, and in several raps since. In some of my earliest memories, her anger was on full display. One time I found some school photos of my mom as a girl while I was searching for the Monopoly board. One time I snuck down from the twin crucifix room, where they made me sleep in the bassinet, to spy several minutes of *The Exorcist* on their TV. Both times garnered smacks to my face.

†

...[P]hysical correction has been practiced for thousands of years and is widely held to be for the child's own good. Almost all parents alive today were beaten when they were young and were unfortunately forced by their parents at a very early age to accept such "correction" as both justified and intrinsically harmless. Accordingly, this false "knowledge" is stored away in their brains and is very difficult to dislodge. Realizing that the opposite is in fact the case would mean doubting the wisdom of their parents, and most people are afraid to do that. They think that such doubt is a punishable offense precisely BECAUSE as children they were subjected to physical cruelty for telling the truth.

—Swiss psychologist Alice Miller, interviewed by Katharina Micada, 8 Oct 2009, translated from the German by Andrew Jenkins http://www.alice-miller.com/en/an-interview-given-by-alice-miller-to-katharina-micada/

†

On the ride up I-95 ("Are we on the Turnpike yet?") to fetch Grandma after Mom's childhood house was sold, we joked about the

"Ice Queen," – within reason, and nothing Mom would consider "crude," of course. Mom's ties to New Jersey, and our shared memories of the crucifixes that had hung on the walls there were clipped off like a hangnail. Grandma came to live near us in Charlottesville. She stayed there till she died.

✝

I'd be revisiting the feelings associated with death, guilt, our missing real family members, and the abyss of death and life beyond Idaho, like everyone else. It was during the holidays that the bonds tightened between the RMA kids and staff.

Even though it was sometimes twenty or forty degrees below freezing outside when the wind blew, we could still have an awesome time. Although I wouldn't have the privilege to ski or snowshoe around at will until the next winter, Santa's Workshop acted to give us a few weeks' reprieve from extended outdoor labor. Main chores got done: Animals at the farm were cared for by Warrior kids who'd been through the I Want To Live, paths were cleared by me and my clan in Brave, and the wood corral would always be managed by the Papooses.

We made the buildings immaculate too. Bookcases in Warrior headquarters were emptied, dusted, and re-ordered. We took small ladders and dusted with bleach water all of the fans that hypnotized and swung with arrhythmical droning during raps. I got a chance to learn more about the Bridge. That's where they took a new kid about to be put on a full-time, or thrown out. That's where they went to call the police if the kid split.

The Bridge was the cockpit of the whole place, so being in there to clean gave me a chance to look around. It was an ordered and tidy room, with a wall of interior windows looking toward the pit and fireplace. The campus medicine cabinet was housed there, where they kept drugs for the occasional kid who really required them – like for epilepsy or something. For the rest of us, who weren't hemorrhaging from a severed artery, they'd just say, "Drink lots of water and take care of your feelings."

A large wooden table in the middle of the room, where staff meetings happened, was ringed with slightly comfortable wooden chairs that had padded cushions on the seat and back. Windows also looked into the kitchen and dining room, so staff could stare at any kid who was in a booth on a full-time. Along the other long wall, more

93

windows looked out at the woods that rose up to Mount Clifty and the smoking porch. Like on a ship, the Bridge was the command center, from which staff could view the conditions in the house, most of the smoking porch, and the whole campus.

The stereo was an important part of what made the Bridge the RMA control center. Whoever selected the music playing through the house set the mood for everyone. Kids weren't allowed to do that, of course, but sometimes, an older kid could make a move to change the music in the house. One time, before he graduated, I saw my big brother Paul Renssalaer do it. He said, "I'm tired of *Memories*. I want to put on Kenny G." He checked with Walter Nemecek, a Brave staff, to get the OK, and just walked in there and changed the tape.

I ripped up potential letters to my parents because I could not tell them how scrambled things were getting. How having to curb my words to them had silenced the essential trust that had always been between us. I mean, even when I got caught doing some dumb thing before I got here, I still believed that my mother and father knew me, at my core, better than anyone. But not anymore.

I wanted to tell them important things. Over time my encoded messages came out the opposite of how I felt. I couldn't tell them how sad I was, or that this artificially seeded agony was not a true manifestation of me. And I wasn't sure how to tell them how confused, tired, isolated, and insecure I now felt. Any pride, confidence, or arrogance, any desire to think about defying them – those had all already left me.

That had been the point.

If I could remind them, with subtlety, of their power for mercy, I thought, there's a chance they'd see this new sheepish demeanor, and pull me out of here.

They were mad that they didn't get meaningful letters. I sent Mom and Dad brief letters that told them basic stuff: I need toothpaste. Raps are difficult to sit through and I hate them. But the food's OK. I really miss home, and will you ask Prescott if it would be acceptable for me to be writing my brother yet? And what about writing to cousin Goldie, and my uncle? Is my sister getting bigger yet?

When it had been almost a page and a half, I wrote a dumb picture or signed my name really big, to fill up the recommended two pages.

Dear Zack,

I love the fact that I can write to you now, though
I've been told it can't be a one-sided operation. I can't
write five letters to your one, so I guess this letter
may be the last until I get another cherished letter
from YOU.

I also understand that there is word-processing
at RMA, so why don't you mosey on over to the
machines and WRITE HOME. Actually, you really
should be working on a word processor because
those skills are the ones EVERYONE needs in this day
and age. The quill pen is gone! Even the typewriter is
obsolete! [...]

—Letter from author's mother, 16 Dec 1988

The two weeks of Santa's Workshop culminated in a huge meal on
December 24th. This night at RMA we gorged on ham. Every wooden
picnic table had a fully cooked chunk, and – as we'd had the month
before with turkey, cranberry sauce, potatoes, cornbread, and gravy –
all the fixings filled the tables with good grub. At the end of our feast,
Nat and Hedwig called for a toast with the little plastic water cups we
used.

Nat took a breath in, got ready to speak, but had to stop and bring
his fingers to pinch the bridge of his nose like he had a headache. He
had already prepped, and as soon as he started remembering / feeling
memory, he was sobbing. "When we first started CEDU with Sol...."

After Nat was done, Hedwig, Tess, Darlayne, Keith, and the rest
of the staff came around and hugged every kid in the school. I never
wanted the night to end. It was even better than any Christmas I'd had
at home, I thought. It was true; as we gave the greeting cards and gifts
we had made to our friends, big brothers, and big sisters, and publicly
displayed the gifts for moms and dads in front of an invitingly large
fire, I knew that the program had goodness to offer.

95

†

[...] Sometimes, Zack, it's hard for us to have you so far away. But we have NO DOUBT that it is necessary and helpful for you. You couldn't have gone on here the way you were, and we couldn't have either. We could NEVER allow you to ruin your life. We love you! And we'll do ANYTHING to see that you develop into the fine man you have the capability to be. ... We don't want to be put into a position of FORCING you to do what's in your best interest, but, if need be, we'll do it anyway....

[...] I think everyone [back home] just accepts the fact that you needed to be away AND, (this is the part I'm sure about) they all believe that given your talents, your sociability, your language skills, and your athletic ability, you'll get IT ALL TOGETHER at RMA so that when you're ready you'll look at all the options open to you and get on with a really good life.

[...] Actually learning that – FOLLOWING THE RULES – is the whole point. I wish you'd just believe me on this, Zack. EVERYBODY HAS TO FOLLOW RULES AND IT'S ABSOLUTELY INEVITABLE THAT THEY WILL, SO YOU MAY AS WELL DO IT SOONER RATHER THAN LATER, BECAUSE YOU HAVE TO DO IT ANYWAY AND IT WILL MAKE YOUR LIFE BETTER AND HAPPIER.

I love, love, love you. And can't wait to see you. We're so proud of your wilderness accomplishments AND how you're growing. When you asked about how a person feels competent, Daddy and I both said at the same time, "By being successful!" Remember? And then you said, "you mean, like the Wilderness." We said, "Yes." That showed you did understand. Zack, you're learning to be successful and you've made us so happy.

Yours, Mommy
—Letter from author's mother, 10 Dec 1988

†

Staff who had their own kids – from cooks in the kitchen to family staff like Tess and Walter – brought them around for Christmas night. Tess carried her two-year-old in front of her in a homespun pouch. It was strange to have a few small children among us. The girls fawned over them. People's little kid pictures were hanging from the Christmas tree, or clutched in photo albums the older kids carried around; we spent hours with these images as we told our stories in big smoosh piles. The music floating from the house speakers brought forth cuddly memories. The lead-up to the big visit day almost made me forget the bitter taste of not having any say or control about my life – down to the minute.

Throughout the magical evening, I witnessed spontaneous tears of joy, and strong feelings of loss. I was not immune to the range of emotions. As powerful as the feelings of abandonment was a feeling I don't have a word for. Special-one-ness. Pain in the heart, but like a sore on the inside of your mouth, when it was formed and taking over your mouth, you couldn't stop picking at it. Some might call this realness joy, but another might label it sorrow. During some combinations of musical notes or lyrical metaphors, I found myself wiping away rivulets of tears. Music, mystical asymmetry, and memory merged.

Balloons floated, matchbox cars mimicked racing engine sounds. Older brothers and sisters, some dressed in elfin regalia like tights or sleigh bells, delivered presents to each of us. The entire population of students was in the house for Christmas Eve.

Crawling over to Ivy across the room, I clawed my way through a carnival atmosphere that was filling joyously with colorful gift wrap. Through the repeating John and Yoko Christmas album, I closed in on Ivy and Tess and George. We hugged one another, sharing the things we'd made and would soon present to our parents. Like a Summit getting out, Christmas at RMA was a monumental experience.

Give Peace a Chance, So This Is Christmas, and *Imagine* with John and Yoko provided the soundtrack. I was letting myself go – like being in the riot of the dance floor when we got to join the celebration after the Summit a half year before – only now it was a state of happy regression!

I felt a magical beam of love shooting out of my eyes as I took in the colorful, loud, special-people-encrusted, wrapping-paper-flooded floor; I felt love because I saw it in this place. It was special, like falling in love. A new love, first love, *"Oh, I love, for the first time in my life...*

97

and my eyes can see." The John Lennon lyric grew into me the way the trees here penetrated up, and grew down, wrapping their roots around boulders.

The tree flailed its cards and trinkets every time a door to the smoking porch opened.

During the holidays, extra tenderness was needed, and it was astutely provided. Maybe we all needed the extra love and understanding since we weren't with family at home. Or maybe it was the stress of knowing we'd indeed be seeing our parents soon, and telling them everything.

Zack Bonnie

TWELVE

Until I saw Mom and Dad, I had only heard a rumor that the parents completed a mini-workshop about CEDU's plan for domination – er, education – before they could visit RMA. In fact, it was an off-campus mini-Brothers propheet with Hedwig and Nat. Only after that were the parents allowed to drive their rental cars, or pile into an RMA shuttle van, and visit their children at the school.

†

"You Are Your Brother's Keeper"

1. There are two elements in friendship. One is truth. The other is tenderness.

2. The only way to have a friend is to be one.

3. The essence of friendship is total trust.

4. The harder the truth to tell, the truer the friend that tells it.

5. Without friends there is no meaning.

6. No man is an island.

—From handout for RMA Brothers Keeper parents' seminar program

†

I wasn't adopted, despite years of my own best efforts to prove otherwise.

However, the intimate doubts that I heard from other kids in raps – the feeling of having gaps in your story line, and a working knowledge of what it is to be unwanted – those I could relate to. Many kids started out by saying that discovering the fact hadn't mattered or been a big thing in their lives. But after enough talking about it in propheets and raps, their story changed. Their awareness of the status as an adopted kid had made them react to abandonment with feelings of inferiority they had discovered in raps. This went also for those whose parents were currently divorcing; everything that had happened in a kid's life could be viewed from new angles. These issues needed to be discovered at RMA. The red-binder part of my mind knew that the artificiality of the relationships we made here, the propheets, and those raps themselves had contributed to our realizations about what wonderful scarred kids we were.

Secretly I longed to be told that I was adopted, or that the folks would get a divorce, so I could have more of a reason, an easier tissue issue. Not being adopted meant that it was all about my original baseline of conceptual uselessness on the planet.

Worse – I mean, thankfully – both my folks were still alive. Needless to say, I felt pity for the kids that had lost a parent, or even one of their adoptive parents, or the kids who had been in the long-term purgatory of foster homes.

My house had been big. And unlike a few of us misplaced here, it hadn't been destroyed by flood or fire. It was a nice brick house, although I preferred not to be in it, back then. I preferred to spend time with myself or old hobo types that I knew from the woods near home. I loved the thrill of sneaking out and being able to bluff my way into the collegiate parties in the neighborhood. I thought porn and fireworks were just part of adult life. Like smoking.

I had been molested, but not raped. At RMA, if a boy – but usually a girl – introspected in a rap about unwanted sexual contact, they might be treated with extra respect that made me also long to have been mistreated worse.

I had been smacked around, sure. Violence was just a natural part of life, wasn't it?

I hadn't been addicted to drugs, had I?

Had I stolen anyone's car if I borrowed it without permission once or twice? Back home, on many Monday mornings in public and private school, the oldest kids had bragged about doing that stuff. I had only borrowed the car from my parents to go around the block a few times my last year there. Okay, I had been taking it around the parking lot when Mom ran into the store n' such since I was about nine. I only got caught once, at age twelve, when someone took the parking spot while she shopped.

Unlike some people at RMA, I'd certainly never set an injured man afire or put someone in the hospital with a bat. But I could understand rage, and therefore violence. Especially when, like a cornered animal, a person feels they have no control over their environment. Just as I'd felt on Survival toward Will Bender, I recognized a blinding rage for my handlers through my whole life so far, and toward Mom especially. Eventually at RMA, I'd be given a tool that was supposed to help me with this, but for now this accrued knowledge just simmered inside of me into a base reduction of guilt and shame.

I was jealous that I didn't have one of those fallback issues like adoption or drug addiction to blame for my problems, or my lug.

My unawareness keeps me alone and unlovable.

I wished for one exact thing to point to, but I didn't know what was wrong with me, or what really had gone wrong at home.

I added a badge to the uniform I was trying to grow into: *Another thing wrong with me was wishing this, right?*

So, if my folks aren't dead, I'm not adopted, or a car thief, drug addict, or a violent offender, instead, my program must be about the existential. The depressive feelings, my Thinking – all the things that would seem to be snuffing out my innocent Rock Bottom kid – were everpresent.

My little kid was corrupt from birth.

When it proved too much, this perpetual searching cored my brain and soul parts, so that I could imagine my patterns of thought as an old abandoned mine. Black. Underground. Inescapable without assistance. Deep down inside and inward, in a search not for what went wrong, but what was wrong with me.

The program had an answer: naturally, my Thinking was to blame. I was primed for the tools that staff would be showing to me, to help me survive the battle skyward out of my thought-mine.

†

By creating an environment where truth is multi-leveled, cult directors make it nearly impossible for a

member to make definitive, objective assessments.
If they have problems, they are told that they are not
mature or advanced enough to know the whole truth
yet. ... If they work hard, they'll earn the right to
understand the higher levels of truth.

—Steven Hassan, *Combating Cult Mind Control*,
Freedom of Mind Press, 2015 (25th anniversary edi-
tion) p 120

†

Maybe my parents would forget the worst moments of screaming
and the consternation that it caused. Maybe I could forget the feelings
and thoughts that I had on those nights. How I wanted to disappear
because of the fights, how even the baby would ball her little fists up to
scream at me, like she, too, wanted me gone. She was learning the way
that people talk to me. I realized the implications of telling my disclosures to Mom and Dad, and I knew I would have to do it when they
arrived. And RMA would provide a witness, to keep me honest.

After we had a rap, George Daughtry, the bug-eyed CEDU devotee
who'd run our Brothers and was most likely to be my next family head
after Prescott, suggested that I write out the disclosures I would confess
to Mom and Dad. He'd be waiting for me when I moved up to Warrior, and I'd already had probably thirty raps with him at this point. So
he knew my dirt. I tried to earn his respect, but even when I thought
I had, he'd be mean the next time I was in a rap with him. But then, if
he was nice to me the time after that, it meant even more.

†

If they remain loyal to their own perceptions about
self and world, they betray the group on which they
have become inordinately dependent; if they remain
loyal to the group, they betray their own perception
of what is real, good, and true. Dissent thus places
members in a 'funnel' from which there is no escape
and which inevitably leads to betrayal, either of themselves or the group.

The result of this process, when carried to its consummation, is a pseudopersonality, a state of dissociation in which members are 'split' but not 'multiple,' in which they proclaim great happiness yet hide great suffering.

—Michael Langone, *Recovery From Cults: Help for Victims of Psychological and Spiritual Abuse*, WW Norton & Co, 1993, p 9

✝

From a Papoose perspective, it could be surmised that parent visits were a transparent attempt by RMA to present the school as a happy work camp where the younger students worked the campus and tried to stay long enough to level up in privileges and the family system, while the older students studied school and how to fight negative Thinking. It doesn't matter to adults like my parents how contrived, in practice, it felt to be dropped into this turbulent current.

Astonishingly, I was now looking forward to whatever my next expedition, propheet, or breakthrough rap would be.

THIRTEEN

Dear Parents:

We are pleased that you plan your two day visit with your child at Rocky Mountain Academy over the Christmas vacation, December 26, 27 and 28, 1988. [...]

Here are some basic agreements that you might wish to review:

If the visit involves both parents, it is important that time be spent alone with each parent.

The students should not be left alone.

If clothing or other ordered items are brought from home, please check with the Floor Manager for approval to have those items marked. [...]

We have spent time with your child emphasizing the importance of sharing and giving of oneself. They have been making gifts for you and their friends as a token of their love. Each of them will be anticipating this visit with a mixture of anxiety and excitement as they set their own goals toward re-establishing your trust.

Have a wonderful visit and a Happy Holiday!

—Letter from RMA Parent Communicator to author's parents, 9 December 1988

RMA fulfilled the need to keep parents happy. One chief way was to make us look healthy but confused, which we were. But they scrambled up the issues for parents too.

Hedwig and Nat had seemingly worked voodoo magic on Mom and Dad during the parent workshop in Coeur d'Alene, a tourist trap / ski town in our neck of the woods. At the resort there, Tim, Griffin, and a couple of other older sisters and RMA staff helped orientate and tenderize our RMA parents in specially secured, big square-shaped conference rooms. I had learned by now that they'd been colluding with RMA staff and administrators before the long-awaited campus visit – as they had been when I was on Survival.

When the ol' parents arrived on our snow-blanketed compound after their morning conference, they were nice n' smiley, and bearing gifts. Along with warm socks, mittens, the newest flannel union-suit, and a thick parka for me, Mom, in a puffy powder-blue down parka with fur-cuffed mittens, and Dad in his dark wool topcoat and stitched leather gloves, also brought kindergarten-level understandings of the lingo and concepts that I lived with daily. From their mini-Brothers propheet at the resort, they had acquired some vocabulary. Mom and Dad were using program terms like "sparkle," "Rock Bottom," "manipulation," even intoning phrases like "working the program," "letting your little dooger/little kid shine," "rap requests," and "Thinking."

"Boy, it was an adventure just getting here from Bonners Ferry! Who knew there'd be this much snow! Isn't this great! Tim says that they ski back and forth from the dorm!" The big smile on Mom's face said it all.

To think that they could spend only one day snowed in here with us, and have any comprehension of what made the fire hot, or the way we all congealed in the feelings of being cast aside and unwanted, was laughable. The juxtaposition was infuriating. Some of the kids from the neighboring PGs surprised me by weeping for joy at seeing parents whom I knew – through accumulated rap and propheet knowledge – they hated.

George, Kelly, and Tess walked up to the three of us during the first moments of our reunion. Tess rubbed me on the shoulder. Like other two- and threesomes of staff, they were wandering around the overcrowded spaces of the main house mingling with pods of rejoining families.

"Mr. and Mrs. Bonnie. Hi! So good to see you again! Zack. You didn't know I met your parents after you split, did you? At the Coeur d'Alene."

107

"Er." I didn't know what to say. The hotel where the parents conference had been held carried the same inviting mystique as the Oxbow
Truck Stop did, when I was dead-dog tired in the desert.

Until this moment, I hadn't known which staff had met with Mom
and Dad when they came while I was on Survival. I considered the
ramifications. This meant that Tess – the family head of Papoose, lead
facilitator of my Truth prophet, and daughter of our famed Sol Turnwell – had already been pumping all the half-truths of the program
into my parents. Worse, I thought to myself, she and George knew all
my PG's misgivings, everything we said aloud that night, and in all the
raps where she or George would then rehash our confessions. The staff
knew things that we'd done, or had been done to us, as kids.

Truth be told, I hadn't seen Mom since my cousin Goldie's sticky
summer wedding in Baltimore, and there had been little said between
us since. My surprise landing here after Goldie's wedding had felt like
such an ambush! Mom's betrayal, her foreknowledge last July that she
wouldn't see me after the wedding, her plotting my sequestration, my
unmanning at Andrew Oswald's hands at Zero Hour Day One, the
final decision on my removal – all lingered like the smell of charred
wood in the house. Her control over my life was asserted with finality.

I'd never seen Mom and Dad so happy. Judging from the facial
expressions of so many other adults, they had plenty of company.

The last I had seen of Dad was after the Spokane airport in July, his
white rental car stirring up a cloud of dust when he took off and left
me with the overgrown Andrew Oswald for my "orientation" at RMA.

Now Mom and Dad had program vocabulary and could intermin-
gle with staff whom they addressed by name.

Things are never going back to the way they were before I came to Idaho.

*Maturity: Prove your belief of the program to Mom and Dad. I have to
accept RMA's program; not as my lord, keeper, and savior, but as theirs – as
Mom's.*

It would have to be carefully done. How would I alert the parents
how much I wanted – needed – to return home? I had to be careful not to inflame tempers. I got them alone during a snowy tour of
the wood corral, the first time we were able to walk away from the
crowded house.

"So, I don't suppose that you're planning on bringing me home with you after this visit?"

My dad started. "Honey, we still don't feel like it's a good use of our limited time discussing that subject. We know you want to come home, but Zack, you're happier here! You're happier and this makes us better and happier. So, let's not ruin it with talking about coming back home just yet. Maybe after your home visit in the spring though...?"

Mom chimed in. "We know it's hard. We know it seems like a long time, but this is the best place. We are so lucky, not only that RMA exists, but that we were able to find it! Now that you're here, ahem, the adjustments are made, right? You fit in. You know the routine. You're being successful, and we're so, so proud. You're becoming quite the respectful and responsible young man."

Of course, Mom and Dad were prepared. They had their answers ready and anything I'd formulated to contest these points melted away. When it ever did come up, I knew this was the tack they would take to calm unsteady waters. Put me off until next time. Placate me with chatter about my evident development. It was fruitless to argue the points I'd planned. I didn't want to be accused of ruining the visit, which would happen if George got wind that I was trying to manipulate Mom and Dad.

We had 45 minutes "alone" with Kelly Grainger down in my dorm – Kelly's first time in a male dorm, she mentioned casually – that changed life forever. It was time to cop out my disclosures to my parents.

At RMA, we gained in status by letting ourselves be vulnerable, sharing our most intimate content in raps and the confessional DMT sessions.

It didn't play the same with my parents.

The grownups sat. Mom and Dad were on the one piece of furniture in the six-bunk room that wasn't a bed – a little boxy blue two-seater couch framed in blonde wood – that no one ever used except for putting on boots and shoes. Kelly sat behind me on the bed where Ari Korta, my new dorm head, slept. It used to be Jasper's bed, but when Prescott and Tess found out in the rap that the two boys who copped out to their sex contract were from Jasper's dorm, he got demoted.

109

I stood under the overhead light in the middle of the room. "Phew. OK. This is going to suck...Remember when ..."

Scenes like this were taking place all over the RMA campus. Disclosures and parents. Accusations of inappropriate touching from family members, pre-RMA sex lives, abortions, drugs, stealing. Wrecked cars, fires, and fights. Fucking, jerking off, the details of shame. I knew how to confess with full personal accountability, from propheets and time spent listening and learning. I listed them all, and pictured all the other kids doing the same.

We confirmed parents' suspicions of sneak-outs, hitchhiking adventures, police chases, violence against animals, other kids, and selves. Mom and Dad must've been instructed that they'd be on some lists of copouts too, so I brought up the worst moments I could remember between us, knowing on some base level, that I would never be going back to that time, house, and age.

The "fact" that I had done cocaine under a bridge with some homeless types in our neighborhood immediately proved two things: One, I was a gullible fool who did anything George, Tess, Darlayne, Hedwig, or another power staff told me to. Two, that by "copping out," I gave my parents all the justifiable proof they needed to keep me here. This was the reward for my honesty. Instead of demonstrating that I had matured enough to come home, I had given them more reasons to keep me here.

The list I had sketched out had seemed kind of innocuous in the everyday life of raps, even the disclosures that were exaggerated, but when the moment of truth arrived, I almost clammed up. Emotionally naked, I couldn't believe I was telling them this terrible shit, but this was why they came all the way from Virginia.

"Well, I thought you knew. Yeah, we'd just pour a little from each bottle. Well, we did it at his parent's house too. When it was full, we mixed it up and chugged it. That's the night that he set fire to the shed – but it *was* an accident."

"I smoked pot on your property. At least ten times, I guess. I'm sorry. I know that it's illegal and I took advantage of that safety. The trust, I guess. I know I had drugs in the same house with the baby. I just feel really guilty about that. . . ." I teared up here, but still had a long way to go.

"I betrayed you also with petty theft of money. Like I'd take a few dollars from your change bowl, Dad. Mom'd sometimes leave her purse around... Chuck and I did that with Baba in France too..."

I sort of mumbled that last bit because Baba, my friend Chuck's grandmother, had invited us to take some of the heavy Franc coins from her purse. But it had become a disclosure in the Truth, so it had become a fact that I was capable of thievery.

Ever since fifth grade, after all my explorations, I had wound up with plenty of years' worth of things that weren't mine. That could have been enough material to confess. But expanding the truth, and taking total – even unnecessary – responsibility for any of my perceived mishaps, had just become part of the ordinary way of trading stories around here.

". . . and like you know about the spray painting and bottles that Jake and I broke, but he shot a cat with a BB gun. No, right through the eye. We buried it by the stream on Dunlop Ave."

After what I thought was the toughest part, I incorporated recent lessons I was learning from the Brothers Keeper. As I told Mom and Dad how lonely it felt to be "on the outside," I sensed a transition from the shame of disclosure into a new kind of discomfort.

I am opening up to them. This part isn't made up.

Embarrassment flooded me.

Particular attention had to be paid to the most personal of my issues. That's why Kelly was lurking around with us – to make sure I told them how bad I felt those nights. Wanting to die. Wanting to run away and never be found. How dumb I felt, not just in school but around Dad, how insignificant.

One time, when I was little, my dad let me put a book inside my pants so when he punished me, at Mom's request, it wouldn't hurt so much. We agreed we wouldn't let Mom know about our book-butt bargain.

Am I supposed to tell them about that, too? Dad already knows, because we agreed to keep it our secret.

Now – like Tess in the Truth, or George in the Brothers – Kelly knew it all.

They don't understand a word I am saying. I went through the Brothers. All they did was a parents' seminar at a resort on a lake at Coeur d'Alene.

111

Since I'd never had a problem making friends, and in fact had always been popular before RMA, they'd never understand how isolated I now felt, how my permanently low status compared to older members of the campus. They'd have thought, "How could Zack be alone with all these hip boys and girls around?"

In no way was I now confident and happy. Mom and Dad wouldn't let me come home, and inside I was crushed because I knew again that they just didn't want me.

They don't want me. What's wrong with my love?

With Kelly watching to be sure I didn't leave out any juicy details, I completed the progression leading up to being here. Coming clean with Mom and Dad. Truth be told, I was sorry about how I acted out feeling so sorry, hurt, and angry at them, when I still lived in Virginia.

All the previous justifications for my actions were melting away. My feelings were my responsibility – my choice – even before I got here, according to the program dogma.

After I took a deep breath and reached for some tissues, Kelly came over and gave me a big hug. My parents rose from the boxy loveseat and joined in this strange group huddle. We swayed there in my dorm for a few minutes, rubbing one another on the back.

In my family, we all knew everyone had been disappointed with me, almost from the beginning. But letting my Dad down, getting kicked out of Pennsylvania's private school, needing to be in Idaho because I wasn't even allowed to be in public school anymore (because of self-hatred, because I didn't care about following rules anymore, because I was too big for them to force me to do stuff now) were abstract details of the grown-up world. The extent of my physical destruction was still somewhat unspeakable subject matter for me – even if it was becoming the primary way in which I internally sought feelings to automate in raps.

As a reward, this was the first time in years that we'd spent 45 minutes together without a fight. Some of it was farce, but some moments were as real as life can be.

I wasn't sure yet how that feeling I kept coming back to during times of "growth" here – that internal quaking with discomfort because I was a crazy pervert who belonged in lumberjack Juvie – was good for my soul. RMA told me that sharing this was "good," but like so many rituals here that I was assured would eventually and permanently assist me, it didn't feel good.

We got closer to others at RMA when we shared disclosures. This contributed to my growing need for program relationships and acceptance. I expected I'd be getting to know my parents as an adult now, too, especially because I was telling them about sexual experiences I'd had. Talking about dark disclosures and deep-rooted feelings of self-doubt with the people I was around daily in this frozen, lusterless, isolated, wooden world, had become so normal. I agreed with the program now. It was necessary for us to be physically removed for this intensive work to succeed. Inviting our parents into this new introspective norm made me – probably all of us – realize that there was even more importance to our emotional growth. Even though Mom and Dad didn't share disclosures with me, I did get positive attention from them. These things I would never have told them, but it was my program to do so. They said how brave I must be to do this emotional and gut-wrenching introspection all the time, they thanked me for my honesty and insisted that this display demonstrated the growth they expected.

After that, my parents opened a shopping bag with wrapped-up presents: a copy of *The Prophet*, a yo-yo, and new work jeans. In addition to the gifts, the fact that they were here in Idaho and had talked to me kindly but firmly about what I was doing here, left little doubt that they loved me – here. My being in Idaho wasn't at all an inconvenience. It was just the necessary method of travel to where I was being transported; not one of us – no parent, no kid or staff, or Summit-committing self – knowing the final destination point.

†

I didn't have any idea of the rollercoaster I had put her on last summer – splitting from Camp Minnehaha, splitting from RMA, getting held back on Survival. Not even gonna think of life as a kid yet. I'm such a shitty person. Unlovable. OR you could say that the problem was my becoming self-reliant. So confident that I would run away. The arrogance that had made me stand up for myself was the thing Mother hated most. She wanted to control me, and I wouldn't let her.

Underneath, I had always sensed an underlying sentiment of distaste, like when I was younger and got that frown for perhaps interrupting grown-ups talking, that was the baseline, and it grew that way with Dad. That's when I gave up.

Before that, the Dad in my youth: "Be quiet. Don't make a spectacle. Sit still! Look like this. Talk this way. The teacher is always right. Stop following me around the house! You don't need any attention — Just go read a book, Zack!"

By about fourth grade, when our misunderstandings and conflicts began to mature, the backstories could tumble into my brain with enough truthful corroboration evidence to damn me forever. This is when the program said my Thinking started taking over.

✝

I chastised myself for any confident, non-program thoughts even while forgiving myself; I still doubted the scratchy feeling of growing into my program uniform.

If I did learn the whole program, my parents would re-take me into the family fold. That was the golden promise for kid and parent alike. Confessing my list of disclosures and deepest regrets would be done in front of the Warrior family staff named Kelly Grainger. She'd be there with us, when I described the times I'd been hurt by people, including the people who put me on the campus. Kelly had made it her mission to "take me on," managing my personal emotional growth program. Now she could get to know Mom and Dad's faces.

What if the program is designed to strengthen my bond to the program, and less to parents, less to home?

Mom linked her arm in mine as we walked through the slushy frozen mud up to the house from my dorm. When we came to a deep mud puddle, I held her so she could walk across the melt-off puddle on my boot.

For months afterwards, she'd remind me of this mini-waltz, and my swinging her onto the other side of the slushy puddle. She thought it was something I wouldn't have thought to do before RMA. But I never forgot things she taught me.

I would have let a lady walk on my boot if we'd ever walked around arm in arm near mud puddles in Virginia.

We walked into a clatter of games and other kids talking to their parents. Lingering in the atmosphere now was the alluring foreign scent of the visiting mothers' perfume.

FOURTEEN

My folks and I claimed the chess nook when Ernesto went off with his dad. Ernesto's face was red, an indicator that he was dreading the process I'd just completed.

While Dad set up the pieces, Mom made notes and applied lipstick. "I'm so curious to know more about the curriculum that RMA has. Sheesh, remarkable. We really are so impressed by what we're seeing and hearing, not just about you, Honey, but about all the wonderful kids here and the changes they've already made."

"We sure heard a lot during the convention with Nat and uh – what's that lady's name?"

"Hedwig, Dad."

"Oh right. What an unusual name. Where's she from? Scandinavia somewhere...." Mom's voice tapered off.

"How long were you guys in that thing? Conference?" I wanted to wrap my brain around what they had done, and how surfacey it was.

"Two or three hours. It was interesting."

Lightweights.

Dad looked at me expectantly. "So, Zack, do you want to tell us about your propheet? What do you call it, Brothers Keeper?"

Without divulging the secrets of the exercises, what was I able to tell them? And how? And why?

†

They'd announced it in front of the house. George Daughtry facilitated our peer group's Brothers Keeper propheet. As the names of kids in my PG had our names called out, and had to stand up front for a seeming eternity, we were supposed to feel lucky, proud, or special for still being there. I remembered thinking that because George once had been a student he would take it easy on us during a propheet. Big mistake.

In the propheet we batted home the notion: "Every time you say or think something bad about another person, you're really only putting that person down to make yourself feel better." Yet I couldn't contain my furtive, judgmental thoughts about him for several more months.

George Daughtry's ability to read body language and "tells" from kids in his propheets and in his family was legend. The cutting, loud indictments in raps that he made were often on point. It was also well known that the street had spit George right back to CEDU after he'd been the victim of a beating and knife slashing. The result was one eye that would wink for no reason, and a bumpy red scar from his eyebrow down his face. Lower school kids could shut one eye and squint, and it was known that, with banned voices, they referred to George – the same way a folded over thumb meant Keith Rios, the Papoose staff. Keith had lost most of his thumb to a circular saw when he came to build the school at RMA a few years after graduating from CEDU in California.

Tess, one of the most upright figures at RMA, who had run my PG's first propheet and therefore knew everything about us, was no slouch when it came to insights about me and my peers. But it somehow seemed easier to hear feedback from Tess than from George in the Brothers.

My superstition pounded. Signs around the propheet room in Walden read: THE ESSENCE OF FRIENDSHIP IS TOTAL TRUST, posted in the most prominent position behind George's chair.

THE HARDER THE TRUTH TO TELL, THE TRUER THE FRIEND THAT TELLS IT.

WORDS DO NOT / CAN NOT / WILL NOT HURT REAL FRIENDS, we were assured from the largest poster.

On the door that exited to the mudroom: REAL FRIENDS GIVE EVEN WHEN TAKING.

I looked to my right and saw another wooden door.

I could still bolt outside.

TRUTH AND TENDERNESS: ESSENTIAL ELEMENTS FOR FRIENDSHIP.

I noticed some empty spaces on the slats that covered the windows; more tools might be hanging there tomorrow.

I truly looked forward to tomorrow.

Alright, let's get this shit over with!

As in the Truth propheet, a candle flickered on the stereo console next to a bright happy looking plant.

When asked, and without protest or hint of an attention game, Ernesto began reading from *The Prophet*.

†

And a youth said, "Speak to us of Friendship."

Your friend is your needs answered.

He is your field which you sow with love and reap with thanksgiving.

And he is your board and your fireside.

For you come to him with your hunger, and you seek him for peace.

When your friend speaks his mind you fear not the "nay" in your own mind, nor do you withhold the "aye."

And when he is silent your heart ceases not to listen to his heart;

For without words, in friendship, all thoughts, all desires, all expectations are born and shared, with joy that is unacclaimed.

When you part from your friend, you grieve not;

For that which you love most in him may be clearer in his absence, as the mountain to the climber is clearer from the plain.

And let there be no purpose in friendship save the deepening of the spirit.

For love that seeks aught but the disclosure of its own mystery is not love but a net cast forth: and only the unprofitable is caught.

And let your best be for your friend.

If he must know the ebb of your tide, let him know its flood also.

For what is your friend that you should seek him
with hours to kill?

Seek him always with hours to live.

For it is his to fill your need, but not your
emptiness.....

—excerpted from Kahlil Gibran, "On Friendship,"
The Prophet

†

"Yo!" George interjected from of his seat. He mussed his hair and
lifted a leg over the arm of the chair.

"I said YO! Psst." Lofting a tightly rolled up index card between his
thumb and forefinger in the air, he spun it in his fingers with purpose
and brought it back down in front of his mouth. He flicked his Bic,
and pretended to light and smoke the index card. Ernesto tried to
continue the reading, a straight-man over the hubbub.

"YO! Wanna hit that shit, Ernie? Shhh. Keep it low, yo! Shhh.
Come on, take it. This is some good weed, DUDE! Don't you want it?
'Ere ya go, take it."

We all laughed uncomfortably as George first stared around the
room like a deranged paranoid, hit the doobie, and mock coughed. He
blew out pretend smoke, and wiggled the joint at Ernie and me. He
expected one of us to come fetch.

When no one approached his chair to take the fake rolled-up
doobie from George, he sprang out of his puffy chair at the head of
the horseshoe shape and walked around our black chairs, laughing,
as if he was stoned. Ernesto focused on reading the end of the selection through the clamor, since that was the original directive. We
could see Ernie's cheeks redden, in both irritation and shame, as soon
as it became clear this interrupting of the sacred reading was part of
George's shtick. Ernie, like Daphne and Narissa, was already especially
self-conscious about former drug use. This made George like them
more. You could tell because of how much attention he showed them.

George wandered to my side of the horseshoe and pushed the
spindled paper on me and pressured me to take the fake joint and take
a toke. Just a hit. I brought it to my lips and took a silent drag and
looked at George.

OK?

"Well, pass it on, man, hahaha, whooweee!" George ambled back to his comfy chair at the head of the broken circle, sat down with his legs spread wide, giggling like a dork. My peer group passed around the non-existent joint as everyone took a hit. Those that said they hadn't ever smoked weed took their first 'hit,' and roll their eyes in a pretend altered state. Without exception, we all forced a fake cough.

Out of the faux smoke-out "sesh-ON," as George called it, we started to talk about peer pressure and exchanged stories from home. For what seemed to be the first time in a while, our lives at home, our friends at home could be mentioned.

"I know you've all been dying to call your friends from home. Some of you did. Ahem. But we're past that now. Here's your big chance to cut up the streets, and cut up your friends."

This gave us all permission to walk around the room and talk about buddies and girlfriends at home. Tess would even ask, "What was that friend's name? What did she look like? What were her parents like? What did you guys do after that?"

For the first time in months we aired out all the good times from home. Andrew Oswald wandered over at some point, trying to make small talk about my adventures as a wayward traveler:

"Hey Zack, I used to hitchhike a lot when I was in my twenties. Did you ever hitch a ride on a motorcycle?"

I ignored him and his seeming desire to wheedle part of my "story" out, and promptly strutted across the room to Wally and Jamie, to join in the growing a cappella rendition of *Rhymin' & Stealin'* by the Beastie Boys. Usually it was against the Agreements to talk about music we used to listen to, or present any drug usage as fun, or even to have an image. The school had stamped that mindset out of us already.

Our group did this socializing around the room while boppy 50s music played loud enough to keep the room's occupants responsive. I realized halfway through one amusing anecdote shared with Ernie, that *this* was an ice breaker. This chance to socialize had been a ruse for George and Tess to spy on us, and to give us a sense of comfort before the evening really got under way. As the conversations dwindled I could see, finally, I wasn't the only one of my peers to notice the subterfuge. Jamie looked to me with a pursed smirk of recognition. Taking in our false sense of comfort, anyone could see that we were already loosened up for the propheet. I had allowed myself to forget for just a second that it was dark and Yukon cold out, and that I would be "middle school" when the sun rose.

Jamie's sly smirk had summed it all up in that one look to me. We were agreeing now to be told what a real friend was or wasn't. We'd never have a word to disagree.

This is what is happening. Whatever principles that RMA wanted me to know tonight, the teaching would be imprinted.

†

Back in the chess nook at the house, Dad and I moved into middle game when he ventured through the center to snatch a pawn. For that he experienced a sudden check, and lost his first power piece to me.

"We're being told that you will have real school classes next year. Academics – yours – are a chief concern to us, as you know. It is distasteful to think that you have already slipped behind on things through the years, so we expect your marks to be high . . . education-ally speaking." Dad's calm voice was measured. Not the pleading growl that was his yelling voice.

At the wooden chess set in our alcove, the Brothers kept tugging at me. I reverted to another section of the last propheet while Dad considered the puzzling gambit he found himself in.

"When we were at the Coeur d'Alene, Nat Farmer said some inter-esting things about how we got the self-concept we have of ourselves. Was that in your propheet too, Zack?"

I went back one month in time again, back to around 3 AM, when we got our lugs.

†

Nearly everyone had gotten theirs, and it was Ernie's time in front of the group.

"OK, Ernesto. Let's take a deeper look at what got you here. Yeah...I bet you do feel disgusted. I would too. That's a lot to carry around isn't it?"

"Yeah, I guess."

121

"So who did that little kid really want to impress, want love from?"

"My dad!"

"YEAH. That's RIGHT."

Right there in front of us something was happening. I could see that George and Tess could feasibly have a reason for all the shit they said to us. It was unfolding like origami. In a demented way, I hoped for another chance to relive my disclosures, to introspect in front of the group. I even felt cheated, like I hadn't gone deep enough because I had gone first.

"And you could never impress him. It was never good enough, right? Never good enough for Dad? You could never make him proud, could you?"

"No."

"What's that feel like? Walking around with that feeling? Not being able to make your dad proud of you. Not ever being able to get that attention – but *always* trying. I mean, he's supposed to be proud of you, isn't he?"

"Yeah."

"Supposed to love you? SO! What's that feel like?"

With growing urgency, staff whipped each of us up when they saw a flash, a recognition of the truth in what they coaxed out of us.

George and Tess were circling Ernie. They didn't miss a thing, picking up on every reaction in his face.

"That's the one! That feeling right there matters! Did you feel that? Say it again. 'I can't impress my dad,' 'He'll never be proud of me!' 'Why won't it ever be good enough for Dad?' Is this sounding right Ernie?"

"NO!"

Tears were slipping down his cheeks. George and Tess were soft-voiced and kept moving closer to him.

"It feels like I'm rotten! Like I'm unworthy...Like I'm a failure!"

"That's the truth, isn't it? Tell your friends that. Go ahead and look at them. Tell them what it's like. They care. They love you. I love you. I care. Yeah."

Ernesto lifted his eyes to tell us.

"I feel like a failure."

"For who?"

"For my dad...I can't fucking make him proud."

"Why?" Ernesto paused here. He didn't want to, but it was his turn to own his disclosures and acknowledge the horrors of his life that brought him to the group. The rest of us had been honest in our vulnerability.

"Because I am an unworthy FAILURE!" Ernesto visibly collapsed without falling.

"Yeah. That's right. Say that again for me."

"I'm a FAILURE! FUCKING FAILURE! Even here in this FUCK-ING ROOM! I can't ever make Dad proud." Ernesto's face crumpled as a wax figure might melt in a kiln. Saline flew out of Ernie's eyes and nose as I'd seen with so many other students at RMA. It was a beautiful, and intriguing, and scary thing to watch my friend, and so many of my peer group, fully surrender.

"Say that again so we all know how it feels to be you, to be trying SO HARD to impress every single person."

"I work so hard."

"Yeah, that's right." George stood there with his hand on Ernesto's shoulder. "It's OK to be vulnerable. To feel what you're feeling. Yeah, it's OK. Just let it out. Do you see the difference between true and not true friends? Yeah. Do you think he's telling the truth, Micah, Zack, Daphne? Yeah, me too..."

"Now let's put all of these feelings together, because this is really important work we're doing. And buddy, I know it feels horrible, but remember the Truth tools. It's worth it to feel as sad and vulnerable as you feel right now. These moments are the moments where you can be a friend, and let others be that for you. So, put it together . . . take all that responsibility for what you're feeling. You impress everybody because you can't make your dad proud of you? Was that it? And we know what it is when we're trying to get them to like us, to accept us. Yeah. Tell us. Right now."

George moved his burly arm around Ernesto's neck while he nodded. The two of them took a deep breath together.

Ernie bawled, "I can't make my dad proud, so I lie to people."

George tightened his hold on Ernesto, who quaked in the public reflection.

"I lie to make my dad proud," George whispered, as he cuddled Ernie.

They stood there and rocked a little while. I could see George's shirt dampen from Ernesto's moist, anguished face. George waved Terrance up to help him console Ernie. It looked a little weird with Ernie in a hug sandwich, crying, but he'd earned the respect of the staff. We all wanted that.

Tess called out, "How long have you been holding onto that, Pig-bug?" Ernesto allowed himself to be cradled closely by George and Terrance, having his back smoothed as he answered.

"Forever. Fucking forever."

"I lie to people to make my dad proud." Tess accentuated Ernie's lug by sweeping her face between Jamie and me at the heads of the horseshoe shape of black chairs.

"Don't you and Jamie think that that statement sums us Ernesto's front up here, in our community, so far?"

Tess summed Ernesto's ordeal up a final time as Kelly wrote it down neatly on a specially sized sticky label. Jamie kept a firm gaze on the stained gray carpet in front of his itchy-looking socks. I could feel the turmoil coming off of him. Normally Jamie was calm.

"I lie to make my dad proud." Tess probed Jamie with Ernesto's lug to see if it would ring true for him as well. To me, it felt like a taunt.

George smiled lovingly at us as he gently held Ernie, even giving him a long kiss atop his head while Ernie continued his breakdown. "I lie to make my dad proud. It's OK, you don't have to lie to me, impress me. None of us, right? Never again. You don't have to lie to be my friend, Ernesto."

†

"Wait a minute, can he do that, Richard? Oh, that's not a pawn, it's a bishop? Tell me what it can do again?"

Mom was pretending to learn chess, so I pretended to teach her. I knew her heart was not in it.

"Yeah, so the bishop stays on his own color and can move diagonally as far as you want."

"It's only two, but it feels like it's getting dark already," Mom said.

"You kind of get used to it, after a while," I replied.

†

Hedwig materialized, as light began to make its way through the window-slats into Walden. Just as in the Truth, she was a surprise guest at our propheet.

In a few moments, her role would be clear to all of us. She handed a large accordion file to Tess, pointed to her wristwatch, and left the room.

Something's about to happen.

Tess began. "Just listen to my voice. After you've found a little space in the room, go to that place you went as a child. Where is that dooger? Where does she go? Where is that safe place for him: maybe it's a tree, or your room, or a closet in your house? I had a patch of woods in back of my house with a tire swing. I'd always go there. Hedwig and George are going to come over to you and you tell them about your spot. How do you feel there? In your safe place? That safe time in your safe place. Be there now."

New music, a song I recognized from many nights of smoosh time and DMTs in the house: "*I need you, I need you. Like the flowers need the rain you know I need you…*"

"And just be in that place. Feel the sensations. . . . Now can you see the room around you. Or the tree. Are you in the moment? There. Good? OK. When you are ready, I want you to think of the person that you would have most liked to join you there. Who can you bring to your special spot? Who can you show that special place to? When you're alone. When you were hurt, this is the person you needed. Who is that person? MOM? DAD? Grandpa? Make it be a person, OK, not your family's dog, adorable though I'm sure he was."

Tess and George were always searching for things to say as they paced the room. The music filled in the gaps in my imagination.

"Who did that little kid want to be there with her? Who made him feel special? Let that person be there for you now. Just be there, allow

125

yourself to be with Mom, with Daddy. Be with that person that made you feel so special. . . . Yeah. That's it, Yu-Yu. Who's with you now? Uh hunh. And let's invite them. To your spot. Remember when those people we loved were our friends? When Mom was your best friend? Dad was your good buddy? Right? Tell your friend how you appreciate, and love them. Good work. 'I've missed you, Mommy!' Tell her, Bianca! 'I love you, Dad,' that's it, Zack. Micah tell Grandma how good it is too see her again. You've got her in a tree-house with you? That's great, my friend. Yeah. . . ."

"Those are real feelings there. That's good work, my little doogers. Who is that person that we love so much? That hero that made us feel that everything was OK. WE were SAFE, weren't we? That person was our hero. Who is that person? What do you really need to tell them? Listen to the music, be with that person now."

Allowing my ears to attune to the imagery of the song, and using that magnifying force of music, I became the vessel that allowed the familiar waves of tears and loneliness to wash over me.

What is it I'm supposed to be feeling?

During Tess's floor-time regression, I let myself feel what I wanted to have felt, magnifying the love I received in my imagination. I was far removed from the years when my parents were hands-on this way.

Mom and Dad weren't as sensitive as Tess or George. Hell, nobody in my family was as attuned to their emotions, their motivations, or their reactions to those feelings, as any staff or student here.

Every time one of the staff would stop by me or my neighbors on the floor and talk, it was with deepening emotion I conjured up photos, or memories. But I was upset, a little angry even, at the whole propheet so far. Did anyone in my peer group feel like I did? They seemed to fall into their emotions easier.

I forced moments of love between myself and family members, especially my father, to come into focus. I could remember the joy of being little, small enough to feel Daddy's big hands on my back, before giving me a loving pat and dropping me to the floor. The infrequent moments of being invited to bed with Mommy and Daddy after a nightmare. I tried not to think about why I might have received love on these occasions, whether it was real or if the memory was manipulated. I tried not to be distracted by the memory of the horrible nightmares that brought me in terror to their bed in the first place.

I had memories of other, warring times, with my parents.

The moments I spent with my grandfather's corpse. The many times my grandmother would hit my brother and me on the fanny with her hairbrush. When it was the brush, the wish for the bristles, instead of the hard plastic back. That first time when Grandma broke a wooden cooking spoon against my ass, and grabbed immediately for another. Almost ten years later, it was one of the ongoing jokes around the dinner table: she brought two wooden spoons when it was time to dole out spankings. There's no way that would play as comedy here, though.

†

Children learn at a very early age what their parents instill into them. So if they experience violence, that's what they learn. As they are prohibited from actually demonstrating what they have learned, they may initially be incredibly obedient and remarkably "good" children .... It is only later that they demonstrate the brutality they have learned from their parents. Artists often express unconsciously what they survived in childhood and later repressed. ...When individuals run amok, EVERYONE insists without a second thought that they have ABSOLUTELY no idea what can have prompted an adolescent to do so.... (Emphasis in the original.)

—Swiss psychologist Alice Miller, interviewed by Katharina Micada, 8 Oct 2009, translated from the German by Andrew Jenkins

http://www.alice-miller.com/en/an-interview-given-by-alice-miller-to-katharina-micada/

†

Staff disrupted or led the mirages of memory with more words. "OK. We're going to say goodbye to those loved ones now. Say goodbye. You'll get to see them again, I promise. But now. Goodbye, Daddy! Mommy's got to leave, now, Yu-Yu. It's OK, Zack."

127

I could hear the mumbling and crying stir around the room. The music came back up, and I was reminded of good goodbyes from when I had been a young boy. Goodbyes to cousins, goodbyes to grandparents that signaled the end of summer or Christmas visits were the first memories to crowd in. I tried to ignore the goodbyes to friends and girls from home that I cared about from recent years. I gently chastised myself: they were not the people – they were not the memories – that should be surfacing.

Next to me, Bianca Taylor said goodbye to an aborted baby, Ernesto cried about a grandfather, and Terrance's moans for his dead mother were impossible for me to block out. The gut-wrenching sobs of the kids around me faded as new music came over the speakers. George yelled over it while I tried to take in the new music.

The malformed noise was purposefully played out of tune, "*Look what they've done to my song....*"

"They're leaving you. You're alone now. Be with that. Feel alone. It's okay to feel sad. To feel empty. That's it. Let yourself be there now, listening to my voice. Goodbye, I love you. Are you alone yet? This is important work. What we're feeling right here is what it's like when you're on the outside, un-included. When did you decide to make your little kid unlovable? That feeling. Right, Zack? Micah? Craig? Yeah, Ivy. Who else? Narissa? Yeah, tell your dad you love him. Horatio? It's OK, buddy, but it is time to say goodbye."

I felt a little vindication now that my peer group was to get a small dose of the loneliness I was to be permanently identified with among them.

"OK, when you're feeling that isolation. I want you thinking about all the things your dooger did to run from pain. That pain made your little kid cover up his feelings. What happened to make you carry that luggage with you? I'LL ALWAYS BE A FAILURE FOR YOU, DADDY! IT'S NEVER GOOD ENOUGH FOR MY MOM! MY UNAWARENESS KEEPS ME UNLOVABLE! I'M INVISIBLE AND CYNICAL AND STARVING FOR ATTENTION. RIGHT, HORATIO? OWN YOUR LUG! I WANT TO HEAR IT, GODDAMMIT!"

"Let it ALL HANG OUT, HERE! BE HERE AND NOW! AAHHH, I'M ALWAYS GOING TO LET YOU DOWN, MAMA!

"Let's GET HONEST! HERE AND NOW! Open that LUGGAGE UP!"

Everyone relearned what it is to feel castigated and isolated. The kids who helped me to understand that I was on the outside, who introduced to me the work uncovering why that was, were now whimpering. Each of us rocked back and forth on our spots on the floor, repeating our lugs, each person in a heightened stage of regression.

My unawareness keeps me alone and unlovable.

We repeated them over and over, reliving all the shit we had done to our little kids. To our bodies, to others'. How we felt in the varied moments. Some talked quietly with bursts of inward frustration at the memories. Some of my friends had been adopted; they talked to their biological parents – as if they'd met before – this was new. Why were they unlovable? Unwanted? Learning, for example, that Yu-Yu had found out she was adopted only the year before, had made me, and others, empathetic to the point of devastation, seeing now the effect it had on her.

Be Here Now. It's OK to feel this if they say so. This is real.

Bianca softly mourned her mother, and at times cried out the words "...so FUCKING ALONE!" Some cried out in the pain of knowing their luggage was true. I stared at the stains in the carpet. Very occasionally I could catch a glimpse of someone looking at me as they paused in their introspection. We each had to be sure that we all were doing it.

My unawareness keeps me alone and unlovable.

The sounds all flooded back in when I unclamped my hands from my ears and ceased mumbling to myself.

"Ils ont changé ma chanson, Ma."

Tess flipped through materials in Hedwig's accordion file until she came to what she sought.

Tess squatted down next to me. She rubbed my shoulder as I stared at what she placed in my lap. Melanie Safka, singing in French now, joined the image with carnival fun-house sounding organ music.

This was a surprise.

"Sweetie, here's who you really are, Rock Bottom. You carry your luggage for this little dooger inside. All the times you've hurt him. And the times he got hurt? Is Spider-man going to be alone his whole life?

Do you think that's what he wants? No way, that's right, that's real. Keep looking. Look at that dooger! Look at Rock Bottom!"

A bigger surprise was how I felt when I registered that that image was my own: Zack's little kid. A photo of myself as a four-year-old stared into my swollen eyes.

He hates me.

He, too, wanted the me that sat on the floor in Walden to be alone.

I couldn't think of anything else.

From Tess, "What is this little dooger seeing right now, Zack? What does Spider-man need to tell you? What do you want to tell this little kid?" And I could hear the voices of my peer group around me begin this conversation, others just a minute behind, while they were themselves being introduced to the photographs of their Rock Bottoms.

I did feel love for the little kid that used to be me, but I didn't see how he could love the fourteen-year-old kid he looked back at.

This feeling ripped me up, and with carnival, youth-reminiscent organ music droning behind my thoughts, I felt as crazy as I ever had in my life.

What if I'm not "right where I need to be"? Am I going to remain feeling this way forever?

It was enough to produce profound terror, even deeper inside.

As staff presented the photos of each kid's little kid, my PG went from bawling to wailing. Listening and adding to the cacophony between breaths, and still trying to shut the language of foreign music from my ears, I felt us all looking into the rock bottom of our souls.

The unconditional love of a child. Wasted on the monsters staring back at the innocent. We, the warped and wicked, peered at the pure soul of our little doogers. We screamed, wailed, moaned, and cried. We held the pictures to our hearts and begged forgiveness for making them carry our metaphorical luggage. For marking up their shooter marbles. For marking other kid's marbles with daggers that we figuratively threw with hurtful talk, jealousy, and automatic reactions to insecurities.

Pretty soon, no matter what was said aloud or thought inside, it was to the cadence of a hateful song. Imagination rampant, music crescendoed and faded into its spacey intro anew. Wails filled the room, ears, brains, and psyches. Zack's voice joined in a chorus of crying into the stained gray carpet. The music tumbled and confused my mind, so I made an attempt to mumble; no matter what I said to myself, it brought worse feelings to me. I recovered my ears so I could hear my own voice talk to Rock Bottom over the carnival music and dissonant lament.

George's shoes paused next to Zack; George's aroma indicated that last night's fresh cologne had expired. The breath of his voice and his mouth was next to Zack's ear, so eyes opened instinctively. Slimy, big dingleberries of snot dangled from the end of Zack's nose. The effort to feel and portray introspection correctly made everything appear blurry.

Does everybody else translate like I did, looking at Rock Bottom?

Is the stuff going on in my mind the same as for others?

It's hard to be Here and Now when you think you may be going permanently insane and bursting blood vessels in your eyes.

When I thought of my "little kid," my "dooger" inside, I didn't just think of the innocent qualities. I thought also of evil me, the shitty me, the me that caused me to do bad things to my little kid. My older self before being sent to RMA had pushed away my parents, literally shoving Mom up against the wall one time, and figuratively made them turn their backs on me.

I was responsible for the things that made my little kid "decide" to grow up. I created that process.

Sunlight was beginning to illuminate the room.

We were all little kids, Rock Bottom.

My little kid represented automatically all the good things, the potentially wonderful things; therefore, Rock Bottom also reminded me of all the sadistic, mean, unlovable, hateful, negative things, the potentially grotesque too.

My Rock Bottom showed me the reality: It was all my fault that he grew up. He hated me for this.

Any normal idea that this growth – physical, emotional, and of course intellectual – would have occurred in my development naturally had just been falsified. Never seeing my own Rock Bottom was now lost to an alternative universe.

My parents had obviously sent the photograph that I stared at. In my mind this reinforced the notion that I was where I needed to be, and that this CEDU tool was important. They were absolutely complicit in making sure I felt this way: Twisted, hateful, scarred, and terrified that I'd warped myself permanently, and would be isolated from people for life.

"What have they done to my mind, Mom..."

†

Dear Zack,

We LOVED talking to you last night, right before you began the [Brothers] profeet. [...F]or the past week Mommy had been assembling this album for you. We wanted to give you a Hanukkah-Christmas present that you'd have your whole life, and we hope that we succeeded.

[...] We knew we were giving YOU a present, but we didn't know that the experience of putting the album together would be a present for US, too, seeing ourselves as children, as a young couple, and as parents of young boys. We ARE your parents, Zack, and you ARE our son. We love you and we miss you.

—Letter from author's parents, November 1988

†

The gag of Rock Bottom was orchestrated wonderfully. I never saw the presentation of the photo coming. Bravo!

I know, my parents know, the staff know, and my little dooger himself also knows, that I've been becoming a horrible monster my whole life.

After naps, after lunch, over new, quieted music, we went around holding our pictures against our hearts for everyone to see who we are, Rock Bottom. Barbra Streisand cried, *"What's too painful to remember we simply choose to forget."* Part of me just wanted it silent in Walden for a few minutes – and to have the freedom and privacy of my own thoughts.

But something happened when we woke up from the nap. I was changed. Instead of being upset at the bruises I'd received from trying to fit in, physically to their circle, I felt an enormous love for my people as I looked at them, their Rock Bottom, their little kids, the way we all were.

Princess, Peanut, Buster, Twinkles, Monkey Boy, Kissnose, Rainbow, and Pig-bug – all the little kids, our metaphorical shooter marbles from the Truth propheet, now had images. We were all there to witness.

Our little kids stared back from within us, not just in accusation, but now too with immediate, real forgiveness.

Our Rock Bottoms can forgive!

To get from my peer group that emotion I'm feeling for them right now, I'll do whatever it takes.

†

Mom broke through my memories again. "Well, I thought it was very emotional, Zack. I have so much respect for the introspective work you and your peer group are doing in the prophecies ... what'd we call them? Propheets? Right. Daddy and I were told we could all share about the recent one, since we had a little mini-propheet at the Coeur d'Alene.

"Tim and a handful of your older brothers and sisters here, one very pretty girl whose mother is also an aspiring writer she told me, were so effective in telling us about what you all do here all day. They answered all of our questions about you. It sounds like Tim, in particular, has gotten to know you in those raps?"

"Yeah. I'm glad I've gotten to know him since we'll be losing that whole PG here soon." I was actually a little saddened at the thought that I'd probably not see many of the oldest kids I'd been learning Spades from this winter.

"Well, they're finally moving on to the next chapter in their life, Honey." Dad made a move that left his bishop open. I didn't even want to go on that square but I had to take it or I'd regret it later.

"Their lakefront workshop was very emotional. Your father is such a softie." Dad grunted at Mom's comment, still focused on creating a good use of his knight on the wooden chess set between us.

They had no idea. None.

From their descriptions, I realized that their workshop had echoed – very faintly – the lessons I learned in the propheets. The staff had mimicked the back-turning exercise, told them about Rock Bottom, and even attempted to regress our parents! Mom would talk to me in upcoming months about things that shaped the person she was. This place never stopped revealing deeper lessons.

Mom seemed to be amusing herself watching the other kids and their parents – probably taking notes for her next book – and Dad gave up the metaphorical fight in front of us.

†

> It is not accidental that many destructive cults tell their members to 'become like little children,' .... Adults can easily be age-regressed to a time when they had little or no critical faculties. As children, we were helpless and dependent on our parents as the ultimate authority figures.
>
> —Steven Hassan, *Combating Cult Mind Control*, Freedom of Mind Press 2015 (25th anniversary edition), pp 99-100

†

Next, we did some more tricks with our Rock Bottom photos. Most appealing was the new John Lennon music; most magnified was the bright pageantry, plus the fact that I wasn't even tired any more. "*When you're crippled inside*," John Lennon sang, goofily, as George introduced us to "eye-mingles."

My PG was to walk the room at different speeds. We were to make eye contact with one another, but to break it when the other kid noticed.

Next, George had us make big, fake, cheek-to-cheek, toothy smiles. The clambering music went back up while we each held our photo over our hearts, face-out, and walked quickly around the room.

Like most new things, they leveled us up with variations.

"Smile big! Let's see the masks! COME ON! That's it, everybody," Tess instructed.

As we passed each other, we first gazed down deeply into the eyes of the little kid in the photo, and then up into the teenaged face with a fake smile plastered on it.

This was another one of those bizarre exercises, like the shoving, that was only going to begin to make sense after the propheet was over. Even if the exercise seems fun for a few minutes, before the concepts have time to mature in your brain, it just keeps going, and it's not fun anymore. The music keeps playing, so you keep smiling.

"OK, now make a huge frown! Let's all change paces. Slo-o-o-w motion. Weight. Let everybody see the hurt. The reactions! Plaster that anger on, Micah, heavy! GOOD! THAT'S IT, PEOPLE!"

After pausing the music, George told us why we were doing the "eye-mingles."

"These are people on the street. You could be sharing with them what you've been learning here, but people look away because they're afraid to be hurt."

The exercise was supposed to demonstrate the ways we betrayed our little kid by using facial expressions to shield ourselves from hurt. Or something.

After the final bathroom break, Tess wound the propheet down with her tenderest voice. As usual I tried to make sense of things with an intellectual reduction. The closing segment of the night/day was meant to reverse any harmed feelings from the night before, and solidify a positive, opposite expression of our lugs. I was skeptical as Tess moved us back into a big circle. But it stayed loose and kind, this time.

We held our Rock Bottom photos over our hearts, as Tess solemnly galvanized for us the idea that a dualistic relationship existed between our negative lugs and the positive. We had to also practice validation in their opposites. We had to see that, like in the Truth propheet's final hours, if we were perceived by ourselves or others in a negative light, we ought to be able to convince people with new perception and action that we were capable of change. I wanted to be viewed as honest, which I felt I was, and self-approving which I knew I wasn't.

My unawareness keeps me alone and unlovable.

"Bianca, all of the truth you'll ever need, and, like we discussed, all the forgiveness, therefore, is inside of you. Micah, same for you. All the loyalty you'll ever need, that you spend so much time testing on me, on others, well, that's really all in you, you see?"

"All the loyalty I'll ever need is inside of me," Micah echoed, with some doubt.

"Excellent! It will take practice, and getting used to. Like Hedwig says, it's like a coat of arms."

The staff laughed at some inside joke.

Tess continued, "Now, we're going to sit down with our cards, and write down the top five things we need, based on our lugs from last night so that we can, uh, manifest those positive qualities. We'll come back to the circle afterwards. Begin."

After we made our lists, we gathered again and read them out.

"All of the beauty I'll ever need is inside me."

"All of the courage . . ."

"All of the awareness . . ."

After about fifty of those, we were done. Hedwig came back to collect the photos for her accordion file, and we followed her out to where our shoes were, for the procession back to the house. Then it was time for sharing, hugs, and dinner.

I wondered what my mother and father's lugs would have been if they'd gone through the real propheet? This thought brought me back to real time.

†

Only about a couple of hours until parents were supposed to leave campus.

Dad's second game was as good as over but he was still concentrating, so I gave him back his last move.

Visits were drawing to a close. The sun set at 3 PM in our arctic asylum, and parents were to be gone by 5:15.

They don't live here. They're only seeing what they want to see.

"OK kiddo, as my Super-D-daddy used to say."

That was Mom's pet name for her own father who'd died when I was ten or eleven. It was also her signal to say, "Enough lollygagging. Get me back to civilization, Richard.'"

Dad held me in a nice long hug, and gripped my face lovingly. "Now, do good. Use your head. And make absolutely sure you don't run away, or 'split' again. OK? Promise me. Trust the process. The time it takes while you conquer your doubts and negative-serving self-concepts of yourself truly does trump all other things. I am proud of you. When you look at time, and how short a couple of years is. . . . The real world will still be out there for you, Honey, it's not going anywhere."

Mom's parting words were actually, "Don't forget to put your balaclava in the cubbyhole."

Puke.

"Your friends and family will still be home in Virginia after you graduate," Dad assured me.

None of us could know that I'd hardly see anyone from home ever again. Mom and Dad took off.

†

> Dear [Mr. Jade]
>
> Richard and I just returned from our visit to Zack at Rocky Mountain Academy and I think the picture says it all. Zack is doing well and we are happier than we've been in years. All of this is in no small part to your efforts on Zack's behalf, and for this we will be forever grateful...
>
> [...]His readmission into RMA– where we hope and pray his progress will continue – was a direct result of his relationship with you. In a very real way, you've "saved" our son.
>
> —Letter from author's mother to [Mr. Jade] (who bonded with Zack during Survival) 30 Dec 1988

FIFTEEN

Dear Zack

I want to tell you what a joyful visit we had with you and how proud Mommy and I are of what you have accomplished.

We're proud of what you accomplished on survival.

We're proud of what you have already achieved at RMA.

We're proud of the mature and thoughtful way you handled your "disclosures."

We're proud of the gift that you made for us. We've displayed it exactly where you said.

We're proud of how well you have mastered chess, and especially of the patience and skill you showed in teaching Mommy how to play.

We're proud of how hard you are working. We do know how hard it is to do everything that is expected of you at RMA, and we are so happy you are succeeding.

We're proud of the way you kept things from getting out of hand when we were talking about the "how long do I have to stay here" issue. (As I told you, I think the best way to deal with this is to keep our goals in mind and not to worry about setting a specific time. The goal is for you to continue to work hard at RMA so that when you do leave, you will be able to succeed wherever you go next. When the time comes, we'll know.)

Zack, RMA has been very good for you, and I think you know this. Keep working hard, and all the doors to a happy and successful life will be open for you.

I love you son. I anxiously await our next visit.
Dad.
—Letter from author's father, 30 Dec 1988

✝

138

In many ways, it was a relief when moms and dads departed from the campus. The stress leading up to their visit, the invasion of our little emo-sector, and all the tears from Christmas night were new perspectives that needed their own time for adjustment and digestion. A familiar discomfort returned as we realized the fun n' games of Santa's Workshop and the lightness of Christmas visits were over. Girls now returned to ponytails pulled back so tightly it looked painful. Many smaller Agreements, like the hair-always-pulled-back Agreement had been spongy during the parent visits because older students – the enforcers – had flown off.

The more emotional pain you had to display, the better a CEDU person you were.

If I wasn't staring into the abyss of my own concepts of Thinking, struggle, and past n' present – and future doomed friendships – I was staring into an older or younger RMA brother or sister's abyss.

I vowed to pick up what staff was putting down for me to learn. And I understood why so many boys and girls were on gender-specific bans. Boys had been users, and we all had been used. But the girls had an added sense of societal shame. A lot of the time it went back to being sexually active, self-loathing, being too material, or having had abortions.

I always felt that girls had it easier than boys at RMA. It seemed that girls could always go to their feelings a little faster than us boys because in the real world that had been the norm. While shame and sexual stuff were metaphors for girls' issues, we boys took out our anger differently. We had other stuff to feel shameful and guilty about. I already had learned from the program to associate the former imagey version of me with accursed sexual or aggressive motivations.

I started to care in, with, and for the program; my PG and the other kids were my family now. The facilitator staff were the parents. The older brothers n' sisters showed me how to be, and how to act, as they had emulated and mimicked the behaviors of kids that had gone before them.

My unawareness keeps me alone and unlovable.

Like a mantra.

139

I took the lug especially seriously. It was as Hedwig and Tess had said to me in a rap: I had a uniform that didn't fit me well, but at least I'd gotten my lug – my first medal – and was working with the thoughts and feelings that came with it, by extension. "You are right where you need to be," she insisted. The more guilt, shame, and doubt in myself I carried, the more meaningful the suit was, and the more the prognoses of the staff seemed correct. The significance of my lug, the quality of it – not to be confused with comfort – changed, and the more it did, the more I could expect others to treat me with respect.

Being in Brave added more privileges, too. I was able to choose a Spades partner during game time on Saturdays. Better, I got to start watching football with Summit kids. The kids in Summit always reserved the seating area ringed with infamous cowhide pillows that left little bristled bovine wisps in our hair and sweatshirts. This area called the pit was situated in front of the hearth – too big and special to simply be called a fireplace. The pit was ceremonial. Nightly last lights, before- and after-propheet sharing, and program graduation rituals all happened there.

I admit to feeling a little wash of special-ness ebb up in me to sit with older brothers like Tim Chalmers and his peer group, for them to know my name. It did give me a privileged feeling, I guess. As a newly minted Brave kid, getting a space with the Summit Grads on a scratchy pillow during the Sunday 7-10 AM TV hours translated to a quantifi-able accomplishment.

After the Brothers, my whole understanding of the program changed.

I could already witness changes in myself and others. I could now credit the program with showing us how to morph, to make the associations I thought they wanted us to concentrate on. The personal growth that the program demanded was almost like science, but not too far a cry from what I would categorize as the spiritual. While there wasn't "proof" of what I was learning, I likened the process to learning mythology, gospel, and the great Greek epics – none of those influenc-ing stories were to be taken literally, yet they explained everything.

My status in the school was also confirmed during the Brothers exercises. The more I focused on being accepted and understood, the more lonely, isolated, and misunderstood I started to feel. As pre-scribed by everyone who'd been in Idaho longer than me, I wanted to use my lug to help me do the introspection I needed in order to work the program best. If I applied myself honestly, I could feel better.

While I was struggling with my issues, more authority was bestowed on me. Being asked to escort a kid down to the wood corral was like receiving an epaulet for my uniform. My struggles based on my lug showed the true mark of quality in my new suit. Now being here wasn't just about how long I'd already been here, it was how I interacted with all the other kids and staff, knowing all the while that I was being viewed differently as months began to whiz by.

My unawareness keeps me alone and unlovable.

For now, I was still concerned with how these revelations from the second propheet affected me, not yet with how I would effect more change in others – or how all of this was even applicable to my personal emotional growth. The program's deepening introspection had only been foreshadowed in the Brothers Keeper propheet. More powerful tools were on the way. Studying more carefully than I ever had in real school, I logged information and sought answers to internal questions.

How to be? How could I chameleon the older kids' behavior while camouflaging my thoughts? How to make use of what I see and learn from the dozens of older brothers and sisters?

But for now: Please don't make me have to feel the pain, don't let me live in awareness that I don't trust my friends, that I'll always be on the outside, and pushing away and being pushed away from those people in my world that matter most. Don't confirm my belief that the vacant chasm inside of me is here forever.

Is my little kid – the real me deep down which is supposed to be innocent – just negative Thinking?

All of this would haunt me more and more leading into and after the next propheet, the I Want To Live, coming in a few more months. I'd join Warrior family after that.

✝

       I'm in another class and I'm stuck so I will tell you where I'm at. I'm in a bad space with myself because this thinking is real strong it's telling me that it's not worth it to live and that I should just finish it all and

141

kill myself. Well anyway, I smoked a half cigarette today and I got all sorts of shit for being a sell-out can you imagine one fucking cigarette.

Also considering some of me other writings I have been wanting a joint worse than I've ever wanted one. I've been dreaming about it. Really bad. Or is it really good. The reason it is good is because it tells me I haven't been changed or brainwashed that much and I don't know if it is better to ...leggo for a while and just trust. Now I really truly in my heart of heart believe that things would work if I went home now. But my parents don't know that. I'm not positive of course but I honestly believe that. I have to share more.

—Author journal 17 January 1989

I haven't written because I haven't had my note-book I thought I would be on a full time because they found it and said they were going to read it til I said that it is not right that they want to read my personal stuff so they asked me what was in it and I said Doors, negativity, badrapping and other stuff so they want me to throw this stuff away so I'm not going to. I am just going to concentrate on being positive. But I don't know what to do. I am getting sick of this place. I am confused. Okay I'm in my dorm now so I guess it's safe. I am way contracted up with [Jamie.] We talk about anything we want to. We do our own program. Something I'm scared of though is that things are going to get out of hand like he is all I have some toxics that we can inhale. This scares me. Because to a certain extent I want to do it to another I don't. I really don't want to see him Die. And those toxants are pretty heavy stuff. We actually went through how we could get dope to smoke. I don't know how long I can hold the contract. What should I do. I've already been informed that I'll go to a lockup if I'm caught. But now I realize how much I don't want to be here. All I know is now I'm definitely going to have to start hiding this notebook. I'm very scared and confused and very homesick. I've only got two minutes left so I'll say again I'm lost and keep thinking now that if I keep refusing and stuff from everywhere I go. My parents would eventually let me come home.

I've got to go bye.

—Author journal 24 January 1989

†

Santas Workshop was fun for me. I learned how to do leatherwork, finger knitting, and normal knitting. The thing I liked the most was working with wood. I had done it before but I had to refresh my memory.

Christmas for me is something I am sure I will always remember. I don't remember many Christmases I've had in the past which leads me to believe they weren't very special.

I got touched when they were bringing and handing out presents because I received a present from my baby sister. The best present I got was a photo album my mom put together. They shared it with me at visits and I learned parts of their story.

—Author, school assignment, from the "Santa's Workshop" page

†

Visits for me were good. They helped me see that my parents really are people. I never knew that they meant anything to me, and that I meant anything to them.

Disclosures were a challenge for me. I thought my parents already knew them but I was wrong. ... Neither of them could relate very well to what I was saying. That scared me a lot.

I enjoyed playing board games with my parents because at home when we tried to have fun I ruined it. I had the privilege on my visit to have a picnic if weather permitted but it was too cold. So during the last hour of the visit my dad drove into town grabbed a pizza and came back with chips and another assortment of food. We then had a picnic in the old library.

—Author, school assignment, from the "Visits" page, December 1988

Dear Zack,

You gave us the best Christmas ever! Daddy and I are still smiling non-stop. It was so wonderful to see you looking so well. And it was great to be able to talk to you without all the anger and sadness that used to get in our way. We love you so much and it makes us the happiest parents in the world to know that you're growing into the fine young man that you want to be. You're starting to take responsibility and getting yourself ready to make decisions about your life. Doors will open for you, there's no doubt, as you keep up the hard work of learning to work, to understand, to communicate. [...]

The film turned out very well too so both [sister] and [brother] got to see you in your snowy environment and on skis. I know seeing you smiling and looking like a fine young man will make them happy. [...]

I love you. I'm proud of you. I hope you're not smoking.

Love, Mommy

—Letter from author's mother, January 1989, after parents' first visit to RMA

It was almost like parent visits and Christmas had never happened. We were back to life as usual at RMA.

Raps after parent visits and about Christmases past always revealed the most detail about what life had felt like for kids back home. This was when we got clear ideas about which uncle had been a perv, or

which cousins got stoned and drunk together, whose folks were separated, divorced, and remarried, who'd recently found out they had
half-brothers and sisters at home, or who'd stolen stuff, as I had, to use
for presents (since I spent my money on cigarettes and the body-fuel of
burgers when I used to skate around town).

Staff could pounce on every detail of visits, and the insights led
us to slowly prefer the program – and life with our real friends in this
bubble – to the hurtful, unaware, outside world. How this perspective
was gained and the pace at which the conscious realizations lurched
out of the shadow depended, like most details we'd bring up in the
program, on which level of understanding about the program we'd
attained in propheets or other program milestones.

I didn't want to go there, but in one rap after parent visits Darlayne
asked about how it felt to take medicine for depression. How it felt to
know that Mom thought there's something wrong with my brain.

"Let's dig around in there. Now concentrate. Tell the rap how it
feels to be you."

I dredged up a memory to keep Darlayne sympathetic and soft,
and to corroborate my growing introspection; I'd do anything to keep
Darlayne happy and not think me oppositional anymore.

There must be an answer for why I started taking all those unnecessary pills. Everyone in the rap now knew that I had taken pills for
depression and ADD, not because those diagnoses were true, but
because I had chosen to develop a system by which I was reacting to
negative attention from Mom and Dad. We had to look deeper. Now
I was gleaning that my Thinking had constructed that self-delusion,
self-chicanery, even though the proper terminology hadn't been taught
to me. I was still aware of my choice to gain the acceptance and attention of my parents by any means, including somehow self-poisoning
my natural ability to learn. This was how I learned to take responsibility for my being such a failure in school.

"Everybody kept saying that schoolwork should be easy for me,
and that I have the 'aptitude,' but couldn't do it." Kelly pressed me on
when and why I chose to become a failure for my dad. My lug in the
last propheet had me realize that I had constructed the role of a spaz in
school, a kid who needed pills to jacket my clowning and resistant – or
in Mom's term, disobedient – behavior.

Because Darlayne and Kelly insisted on probing, I looked at a memory. Instead of a microscope, binoculars inaptly came into my head, and it wasn't a Mom memory like I expected. This Dad memory surprised me, and came spontaneously – so I knew it to be important to bring up.

✝

College football. It's UVa's game day. I'm lucky to be in the memory. It's a real privilege to go to the game, and even jollier because I get to go to the game with Dad.

Wait! I tried to shift away from the thought, like I used to juke kids on the soccer pitch at home, but Darlayne and Kelly were there to turn me back into it.

On what should have been one of the most special times I could have early in that fifth-grade year, Dad invited me – by letter – to share one of his two tickets to the game. He drove us down the way I knew so well from my bicycle and skateboarding adventures. Past the "Corner" and past first-year Grounds, past the hallowed former brick chamber of Edgar Allan Poe, and all that Jefferson hoohaw, or Wahoohaw, at the Rotunda, and past the church where Chuck's dad's funeral had been, we found a place to park the car. Now we started following all the pretty girls, and Frisbee-tossing boys carrying their beer to watch the home team at a very familiar part of the UVa Grounds. I knew the area well, and had discovered secret hide-out retreat spots since this very stadium was vacant and fun to explore late at night.

An old guy dressed in a bright orange jacket and khakis ripped our tickets and handed us the stubs. Dad and I nestled into our seats. I was sitting where Mom or my brother usually sat with him.

During a field goal attempt in the first quarter, Dad and I got in a tugging war over the binoculars. It happened in just one hot moment, like a number of the fights we had. Fast fights. In this second of excitement I thought I was in charge of the binoculars.

It was his flash to anger. A quick cock of the head, a flush of air to pursed lips, and a bugging out of his eyes behind glasses. He was furious. If I ever need to reference them, my parents' faces in moments of acute distress are forever inked onto the lids of my mind's eyes. At RMA, I needed to remember. And that look on Dad's face was one of his most memorable expressions.

The strap for the black binos was hefty around my neck, and Dad was grabby. He started to snatch the clunky shaped heavy object before the strap was free of my head. It happened fast. Briefly, without knowing why, or intending it — like so many of the ways I usually fucked up — I held onto them. The binoculars weren't the issue. I wasn't done with them.

Dad yanked the binoculars out of my grip as he stood up to watch a play on the field. At the same time, the man on the bench behind us also rose up. In the enormous crowd that engulfed us, Dad couldn't see or know about the man behind us.

The man's head collided with the binoculars which were now in Dad's hand. The guy clutched at his head while the Cavahoos took positions to protect the kicker behind the scuffle. One man held his head, while everyone around us cheered at the spectacle. The other, more familiar, man grabbed my arm and dragged me to the parking lot.

"Don't leave the car. I'll be back after the game."

What was my responsibility? What happened to my Rock Bottom?

I was starting to understand. Variations on these themes — with varying degrees of "blame" — were my life. These steps, repeated, led my Thinking to take over my innocent Rock Bottom.

By program theory — which I was buying into — it was important to look. Denying to look at what made yourself tick — now that we were convinced that there was something wrong with us — would be even worse. Many of the "whys" of my shitty behavior and personality had already been examined by others and myself before RMA. Now, with the program's help I could discover more.

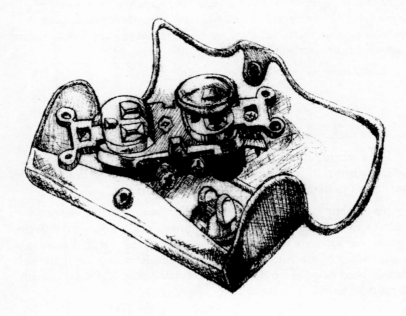

SIxTEEN

Dear Mom & Dad

I love you. I am in a very peaceful mood when I am here. You should be very proud of me. I have caught The Bug, The Reading Bug. I cannot stop reading. By the time you get this letter I will be done with every book I brought and that you sent me. [...]

Would you please send 1,2, or 3 more books and the Hill School's address and reading list..... I am very confident I will do well at school.

Your wonderful, beautiful, gracious, loving, tender, Modest, sensitive, kind, Smart son.

—Letter from author to parents, from Garlan, France, summer 1987 (One year before going to RMA, one month before briefly attending the Hill School.)

†

Dear Zack,

I've never received a better letter than yours. I've never been so happy to read a letter. To learn that you've caught the reading bug has got to be the most wonderful news. Or maybe, the best news is that you love us, or you feel confident about your new school year. All those bits of information made your parents so happy. We were on a happy cloud for days. [...]

—Letter from author's mother in reply to author, summer 1987

†

Dear Zack

[...] After our wonderful two days with you, it was interesting to talk with [your brother]. He could use

149

some of those skills you have learned. I wish he could go through a PROPHEET and even take part in some RAPS. [...]

Please read. Next to what you're doing in raps and at the school, reading will be the next best thing you can do. I mean this. I'll send your glasses.

—Letter from author's mother, January 1989

†

The best part of a good book is the part you are engrossed in, when you're right there in the moment. Both of my parents were obsessed with reading. In my parents' house, reading became the unique force that could settle me, and make me be still. The quantity of my mom's approval had been proportionate to the amount of knowledge my eyeballs bounced across and took in. If I could memorize text, anything historical, that was a bonus.

†

The books I sent and which [Prescott] will give you as you earn them are: *Rascal, Sounder, Day No Pigs Would Die, Hatchet, Swiftly Tilting Planet, Island of the Blue Dolphins, Of Mice and Men.*

I'm not familiar with all of them, but they were on a list I had and two young men in the book store said they LOVED the books and had read them when they were about your age. I don't know which one you'll earn first, but get to work. ...

—Letter from author's mother, 28 February 1989

†

It couldn't have been predicted; Prescott Freshwater wasn't proud or happy that I was reading. In fact, reading had the opposite effect on him. In Prescott's opinion, I was jailhousing, not looking deeply enough at my issues. He did not approve of what I thought to be my increased level of awareness in the program, and how it applied to my past, present, and future. To him, reading meant I was hiding from my inner child and encouraging my intellectual inner demons.

"It's even worse than playing games, because you aren't even spending time with another person. You're isolating and distracting from the real work. If you're actually conscious of it, then it validates us both. Let's work on you."

Prescott banned me from reading.

The lack of quality time with other people was Prescott's reason for banning me from books, because they distracted me from the real issues that staff thought I needed to talk about in raps. This would come back to haunt me in the future, but for now served as a way for me to get to know Prescott. He requested that I be in his raps a lot.

I had to be honest with more people. I needed to use the Truth and Brothers tools, and combine that knowledge with my awareness. Doing so made me mimic George and a handful of older students; this all made me a growing player on the indictment-making stage in raps. I was becoming a ferocious CEDU monk.

I hid out in the chess nook a lot with Terrance. People left us alone to concentrate there. At first I was just staring off. I could beat my parents because I knew which way the pieces moved, but I often lost to the better players in the school, until I began to pay attention. Terrance was flashy, but he almost always won. It was indisputable that Terrance was the best chess player in the school, and after a month of my reading bans, I was the second best. This was because after cowboy coffee one morning, Terrance told me a few of the real rules and how the game is normally won:

"Alright dude. So. First, the opening is the most important part of the game, and even if it looks like you're losing pieces in the setup of your pawns, Do Not Worry. Second, see first rule – time is of the essence in controlling the center four squares of the chessboard. Whoever 'owns' that territory 'should' win the game. Notice the quotations around should and own though; we'll get to that. Rrright. Thirdly, winning the game is only possible in not losing the game; once your dominance is established watch out for crafty opponents, and always make the mate as soon as possible."

That was it. The last part about getting an opponent into checkmate is the most challenging of the basic philosophy. Most of the time in opening game, I knew what my next move would be, regardless what my opponents opted to open with. So I got good at playing catch up, and colonizing the middle four squares.

When Prescott then put me on bans from card games, sports, board games – even chess – I was sure that there was conspiracy at play. Prescott didn't want me to be the best chess player in school. The one confidence I had going, being good at chess, was diametrically opposed to the demand for emotional growth in the program! Worse though, Terrance Whittlemore – the only other kid in the school who could consistently see one further damn move past me, inevitably leading toward skirmishes for the middle of the chessboard – was put on bans from me. It was his punishment for "hiding out in chess and books" – for hanging out with me.

That was to be my last infestation of the "reading bug" about which my mom and I had corresponded. After I had to move back in with my parents when the Hill School kicked me out in eighth grade, the steady decline accelerated.

I stayed awake late at night – now deeply concerned about my approval ratings, and how to be a better chameleon of the staff and upper-school dudes. I thought about the parent visit. I thought about my lug. I thought about how to put opponents in gambits.

My unawareness keeps me alone and unlovable.

I am attached to the rest of my PG by only the thinnest of membranes. I am unnecessary.

Without finishing the program and knowing the secrets revealed in the Summit, life would be less meaningful. But consider the potential if this were true, of having abilities and awareness that few others knew, and tools that almost nobody else used – the life that could only be attained through CEDU!

I wanted meaning, I wanted knowledge unique, I wanted more than all to have the completion of the program be the means by which all the things I'd failed at in the past would be forgiven. The necessity of having to be sent away for my own good, the programming that I was receiving here, guaranteed all of this, didn't it? Didn't it promise to restore the admiration from Mom and Dad, satisfy the systems of school, and outfit me with special tools in the future?

†

One brick for pain and here is my wall.
One pound for guilt and I will carry the world.

152

Give me a feast and I will starve myself.
Give me a friend but don't let them touch me.
I'll let you in but not far enough to know me. See my
love but don't tell me. See my beauty but don't look
at me.
Respect my power but don't listen to me.
Listen to my thinking, but don't believe it, as I do.

—Author journal, 1989

†

Dear Zack,

Now, I think I've got guilt. I think I SHOULD have put
off the darn t.v. that was in the background so I could
better hear what you were saying. [...]

Happy Valentine's day!!! [...] You've been given a
good role model (with some flaws I'll admit) in Daddy,
and I see that NOW you're able to appreciate him. I
love you and I love the young man you are becoming.
[...]

—Letter from author's mother, February 1989

PART TWO RESOURCES

We need to think of brainwashing [...] in secular, scientific terms, as a set of techniques that can act on a human brain to produce belief change.

One striking fact about brainwashing is its consistency. Whether the context is a prisoner-of-war camp, a cult's headquarters or a radical mosque, five core techniques keep cropping up: isolation, control, uncertainty, repetition and emotional manipulation.

In Maoist China, ... groups of students engaged in a process called "struggle": one person was accused of, or confessed to, having "wrong thoughts" or beliefs; then other group members showed their loyalty by competing to challenge and condemn the unfortunate victim and reiterate the communist message. Students also had to keep detailed, publicly available diaries of what they were thinking: lengthy confessions of thoughtcrime, in effect. Diaries, struggle groups, lectures, debates – and always the same message, hammering into the skull again and again, breaking down resistance.

[...] The contrast between the complicated, fragmented muddle of the unbeliever's life and the pure simplicity of true belief is often emphasised by ideologues who understand the power of uncertainty to frighten and unnerve people who may already feel that their lives are out of control.

—Kathleen Taylor, PhD, "Thought Crime," *The Guardian*, 7 Oct 2005 http://www.theguardian.com/world/2005/oct/08/terrorism.booksonhealth

†

The winter holiday celebration at Rocky Mountain Academy, one of the highlights of the year, is just around the corner. It seems an opportune time to acquaint you with our observance of the holiday season.

The focal point of the festivities is the decoration of a huge fresh-cut tree. Students make ornaments from fruits, cookies, candy and natural materials taken from the forest; the lodges are trimmed with wreaths and holly boughs. Carols, poems, and stories relate the origins and meanings of the various holidays observed during this period. It is a very special time of giving; gift items exchanged among students are handmade tokens of care and reflections. Downhill and cross country skiing trips, wilderness expeditions for some of the students, baking and cookie decoration, special craft instruction and gift making activities will make this a full, rich time.

Due to the increased activity and, of course, the emotional nature of the holiday season, we shall not schedule parent visits between November 23 and December 25. We invite you, however, to visit with us and your child on Monday, December 26, and Tuesday, December 27, 1988. Most of the students in the upper school will be embarking on home visits at that time. This should be an intimate, personal time for you and your child, please do not bring guests. [...]

The enclosed list of gift suggestions will guide you in selecting items which are tokens of love and supportive of your child's activities in the school.... [W]e ask that there be a maximum of seven presents sent to your child. With the exchange of gifts between student and faculty, plus those sent from home, there are in excess of 1,000 presents. You can imagine the logistical problems surrounding the gift opening. We strongly recommend that the total cost of all the gifts sent by the whole family (inclusive of siblings and relatives) to your child not exceed $300.00. we emphasize, above all during this season, the joys of giving oneself.... We will be returning all gifts received beyond the seven maximum to parents. [...] Please do not bring presents with you when you visit as the time of gift exchange will have passed and the visit can focus on family time. Your Parent Communicator will be happy to assist you in making your holiday arrangements.

We look forward to sharing the holiday with you and your child and send our warmest regards.

—Letter from RMA director to parents, 29 September 1988

†

The most basic feature of the thought reform environment ... is the control of human communication. Through this milieu control the totalist environment seeks to establish domain over not only the individual's communication with the outside..., but also – in its penetration of his inner life – over what we may speak of as his communication with himself.

—Robert J. Lifton, *Thought Reform and the Psychology of Totalism: A Study of "Brainwashing" in China*, Martino Publishing, 2014, p 420

†

[...] 6. In keeping with the "Draft Body of Principles and Guarantees for the Protection of Mentally Ill Persons and for the Improvement of Mental Health Care" of the U.N. Commission on Human Rights, the treatment environment of the Special Psychiatric Hospitals [in the Soviet Union] should be rendered less restrictive and patients granted more rights and opportunities to engage in normal activities. There should be fewer deprivations and restrictions, such as restriction of access to writing materials, censorship of mail, close supervision of visits, and the absence of personal possessions.

7. Hospitalized patients should be informed of their rights, and these rights should be guaranteed in legislation and regulation. Patients should be invited to participate to a greater extent in treatment decision making. Grievance procedures should be instituted,

and patient advocacy services should be imple-
mented through ombudsman or other types of rights
protection programs.

—*Report of the U.S. Delegation to Assess Recent
Changes in Soviet Psychiatry to Assistant Secretary
of State for Human Rights and Humanitarian
Affairs*, U.S. Department of State, July 12, 1980,
Executive Summary Part C. Prepared by Richard
J. Bonnie, Esq. Legal Process and Patients' Rights
Recommendations, pp xiii–xiv

Adolescents subjected to totalistic reform environments are often witness to a heartbreaking cruelty,
but their stories combined tell a larger story of an
invisible monster, sold to parents and the public as
therapeutic growth. Institutionalized persuasion is
not therapy, it's orchestrated assault, indoctrination
and reconditioning. The practices of many programs
can be defined as torture, and according to international law, the [United States] federal government
is criminally negligent in its failure to provide safe-
guards against these practices.

—Marcus Chatfield, *Institutionalized Persuasion: The
Technology of Reformation in Straight Incorporated and
the Residential Teen Treatment Industry*, 2014, p 275

PART THREE

159

Zack Bonnie

SEVENTEEN

In the real world, people would never see the value of being so into their own emotions that they scheduled time to cry and yell all afternoon. They wouldn't see the value in continuing to indict a person who hurt your feelings or made you mad, just because it was therapeutic for you to do it, even if the person had already been reduced to a sobbing puddle. In the real world, parents, dead relatives, former teachers, and all the other various past transgressors would never actually sit in the vacant plastic, black, rap chairs we screamed at to prove we were growing.

When we felt, we believed, so the growth was real. So we trusted the program more.

It was repeated ad nauseum that the system called CEDU, which our RMA was part of, was invented by Sol Turnwell, Tess's dad. He owned us and the campus. He ran the financial headquarters, and managed the two headmasters of the efficient California and Idaho campuses. They relayed whatever it was to the various family heads, and from there, messages traveled down the line to students about how to be, act, and strive to become a good emotional warrior.

Success here was not what it would look like outside of the program.

Sol designed his pseudo-religious belief system around three major principles – the big three Agreements. No violence. No drugs. No sex. They were seldom broken – on the surface. Any public infractions would likely be punished by a full-time, or expulsion. No matter how petty the infraction, if it had to do with sex, drugs, or violence, major consequences would have to be expected.

CEDU's unique approach to emotional growth evolved into pretty much its present form during the seventies. The school shies away from rules, believing they have a tendency to be rigid, and can foster divisive hairsplitting on the part of verbal and manipulative students. Instead, each student starts with a

> set of agreements which is explained when a student
> enrolls. The school believes agreements can better
> get to the heart of an understanding of expected
> student behavior without being as vulnerable to
> distractions over the precise meaning of words. Also,
> agreements are more conducive to modification on
> an individual basis when the student's behavior earns
> less structured agreements.
>
> —Lon Woodbury, "Schools, Programs, & Visit
> Reports," *Woodbury Reports*, June 1991 (reviewing
> his April 1991 visit to RMA's sister school, CEDU, in
> Running Springs, California)

†

The "good" outside world – girls, good times, and friends before Idaho – ceased to exist except in a fantasy freedom that I kept reserved for moments of mental and physical masturbation. They usually had to do with the few "good" times I'd had on my own: splitting from camp, beers in the woods with friends. Sex, obviously. The more time that went by, the less I could remember the bits of freedom I came to associate with my negative life before coming here and starting the program. After the I Want To Live – coming up next in the propheet sequence – I would begin to identify and frown on each of those thoughts, and keep a different style of notes and musings in my journals.

Already, it was easy to recognize since the Brothers Keeper propheet that the conversations in my PG, or with my older RMA friends, didn't have the same surface content like when I was a Papoose. If I had a few minutes walking with Ivy or Ernie down toward the farm, we shared about our feelings, or if we were purposefully keeping it light, about food and the upcoming expedition. We talked about gear we wanted to use, and possible adventures in the future together scaling Kilimanjaro or Denali, as Chet Lively had done before settling here.

Usually after a week or two, rumors of a new campus drama assisted in squelching even the wackiest reports of split/sex contracts among the youngest cadre. In raps, counselors reminded us that we were the ones still here, still learning, so we should concentrate on ourselves. Over time, we stopped talking about people who left and kids we wouldn't get to know because a scandal got them removed. The scandals sometimes affected those of us who stayed, too. When two boys got expelled for a sex contract in our sleeping space at La Mancha, Jasper Browning slipped in status because of his failure to take a leadership role in his duties as dorm head. He still blamed Andre and Geordi for his demotion, even though it was several months ago, and those guys were both gone.

I heard the rumor that Geordi made Andre do it – that it wasn't even consensual. But they were both thrown out. This was another piece of why I had been sure my decision to split the campus last summer was sound. I thought something might happen to me if I stayed. It was all so new. I wasn't even supposed to look at the hot girls here. They said, "Smooosh with these boys over here. Don't talk to girls 'til you've earned that privilege." Then something would happen, like with those boys, and before they were thrown out, Andre and Geordi were in a few raps, just so they could be publicly humiliated. I could not figure out what they wanted from us. Anything sexual – even kissing – was severely punished. And if the other person had been molested in the past, that meant you were taking advantage of someone and you were a bad person and a horrible friend.

Sometimes a new scandal came as a complete surprise – like mine would, later. It turned out that just after my third home visit, when I was applying for entrance into the Summit family, I would be accused of being seriously out of agreement. When that hit the fan, I would be put on my very own full-time. Stuck in a booth all day every day, not looking at or speaking to anyone, making lists of all my dirt. My natural life depended on deconstructing what an honest, tender friend is, and what a lonesome miserable shit I'd let myself become. The very Thinking that made me question the program dogma would become the topic of the ceaseless writing assignments that Kelly prescribed as part of my punishment.

Change was underway. At first it was play-acting, taking on the roles I was expected to portray, but it helped alleviate some shit-slinging at me in raps. In this role, I pretended I was in for the long haul, and was greatly interested in stuff that Summit kids and facilitating staff said to me in raps. I applied Method Acting, the better to emulate my older brothers and sisters. But with all the perspective I'd garnered, I wasn't ready to shut the side door in my mind that voted for splitting, or arranging my own disappearance, or worse. It couldn't be slammed shut and boarded over. Not just yet.

I had to begin to live and breathe and believe like I knew RMA was saving my life. What's worse though, I had to act this confusing farce out – believably. My resistance had been volatile. Because of my refusal to accept my need for the program, or even come back here voluntarily after splitting, it was a forgone conclusion now that everyone expected something deep would be happening within me – transforming me into one of their pidgin-English–speaking emotional puppets.

I won't not look anymore. It can't be done now – I can't un-ring the CEDU-growth bell.

Fake it 'til you make it. I'm having a more difficult time differentiating the fake from the act, and what was me compared to the expectation of what I should become.

Maybe a little bit of me yearned to eventually command the respect that the Summit Grads did. I didn't yet know that this respect didn't translate out in the real world.

At RMA, they told us, your social status back home didn't matter. We didn't have much racism. Most kids were well-off, and knew it, so it was assumed we could all become doctors, pilots, lawyers, shrinks, and the like, by inheritance. What mattered here was whether you did the Summit Workshop and graduated from RMA with program knowledge. If someone split, got pulled, or even left permanently due to private family or health issues, it was because "they weren't ready to be here yet." A subtly layered phrase, it was applied when anyone would leave here suddenly. This always suggested that some people might return. We couldn't write to friends who left, unless they graduated from the program.

Kids came to RMA and left without warning. That, I resented. People left all the time. Maybe a mother decided she disagreed with the program, or the father couldn't afford it anymore. Kids got pulled sometimes if a parent divorced or died. You never knew when someone would split or get pulled by their guardians.

When people, my friends, left unexpectedly, it always felt like a low blow. They would not be graduating from the program. They would never know the tools of the Summit. This lack would separate us from them; we'd outgrow them the way we'd outgrown our pre-RMA friends.

Who was next? Jamie? Of the many short-term friends I'd made the last years and months, who would be next to be forgotten? I'd have been gone; if RMA hadn't taken me back, I'd be at a lock-up. I'd probably have gotten shanked in the carotid artery or raped by now.

Someone could suddenly go to a hospital for "attention games." That's what RMA called suicide attempts. It hadn't occurred to me until they said it: If you were as committed to dying as you were to tying a shoelace, you'd follow through, wouldn't you? Anything else was really an attention game. Wasn't it? I mean, it's an extreme act to begin with. My logic came to believe that the program had made a good point. This prepared me to soon better understand the meaning of "choice" according to the RMA program standard.

I would never jump from half a cliff.

Besides split/sex contracts and "attention games," the spectrum and combination of things that kids might do wrong was a mosaic:

One kid brought seeds of weed home from a visit and the little plants took hold in a patch near the tipi. One kid (me, as what started as a prank one day) took the phone from the Bridge and smuggled it the half mile down to the farm and stuck it under one of the chickens at roost. Several girls had been accused of shower power – a way for them to masturbate – that started out as an issue about long showers and a special nozzle being shared between girl's dorms. At sundown after a late-fall Darlayne rap, Christopher, a kid from Bart's PG, got kicked out for fighting. He tripped a Warrior kid named Henry and whomped him, not in a playful way, but as hard as he could. I imagined the scene as his Sorel boot impacted against ass. I'd felt like doing that to my dorm head when I was new.

We heard how Keith Rios hustled Christopher roughly to a booth, via gossip that washed the campus like a rogue wave. Violence was simply intolerable to staff, and to me, too, now that I saw everyone as little kids inside. The booth where Christopher sat until the next day was the object of many an indirect glance. He was on campus-wide bans, so not even staff were allowed to approach.

A few months later, Donald, a kid in only his third rap, had punched George in the neck during an indictment. It particularly bothered some older students on the issue of "safety," in many of the next Monday and Wednesday raps. I got wind about how freaked everyone in the room had been, but no exact details on what had transpired to cause the ruckus. I didn't find out how he was shuttled off campus that evening.

A few weeks after that, Galen Terzian was out. Galen originally had been in our PG, but was dropped back a PG, so he hadn't been in the Brothers with the rest of us. He'd knifed a gash into his arm and bled all over the floor in the Share Shack, one of our dorm houses. I only knew it happened because he slept near Horatio in their dorm, and I got the skinny on it during the second propheet when Horatio described the terrifying scene.

Around the time Galen cut himself, Nat and Hedwig took the forum together at Monday Morning Meeting. This boded that something important would be said. As he got in front of us, Nat looked like a champagne bottle, mid-pop. He grabbed both sides of his head and, rocking on his heels, began to weep. When the house was silent, he roared into our assembled student body: "We DO NOT HAVE CRAZY PEOPLE HERE! You GOT THAT?"

The reason, even while it was happening, that I knew I'd remember this moment for the rest of my life – was love. Love for the program, for respecting the process. Nat's display showed us all how hurt he was, how angry and moved he was when he got in front of our congregated forum rocking on his heels, in imitation of the self-soothing mechanism that Darlayne used. Tears of aggravation, like he wanted to shake sense into the whole world, squirted down his face and got lost in his beard. He wrung his hands together and they trembled.

"WE DO NOT HAVE CRAZY KIDS. WE DON'T HAVE VIOLENT KIDS HERE! WE HAVE GOOD FUCKING KIDS HERE! GOT IT?"

We all felt like we'd upset Dad, or the gods.

Generally speaking, the most scandalous things were hushed up fastest.

A girl named Tracy had split, and as with so many others, we never again heard anything from her. A dude named Abe gave himself the ugliest tattoo with a stolen scrimshaw needle and shoelace saturated with ash and ink. That was quite the scandal for a time. I was a tad pleased when the fallout from that affected a few other kids I viewed as look-goods. Jennifer Oyama, a frenemy in Warrior, got a week's WDs when staff found out she'd been altering girls' appearances in the dorms, cutting hair for as many as seven girls over the weeks.

Boris Vlantimir had either split or gotten booted just a few weeks ago. And before disappearing, since he was under intense duress and scrutiny from a full-time, he explained why he'd snuck into girls' dorms and took their panties. I had been in one of the follow-up raps to hear from the girls how violated they'd felt. Obviously, this led to a pretty hairball rap or two about the campus girls being violated. We could all relate and hate Boris together.

Other kids got pulled for "financial reasons," another loaded phrase the program used to blame parents of kids who were being non-committal. More new kids vanished for reasons I wasn't privy to.

In Papoose, I got a daily point just for staying. Now, I was earning leadership points for volunteering in raps, and being a big brother.

†

Dear Zack:

[...] I think I really won't write you again until we get a letter. I'm even going to include a stamped addressed envelope to make it easy for you. Zack, we're so eager to hear about what you're doing and what's going on at RMA. Give us some details, gossip, work activities, fun activities. We think about you all the time; we're so proud of how you're getting your life together and developing all those skills. Please share some of your feelings with us. We love you, honey. [...]

Honey, we had a neighbor once, who before she left town told me I was the most "safety-conscious" mother she knew. It was quite a compliment. I am safety conscious, and it hurts to realize I couldn't protect you from some unsafe influences. I know at this stage of your life you must be thinking about some of those influences – false friends, harmful attitudes and behaviors – and you probably know YOU'RE THE ONE WHO HAS TO PROTECT YOURSELF so you can grow strong and healthy. But Zack, I want you to know, if I could have protected you from anything bad in your life, I would have.

You'll have to choose because parents, no matter how much they love a child and how much they WANT to protect him, can't keep the bad parts of the world

167

Zack Bonnie

away from their child. Daddy and I sometimes fan-
tasized about taking our children to some rural spot
in Kansas (or Idaho) and living AWAY from all the evil
influences in the world, but . . . . here we are . . . and
there you are. [...]

—Letter from author's mother, 20 May 1989

EIGHTEEN

I could now identify the different reasons and qualities of tears. Tears of love. Pride. Ownership. Envy. Empathy. Sympathy, understanding, forgiveness, and something like a snotty mixture of fear, anticipation, and grace. The frustrated ones, in the first month or two, that got uncorked only during fits of rage. I could get there when needed, most of the time. I had almost trained my eyes to rain – but I had to train my brain to get me there. Music helped.

The hymns at RMA functioned, in many ways, like a person. You got to know the songs better and better as you went through the program. The wrinkles in the recording, the strain of a voice, the lyric that was written just for you, and that you waited with masochism to hear until you felt the satisfying flush in your cheeks; music elicited a Pavlovian conditioned response.

Certain words and phrases inside of the songs from the propheets, reunions, and warm-ups sent immediate coded messages to my brain, and I would start to feel all weepy and decrepit inside. Of course this was proof I was transcending my own mental limitations: the limitations I'd put on myself because of Mom and Dad, plus the limitations of the real world that mis-created us all.

I knew now why it was that when a PG "got out" of a celebration, the rest of the older students who had completed that level of the program, that achievement, would also appear to be so moved.

Sometimes I could get to the point where a few tears would squeeze out, but my response felt dependent on my reaction to the music in the house. I also needed the chemistry of other kids in the room believing their emotions, before I could allow myself to break down.

✝

The discovery of shared circuits [in the mirror neurons of the human brain] changes the way we have to think about human nature. We are not strictly separated from the people around us. Many of the brain areas that were thought to be the strongholds of individuality turn out to be theatres of our social nature. .... In all these shared circuits, neurons that deal exclusively with the self coexist with neurons that respond similarly to self and other.

How much of us is purely private, then? How many of our bodily skills are ours? Shared circuits blur this question and distinction because the moment I see you do something, your actions become mine. The moment I see your pain, I share it. Are these actions and pain yours? Are they mine? The border between individuals is softened through the neural activity of these systems. A little bit of you becomes me, and a little bit of me becomes you.

—Christian Keysers, *The Empathic Brain: How the Discovery of Mirror Neurons Changes Our Understanding of Human Nature*, Social Brain Press, 2011, pp 221-222

†

The noises of a girl crying or the crumpled-up face of any person I cared for was enough for my sympathetic brain parts to lead me where I had to go. We were all in such great pain; we all needed to be loved unconditionally and know we weren't judged. This, now instilled in me, brought on a new level of understanding about the clockwork-like inner mechanism of CEDU.

I should become what I resisted.

I had been wrong: emotions were good, the program opened us up like tin cans and filled us with all the warm squeeziness of a can of sun-heated peaches.

My memories from Survival in the Owyhee Desert faded. They became just part of my life before I believed what I knew now. On Survival, I needed to be silent. Here, up north in the panhandle, we were allowed, even encouraged, to express our feelings to the point of whining.

My memories from the Brothers were surfacing all the time lately. Impossible to ignore, they caught me off-guard when I'd be walking back to the dorm after a rap, or in the middle of chores. I carried my lug with me everywhere.

My unawareness keeps me alone and unlovable.

Here's how I got it, back in November, before the Brothers propheet got physical.

✝

"How'd that make you feel?" George probed Micah.

"It just pissed me off."

"And what about it pissed you off, Micah?"

"He got off easy. You got off easy, Zack! You left for a month and I didn't even think you could come back. I thought that wasn't fair. He's either a look-good or a kiss-ass because he – you don't deserve to be in this peer group!"

"You totally act like a goddamn snake! I heard about that drawing that you made in Papoose."

"You know what I'm talking about. You are going to have to take a deep look at that, Zack. You've got a lot to learn about yourself."

"You pretend your shit don't stink, but it does. I was in the rap you walked out of with Darlayne. Where'd that get you? Survival. Hunh?"

"Hold on. Let's back up. Let's talk about you getting kicked out of schools. Let's talk about the FACT that you're always running away from your problems. You never look at your shit. The real hurt that got you here. So, let's hear it."

I won't respond. I won't respond. I won't respond.

"You know, I'm thinking who in this room are you even really friends with? I wouldn't even count Ernesto. You can't even count him because you'd huff gas with him the same way you'd share a baggie of heroin, wouldn't you? Yeah, ERNIE'S EVERYONE'S FRIEND; KEEP SMILING, FAKE-BOY!"

George stopped looking at me and drilled a look at Ernie. My peer group picked up where George left off.

"Zack, you were mentioned in everyone's dirt for a reason. Take a look at that, dude."

171

"Now that we've busted your negativity contract with Jamie wide open, you really should look at how you bring people down. How you take!"

"Why don't you talk about the feelings that lead to your always setting it up so that you are alone!"

"How am I alone?"

"Well, Zack, you spend a lot of time reading, don't you?" That was the first indicator that I would be put on bans from reading later that winter.

"SO FUCKING TRUE! You're always doing the loop, just a-walkin' around the Quest trail looking for someone to talk to, someone who 'gets' you! You're FUCKING PATHETIC!"

"I do?"

"You know what I think is going on with you? It's like you just can't make up for the mistrust you've cultivated from splitting, and the lack of safety you seem to bring everywhere you go."

"That's true. And you are a sarcastic bastard, and that's why I love you. Tell us what's really going on? And it can't just be about hating it here anymore. Or that you can't talk to people 'cause of bans." Ernesto, being a true friend, waylaid and temporarily altered the escalating course of diatribe and cued my not-so-profound response.

"I just feel like, you know, nobody knows me here. I mean really knows me since I was on bans so much, and I wasn't here when the peer group below us was forming." I made sure to sound sincere, not snitty.

"That was your choice though!"

Ernie added, "That's a copout, you know."

"When are you gonna get real? There's nothing preventing you from BEING REAL!"

"Talk about how you hate YOURSELF!" This was Mariah's cutting insight.

The room swayed and bent, just as it had at times here during the Truth propheet. It felt as if the floor of the building called Walden was dropping in the corners. Were the pylons that held it up failing? Was this what "getting real" felt like? Rain started pattering on the roof.

"Yeah, you always are saying in raps how 'betrayed' you feel about being left here. You could go into that."

"I can relate to that, you know."

"I have something I've been waiting to say. Is it true that you drew a cartoon of somebody taking care of their feelings in a rap? Or something like that?"

"Yeah. In Papoose. I already did some Work Details for that."

Three people yelled "BULLSHIT!" They shared their reasons why they felt that way, while George and Tess yelled over them until only George's and Mariah's voices sustained:

"...be THAT FUCKING UNAWARE? that fucking unaware. I mean, even in the way you tried to distance yourself from the action "I 'ALREADY' did Work Details! It all just shows you're not taking full responsibility still."

"...it makes me feel personally disrespected! FUCK YOU for treating this place like your personal warehouse. This isn't a place for you to just count days on the calendar. Maybe when you were new that was to be expected, but not now. We're not jailhousing, wasting our time. The work we're doing is FUCKING IMPORTANT. You drawing a sarcastic cartoon or whatever the fuck it was is counterproductive to what we are doing. Just like you've already fucking heard it in this propheet all night, dude!"

"It does all go back to awareness and if you were just a little more aware you'd see that, Zack."

Oh, I get it. Showtime.

"It's true, I am alone. I feel hated. My parents keep telling me I can't come home, and they keep saying that they don't want me 'right now,' whatever that fucking means? WHEN ARE THEY going to WANT me?"

"That's it. Own it. WHEN ARE MY PARENTS GOING TO LOVE ME? Let's hear that again, Zack! How real is that going to be, when they're here for parent visits next month? ARE YOU READY to have those buttons pushed?"

"WHY goddammit am I so alone? I was so alone on Survival and I don't FEEL ANY FUCKING DIFFERENT HERE!"

"You just want to join in the clique, right? Fit in somewhere? Tell us what it's like to not fit in!"

"Yeah, I guess I've been unaware all the time. . . . When I really slow down, I just don't want to feel my pain."

"It hurts too much to look, right?"

"I've felt alone my whole life. I just want to be little again, to feel loved by them."

"Who?"

"My fucking parents!"

"WHO REALLY?"

Pause.

"What's coming up? Right there? Name that feeling for us."

"Pissed."

"Well, what is that? We've talked about this."

"Hurt, I guess." I had to concede.

"Yeah. Name that feeling – that hurt."

"Unlovable." I could feel my chin sink toward my quivering chest.

"Just feel it. Do you feel unlovable?"

"Yes."

"Own it."

"I'm unlovable.

"Tell us about it, then!"

"I AM! I FUCKING HATE IT! I'm in 'hate' with myself. UNLOVABLE. I AM UNLOVABLE!" I no longer could resist the urge to wipe my flushed and wetting cheeks.

I wondered what I looked like up there, in the hot seat, stomach clenched so it felt a bowling ball was stuck in my belly button, heaving in the chest like a capsized raft, heart pounding like a jackhammer, and brain obsessed with the image of being young and "loved," held, trusted, held, wanted, held, and needed by Mother and Father. But Mom and Dad don't want me anymore. Sinking in to the truth of how that felt, I would not allow myself to feel it deeper still. Talking about it all started to jumble me up; I could not distance myself from my words despite any previous plan to do just that.

"Do you think you deserve their love?"

"Well, no, yes, I don't know. I can't try any harder."

George and Terrance came up and rubbed my back as I wiped at my nose with some tissue. I had done all right. Kelly joined me and the others at the opening in the horseshoe; the song filled the room with appropriate feeling. She pressed a big sticky label to my chest.

"MY UNAWARENESS KEEPS ME ALONE AND UNLOVABLE."

I was aware of how alone I felt and had a good reason why: I'm unlovable to my family, I'm unlovable to my peer group, and I'm unlovable to the program. It wasn't ugly luggage; I was becoming proud of it.

I am alone because my parents won't love me. It's simple. I have been carrying my luggage my whole life. There's truth in it:

My unawareness keeps me alone and unlovable.

Exploring the intricacies of this self-identified, yet co-facilitated realization, would take much thought. What I didn't know was that it could define me forever. Even though the inscribed sticky label would come off at the end of the propheet, I would keep carrying my luggage.

It joined my accumulated knowledge from the propheets, or what RMA called our "toolbox." Like the uniform I likened my chameleon growth to, the toolbox was both award medallion and ball and chain. Like my word, "LIAR," had been in the Truth, this label was put over my heart to remind me of issues that I'd be expected to work with long after the Brothers Keeper propheet.

It was my lug. I owned it now and into an imaginary shrinkable file-box it was filed it away with my Truth. Honest.

I'm starting to have an actual reason to be here.

NINETEEN

"H'vrey one een dis room will do whork today. Less have a rap!"

Hedwig Farmer had the confidence of an avalanche. Her words, put so passionately into our freshly seated circle, without even a hint of razz time, ought to have terrified me. She took the cushioned chair. As she exhaled, the smell of mint tea emanated from her steaming mug.

She's a boss. So's the co-facilitator for this rap, Darlayne.

"Today we harr goin' to ghet to de bhottum of alliv' de chit going on 'round here! OK children?" Hedwig could have been referring to any number of incidents since the weather had started to break. This was the beginning of what local staff called "mud season."

Darlayne followed right on her heels: "The level of unawareness on the campus is totally unacceptable."

I felt my stomach flip when I heard the word "awareness" come up, and her eyes fixed on me a moment later. Its word use certainly pertained to me. How would this come into play with Darlayne in the room?

What does Darlayne know about my lug – my negative contract – from the Brothers? Hedwig makes it her business to know everything about everyone.

Awareness equaled my luggage from the Brothers Keeper.

My unawareness keeps me alone and unlovable.

…and everyone can see this. How I sit, where I sit, what I wear, how and why I wear it; these people know Rock Bottom too.

I immediately considered ways to be a better friend to the approachable people in the room.

I could sense the subtext that accompanied every word spoken or thought in raps. I was also very aware of my appearance as a person with no self-confidence. I sat up a little straighter.

Darlayne and Hedwig were as observant as raptors. Instead of me, they targeted Dirk Morgan, the baby in the room, to bring the rap to the appropriate temperature. He hadn't been through any propheets yet, so that made him the only one who didn't know about his little kid shooter marble, the Truth propheet concept that had been magnified and personalized with photos in the second propheet.

"Whass' hup? Dirk, right? Whass jur surname?"

"Dirk Morgan."

"How old are juw?"

"Sixteen."

"What do you want to share with the rap today? You've gotta say something. You're part of the environment now." Darlayne sounded chipper.

"I don't know."

"Come on. Let's get in there and find out what makes Dirk tick!"

"Why juw laughing?"

"I don't know."

Here a few voices chimed in with our assimilated knowledge.

"Laughing is a fear reaction!"

"'I don't know' means 'I don't WANT TO LOOK'!"

"Let's give *Mr. Organ* some space."

"Yeah, I'm from Encinitas too, welcome! Share something with the rap?"

A lengthy pause so we could watch Dirk look at his twisting hands for answers. He snorted a quick laugh when the focus of the rap did not shift from him.

"I dunno. You know, I just hate it here."

"That's OK. We're going to talk about that."

"We all did."

"That's normal."

"That's a fucking understatement. Ha, er –."

"It shows."

"I just don't want to be here."

"I don't want to be here either, Dirk. None of us did, but you have to give it time."

"And, it was your choices that got you here. Time to try something else yet?"

Dirk grabbed at the bait – an ancient predicament. Raps always reminded me of primitive hunting or fishing.

"I didn't choose this."

"But the fact that you ARE HERE, and WHAT YOU DO WITH IT, IS!"

"I totally relate, Dirk. But once I got used to the fact, and became aware of how to apply what's true here, it became a little easier."

"Why'd you get sent here, Dirk? Share your story with us."

"Nobody does make it alone."

"Yeah."

"What's that feel like?"

"I just feel trapped? I guess."

"And how long have you been here now?

"Twelve days."

"You feel trapped."

"Yeah."

"What does that remind you of?"

"Is there another time you felt like that?"

Dirk and the rest of us stewed a few additional moments on the clock.

Darlayne disrupted the hanging moment of stillness.

"OK. Talk a little more about how you got here."

"My mother brought me. My mom is with a new guy. Like, he's my stepfather now."

"How's that relationship?"

"We had some problems."

"Evasive."

"Give him some space, he's new! Like a pack of fucking wolves!" Darlayne hypocritically chastised us. A few more seconds off the clock while Dirk simmered instead of answering right away.

"And how long have they been together?"

"They've been together eight years but they're . . . got married."

"How long ago was that."

"I don't – three years or so, I guess."

"Did that make you feel trapped?"

"I guess."

"Why?"

"My mom moved out and took me with her. It's kind of sucked ever since. I can't see my dad any more. Custody stuff, I guess."

"Are you listening over there, Jacob!" Jacob was a kid with a permanent grimace, two PGs above mine, who was on a full-time.

"You don't have to guess. Right? Does it make you feel trapped?" That was Griffin, being a look-good, as usual.

"Do you blame your stepfather?"

"What's *his* name?"

"Ross."

"Ross."

"I'm getting a little anger here. Hiss' easy to sense, juw think you've got a lot of anger for Ross. We're going to get into that today." Hedwig spoke to Dirk with Nordic, breathy, "H's" and dulled "T's."

I listened with one ear, while concentrating on how to astral-project myself out of the room.

"ASSHOLE!" This came suddenly from Jacob who'd been in the graduating class, but now had six months tacked on to his time in Summit, for splitting on a home visit. "Keep blaming others for your feelings, Dirk."

"Dirk, did Ross have to call the cops on you...why was that?"

"We got into a fight."

"You're an angry little fucker ain't ya?"

"We're going to get there. I know you're just figuring things out."

"Is there anything you'd say to Ross if he were in this room?"

"Ha ha! No let's have some fun with this! What would you say?"

"Fuck you, I guess." Embarrassed laugh, but Dirk was miles more animated than he'd been forty minutes ago.

Darlayne subtexted his thinking, just to show him what raps were all about. "I just FUCKING HATE IT HERE! I HATE IT. I CAN'T TAKE IT – and I DO FUCKING HATE ROSS!"

Then, Darlayne's voice notched down. "Tell him." Others spoke up.

"It's OK."

"This is good work."

"Show us. Pretend he's right there!"

"Fuck you, Ross!"

"'FUCK YOU ROSS!' Like that." Darlayne showed Dirk how she'd make the sound leap out of her belly.

"FUCK YOU ROSS, MOTHERFUCKER! You fuckin...RRR. no."

"You can trust this process, DIRK! I AM so much LIKE YOU, dude!" I joined in, to encourage the Papoose, to show him I cared, and to be part of the rhythm of the room.

"It's OK to tap into that. This is a safe place for you to explore that anger."

"FUCK YOU ROSS! Fuck you Mom! Let's HEAR IT!"

"What's this kicking up for you, Zack?"

I remember. When this was new. Before Survival taught me the workings of this ancient, primitive trap.

"Why'd you BASTARDS LEAVE ME HERE? Right?"

"I'm just totally relating to feeling trapped. I can totally relate to Dirk's feeling trapped. Like how I never could make anyone happy at home. Even teachers hated me before I dropped out, so. I guess like five years ago, Dirk, I started to feel trapped. Then how I felt at home became a trap, and I was just fucking miserable. I hated my parents."

Griffin added some more, finishing with, "This place is becoming my family now. I know it sounds corny, but it's as true as it gets. Love is real, and I can't get that from Mom."

Darlayne and Hedwig nodded at Griffin, and swung the focus back to Dirk. I could sense this rap gearing up to another incline, like a roller coaster chugging slowly up to a g-force drop.

Dirk looked perplexed, but we all knew he'd done pretty well. He'd survive. He was willing to introspect, I thought, as he exchanged quieted words with Hedwig.

From here Darlayne did her famous switcheroo. "Stay with that feeling right there, Dirk. NOW! There's SOMEONE in here I was hoping to have heard from!"

We'd been lulled into chugging along with Dirk's life, and now Darlayne skipped fourth gear completely by keeping her stony brown eyes sparkling at Dirk at her ten o'clock but her voice went to Griffin at one o'clock. The rap remained in highway mode from here until the weepy smoosh pile at the end, with various happenings and motivations for each of us as the moments whizzed past.

"Um, let me take some space. Um – I need to clean up something." Griffin begins.

"Less' hear it, baby." Hedwig over mint tea.

"Well, I'm struggling here. I don't believe the changes in me are real. It's just another game I have to play, a dance for my mom."

"Come on! This isn't really about her, IS IT?" Just like that, the rap became all about Griffin's life before Idaho.

"I feel so fucking fake. Plastic for Mom."

"THAT'S THE FUCKING TRUTH, ISN'T it?"

"Yeah."

"Say it again: NOBODY WANTS ME AS ME!"

"I'm unwanted."

"NOBODY WANTS ME! NOBODY NEEDS ME!"

"NOBODY needs ME!" Darlayne at her very loudest.

"GOOD. Feel that?"

"It feels like shit."

"I'm sure IT DOES! THAT'S WHAT YOU WALK AROUND WITH EVERY DAY!"

"Feel how heavy it is. FEEL THE WEIGHT!"

Darlayne pressed her hand to Griffin's back.

"Less' keep gohin'!" We were in the final quarter of the rap. This room's attention stayed on the pretty girl.

"Griffin, let's go back to WHATEVER THE FUCK you were doing on the climbing wall Saturday?" On her word, "Saturday," Darlayne's chubby thumb flipped up on Dirk's back.

"I know, I know it! I saw that, that was so UNSAFE, girl!"

"Tina and I wanted to just boulder a little."

"That's why you even wanted to make space here a minute ago! So you wouldn't have to hear it! So you blame your mom? Totally fake in itself. What a lame game."

"Dude, that's part of your game. Shifting responsibility again!"

"What's sad is that you were on the wall to begin with though. Just another example of what is being said to you. But back to the climbing wall: You know that's out of agreement, seriously! What the fuck, Griff!"

"Since the Wilderness Challenge is coming up, I needed to support Tina in getting into better shape...."

I risked a glance across the rap circle at Bianca, the head of my peer group, as she was making an indictment. Bianca had been seated next to Griffin when she began her sentence and plopped down in the row of five pretty girls from chairs on my side of the circle. They wanted to be friends with Griffin too. I moved, trying to stay out of a seat next to, or across from staff, but disappearing in plain sight was as impossible as the astral projection I'd read about.

"...and you made it like a big deal that you were going to train with me, but you turned your back on me! You didn't show up to our jog on Sunday. Well, I'm just saying that hurt my feelings."

"I know Bianca. I'm sorry."

"Come on, ghoos got sunthin' to say? Was' next? Les' ghet real!"

"You know, what's the deal between you and Tina, anyway? You two are always the last ones to get your lights off and I'm fucking sick of it! I need my goddamn sleep."

"THASS RIGHT, TELL HER!"

"...yeah, that's why I made the rap request for you and Tina, actually."

"Who else lives in Garden house? Where's Tess? My Papoose girls tell me that there's some shit going on that needs to come out here today!"

"OK, for me, I'm not like angry or anything, but you keep using my soap. I had to wait until Warrior to get permission for my dad to send it. I wasn't even allowed to use it on my home visit! Please stop using it without permission."

"WOW, GRIFFIN, I CAN'T BELIEVE THAT! SHE – YOU DID THE SAME FUCKING THING TO ME BEFORE I MOVED TO SUMMIT GRAD HOUSE! THAT REALLY PISSES ME OFF!"

"What else? Who gives a shit about soap?"

"It's not that, it's the privilege, and besides, your hygiene isn't up to par."

"There's a FLAG, right THERE! Hygiene."

"Yeah, for an upper-school student, you should really know how you represent yourself better, I think."

"She's not listening. Nobody's going to listen to you! EVER! MAY AS WELL GIVE UP, RIGHT? Go ahead. Let's get it out now!"

"You too, Zack, baby. Let's hear some more from you here!"

"...no, NO! It's about not treating MY HOME with RESPECT! That's a big word for me! Respect ME!"

"You don't have ownership of your issues either, take a FUCKING LOOK! So the respect thing totally makes sense."

"Well, for me, I think you don't respect yourself. You play a good game, but inside you're always looking for acceptance. What you did in the dorm with Tina was an acceptance game."

"OHMIGOD that is SO TRUE! On Sunday, when you put your sheet up you called it a 'frig rig'"!

"I heard about that! That was you!"

"WHASS DIS FRIG RIG?"

Pause.

". . . well, you know how the boys have their beat sheets on Sunday sleep-ins?"

"...yeah"

"Well, it's the same thing..."

"OH no no no no THASS' DISGRACEFUL! WHY YOU DEED THAT, JUW THEENK?"

". . . I dunn – to show off for the dorm, I guess. It was acceptance! It was just something to say like I wasn't like being crude or anything, I just thought it was funny?"

"FUCKING FRIG RIG! DO you know HOW like, OUT OF TOUCH that is with what we're doing here?"

". . . I know I'm sorry. I am."

"Boys are like, you know, pigs, so we kinda have to expect that shit from them. . . ."

"I shouldn't have drawn any attention to, you know. . . ."

"No, you're not! You're not being honest right now, I can tell!"

"What kind of person needs acceptance that bad? Hunh Griffin? You need to masturbate NOT TO FEEL ALONE! THINK OF HOW FUCKING SAD THAT REALLY IS. WHO DOES THAT? ANSWER ME GODDAMMIT!"

"A desperate person. A TAKER. A FAKER. Just a desperate fucking brat, I guess."

"That's RIGHT! What else is going on IN YOUR THINKING?"

"THE THINKING GRIFFIN, COME ON! YOU'RE ABOUT TO BURST. JUST LET IT GO, KIDDO!"

"I NEED LOVE! I miss sex, my LITTLE GIRL IS A FUCKING SLUT! I MISS FUCKING SEX. I MISS HAVING LOVE! I'M SO AFRAID I'LL NEVER GET TO AGAIN. NOBODY WILL EVER LOVE ME! I FEEL FAT, I THINK I'M FAT. I'M FAT, OK?"

"Go on."

Nobody moved to stop her even though she'd slammed the floor with a fist at one point on "slut," and it was all rushing out with an enormous tangle, like the exposed root system of a big fallen tree. Griffin was beautiful. She wasn't fat.

"I miss sex, I WANNA BE NORMAL. I don't want to be here still, but I am! I fucking hate it! I HAVE ISSUES I DON'T WANT TO DEAL WITH. I'm tired of looking at them. FUCKING NOBODY. NOBODY WILL CARE ABOUT ME IF..."

"WHO, Griffin? WHO IS IT YOU CAN'T DEAL WITH?"

"MY DAD! MY MOM! YOU! I FUCKING HATE THEM. I'M TIRED OF BEING THE ONE BLAMED FOR DAD LEAVING. FUCK YOU! WHY DO I TELL MYSELF THIS SHIT. FUCK! FUCK! FUCK! I'LL NEVER BE NORMAL! NO GUY WILL EVER LOVE ME FOR WHO I AM!"

"THAT'S RIGHT! THAT'S WHAT IT'S SAYING. FIGHT YOUR THINKING BABY! USE YOUR TOOLS! Who's going to join? WHO KNOWS WHAT IT'S LIKE?

"WHASS'AT FEELING RIGHT THERE RIGHT NOW, hunh? STACY? ZACK? BIANCA? WHASS THIS KICKING UP FOR YOU?" This and more transpired over the now-furious high-pitched screams of Griffin, who clutched both hands around tufts of red hair, and sucked in air as she introspected.

Hedwig turned to our PG head. "What is that you are feeling? Right now, that feeling right there, Bianca?"

"I'm embarrassed."

"Whass' that burden juw carrying? I can see feelings coming up for you right now?"

"I'm uncomfortable with talking about..."

"You're...YOU are NOT HERE to BE COMFORTABLE! YOU'RE HERE TO TAKE A LOOK AT YOUR ISSUES! If YOU DON'T LET GO, YOU AIN'T GONNA GROW HERE, BABY! I've been where you're sitting. I know what you're feeling. And being out of your comfort zone is how you grow."

"You put that shame in your luggage and you feel it, right? It weighs a ton, doesn't it?"

"Yes."

"Tink habout hall the messages. Your luggage. Really take a moment to think about what that little girl has done. I can see shame written on juw as juw sit dare! It's like in your acne. Thas' your body telling juw baby, DON'T hold on to the dis-hease, the shit going on IN Juw! Juw see?"

I prayed Hedwig would not mention Mount Vesuvius on my forehead.

"That's not my fault."

"But keeping yourself CLEAN is!"

I had an idea. If I saturated the rap with Bianca's important issues, I could skate through this afternoon without working.

"Bianca, I know you are just starting to deal with the abortion stuff, but if you want, here might be a good place to talk about that?"

I'm not sure if I was using triangulation or projection, but it was definitely deflection, and it worked for me for a little while.

"It isn't really your choice or not to deal with your problems now or not, you see. It's running you whether you want it to or not. That guilt. That Thinking! Don't you think that's fair? A fair statement?"

"Yeah...I am guilty..."

"Guilt blocks all growth, Bianca. I'm sharing a secret with you right now. You've got to face the FUCKING GUILT, Honey. It's eating you up isn't it?"

Bianca's face melted into the dramatic expression I'd seen in our propheets together, and I felt a stab of love for her despite her struggle: "Yeah. FUCK, I just...I Fucking...I FUCKING KILLED A BABY, MAN! FUCK!"

"WHAT does THAT FEEL LIKE?"

"LIKE SHIT. I'm fucking crazy – I feel like I'm going crazy having to think about it all again, understand? FUCK!"

"You betcha. I bet that sucks for you. I've done this work myself, Bianca. You know that. That's why I'm here for you...shhhh. Yeah. Where's that feeling, baby? Where do you feel it? Yeah? In your gut?"

Darlayne placed a puffy hand on Griffin's belly.

"Yeah." Sniffle.

"What do you think that feeling would sound like if it made a noise?"

"OHGODDON'TMAKE ME. I CAN'T AGAIN! WHEN'S IT GOING TO LEAVE ME ALONE! Aaaaahhhh."

"AAAAHHHH! COME ON LET ME HEAR THAT NOISE IN YOUR GUT!"

"AAAAAAAAHHHHHHHHHH AAAAAAHHHHHHH!" Hedwig was taking the intensity level of this rap to propheet-level histrionics.

"That's it! THAT'S RIGHT, GET IT OUT, BIANCA! SEE THE WORK GOING ON HERE, JACOB? THAT'S WHY YOU'RE ON A FULL-TIME! YOU'RE WASTING THEIR TIME! HOW MUCH LONGER ARE YOU GONNA LET THAT FEELING EAT YOU UP?"

This rap was becoming hairball. Hedwig would have almost every person in the circle crying or voicing their Thinking, over escalating wails, that final hour. Dirk, freshened from opening the rap, now gripped his chair in terror. I tried to remember witnessing my first month of raps.

"Zack, why don't you share what's going on inside of you right now?"

Shit. That's me.

"I dunno. I mean, I just feel lonely."

Maybe if I talk about my lug from the Brothers, then she won't ask me to run my Thinking, which I might not do the right way.

"OK. Let's go deeper into that. What does it feel like to be lonely?"

"Empty. Like I'm doing the loop all the time. Looking for an older brother to share with. I'm afraid to smoosh with the girls, everyone will think I want to fuck, or like corrupt them, or something."

"You don't feel trusted? OK, that's honest. But that's just a reaction. Automatic reaction to your loneliness. Being on the outside, right? So it's not a surprise that you think people think you're untrustworthy? You know that, right?" This was Darlayne being sensible with me. And it told me the propheet staff had been talking to her about my exclusion that night.

What to say?

187

"Yeah, I mean, yeah. I'm trying to be more aware of how I isolate. How I isolate myself from my real friends here."

"Can you remember another time you felt this way."

"One time when I was young I was in the bedroom."

"How old do you think that little dooger is?"

"Like five."

"Only five years old?"

"What's he doing?" Hedwig looked at me while she stroked Bianca's back softly. Her wails had melted into sobs.

"Yeah. And I was climbing the dresser where my clothes were...and then the thing fell on me..."

"It fell on you! Oh no! You felt alone then?"

"Yeah."

"What else did you feel?"

"Trapped."

"Can you remember another thing from that time?"

"The drawers' knobs had different colors."

"The drawers. They did."

"Yeah."

"And you were climbing up and the dresser fell on top of Spider-man?"

"Yeah."

"Can you be there now?"

"OK."

I knew she meant for me to revisit the guided imagery exercise in the Brothers, right before we stared into our Rock Bottom's eyes. I found it was easy to go back to that hypnotic dream state.

"And you wanted your mother?" Hedwig coaxed the memory I'd chosen at random from ones that I knew better than to bring up – yet.

"Yeah."

"Where is she? In the next room?"

"Yeah."

"Call her. She's right in the next room."

"And then she came in and she picked it up off me."

"She did – be there now."

"Yeah."

"But she didn't see if I was OK. I was hurt and scared. She just walked away!"

"She just walked away? She left Spider-man there all alone?"

"Yeah."

"And he was scared and hurt."

"Yeah."

"Yeah? What did that little boy want to say to Mommy?"

"Come back! Come hold me."

"Come hold you?"

"Yes. And she won't."

"She turned her back on you."

I knew she meant metaphorically. But that was exactly how it had occurred. I think.

"Tell her to come back!"

"COME BACK!"

"COME BACK, MOMMY!"

"COME BACK, MOMMY! I LOVE YOU. DON'T LEAVE ME HERE! I'M HURTING! DON'T YOU LOVE ME?"

"That's it. Keep going until it comes up."

"Hey, Dirk. Don't forget to spend time with Terrance tonight after you finish dish crews. He'd like the chance to share his story with you. Are you going to make the I Want To Live scrolls with the Purpose Committee this weekend? Good. Keep going Zack, I believe you. That's right! You don't want to feel this alone forever do you?"

"MOMMY. DON'T LEAVE ME HERE! COME HOLD ME LOVE ME CARE for meeeeeeeeeeeeeee." Sobbing for real now, Zack's nose runs. I need to impress Darlayne and reciprocate the vulnerability that Bianca and the rest just shared. Like with Yu-Yu and Ivy, who weren't in the rap, I felt a special kinship and protective vein for the girls in my PG, and for Griffin and Mariah, and for every girl I knew in Idaho. Snot-ripper songs played in Zack's subconscious. My subconscious, I mean; but for now I was content to let my personalities meld and fracture, since everyone in the room was watching with love.

I hope Hedwig, rather than Darlayne Hammer, will stroke my back soon?

But I felt guilt for that thought, and knew my negative Thinking was to blame.

Ignore the tissues, let yourself feel it. Feel bad for that manipulating thought. Know you're alone, be lowly and meek and vulnerable, for the rap.

I'm doing great. I must be, since I can't use my nose to breathe.

Darlayne wrapped it up. "I think you guys are the greatest. This is the most courageous work you can do. Let's be there for Zack for a few minutes of smoosh time. And everyone, remember to be slow tonight."

The chairs were stacked into a couple of messy piles. I was invited to smoosh on the floor with Darlayne, Hedwig, and the kids.

Were puffy eyes gateways to what was truly real?

Would expressing my hurt prevent the heart-stabbing loneliness when I thought of Mom and Dad? Or when Griffin, or especially Hedwig or Darlayne, touched me on the chest or head?

What should I feel, when hugging makes me feel more hollow, the longer a person wrapped their arms around me?

A child must be surrounded by people with vitality, people who live with their work, who are healthy, interested and growing. It's more than providing good role models. Children have an unerring ability to sense hypocrisy.

—From CEDU (California) printed brochure, late
1980s, quoting Brigitte Wasserman (married to CEDU
program founder Mel Wasserman)

✝

*Would getting to know what drives an individual – the very heartbeat
of someone's inner psychology – reveal a secret to me?*

*How lovable is my Rock Bottom? Instead of little doogers, Rock Bottom,
were we all just walking misery, perambulating Thinking that wanted to
kill us? Were we finally then slaves to the reactions to that Thinking? Our
image? Are we what we project?*

*Did everyone's intense interest in what everyone else said or did – so it
could be then dissected in raps – make the stuff rise to the level of importance that was ascribed to it?*

*What would anyone else think of RMA and raps and propheets and
Thinking and my crazy new language? Would I learn to silence doubts,
and some of that Thinking, after the I Want To Live propheet, the way the
program promised?*

Zack Bonnie

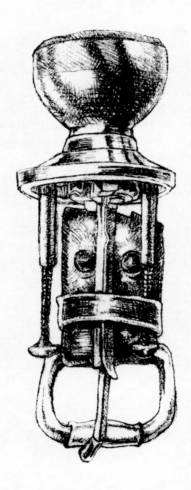

TWENTY

My parents' trust in the program was absolute.

My older brothers and sisters at RMA felt that way too, and as for the staff, I knew they'd drink Kool-Aid with Sol Turnwell's piss in it. The most important thing was to be able to go into my emotions in raps. It didn't always work, though. It depended on the corresponding personal friendships, how my previous rap had been, and the mood of the individual staff facilitator in the room that day.

I was instrumental in, and aware of, the entire process. I was changing.

Am I changing just to please everybody, or is it real?

> We are deeply and inevitably social. Our societies, our culture, our knowledge, our technology, and our language – everything that makes us truly proud of being human seems to be a logical consequence of this brain architecture that makes us share each other's mind.
>
> [...] Our decision to do an action or not is a balance between the benefit this act will have for ourselves and the vicarious consequences shared circuits make us feel.
>
> —Christian Keysers, *The Empathic Brain: How the Discovery of Mirror Neurons Changes Our Understanding of Human Nature*, Social Brain Press, 2011, p 222

As part of our progression in Idaho, we'd all gone from not believing, to starting to believe the program, to needing the propheet secrets revealed to us, to relying on added positive attention and respect from staff. We were now becoming enthusiastic about the program itself. It felt like these stages occurred for the members of my PG and surrounding ones at about the same time, as we all began to appreciate the time spent digging into our issues in raps.

The tools I learned showed me how rap yelling, when reserved for truer moments, helped to get in touch with whatever feelings I should be feeling, so it became second nature to point out my own issues in another person. We called this "triangulation." When I did this shamelessly in raps, it was with the hope that this might also kick up feelings I could run with myself, when a counselor missed a beat. That behavior would impress the facilitating staff, and word would get to my Brave family head, Prescott. It was George I wanted to impress most, since I'd be in Warrior soon, and I knew Prescott and he were friendly, so I banked that any good deeds could serve me twice – much like a good chess move.

There was no escaping the program's required intimate bonding, smooshing, and hand joining. There was no escaping the effect it had on me, either. Working the program meant touching others, and being touched. The facilitators were emotional coaches, even if at first I perceived them to be guides into insanity. And I now looked forward to smooshing, to being expressly noticed, tolerated, and even appreciated by my older RMA counterparts.

Now, instead of scaring the bejesus out of me, it comforted me to know – to believe – that I was doing something right for a change.

I reduced it down:

Go to a lock-up until I was eighteen, or trust that the changes that were clearly happening to me and my PG were good, and right.

Continue to surrender my soul.

Anything this uncomfortable surely constituted "growth" in the program's eyes. I was learning to believe all that this growth implied: an easier and easier justification for my growing self-caused consternation.

I was completely in the machinery of the place. What my PG and I would be doing the next day was rarely a surprise, except when my family or PG would suddenly ship out for a day's canoeing to train for the May expedition, or an overnight camping trip with only a few hours' notice. I wouldn't be leaving the campus much – like for a ski trip or getting to take in a movie in Bonners Ferry – until after my first home visit. Then the extra privileges would come rolling in – that is if I couldn't convince Dad to keep me in Virginia.

However, I had a certain love for the place now, and for every single person on the campus – except the Papooses. I didn't feel anything for them, except a twinge of disdain for their self-ignorance. And with that twinge came a ration of negative-Thinking: that Thought was bad. It was somewhat OK to "judge" Papooses, but I should be supportive of them regardless of their ability to acknowledge the good of the program.

Wait! Did I just think that?

Instead of rebelling, I began to revel in the precision-tuned, water-mill essence of Hedwig's handiwork. I gloried in the well-made, quarter-bouncing, hospital-cornered bed I could make. I liked outper-forming people at labor. My labors were – as the program suggested, quoting Kahlil Gibran – my "love made visible." I pursued the voca-tion of identifying problems inside of me, exposing them to light so that it appeared I was growing ready – on edge, as expected of me and my PG – for the I Want To Live. By many program standards I was thriving. I didn't even think about home any more.

Next to impossible to believe, in just a couple of months, I was going to take an airplane, by myself, home to Virginia. This was all supposed to occur at some point soon after the I Want To Live. One of the requirements before parents could book flights for us was that we had to have successfully entered Warrior. So I knew I'd have to suck it up and write Mom a few more times after the propheet. I thought about how much time I had put into my letters home from my inde-pendent travels in France the summer before RMA. That seemed so long ago.

I couldn't remember the person I was when I was thirteen. A recently minted fifteen-year-old, I was turning into a different thing, entirely. Half lumberjack, half I dunno what.

Of course there were things to keep hidden, but I could work on them in the abstract, or so I thought. Now it wasn't about how I could survive here, it was how I could make the absolute best of it, how I could thrive. My last hurdle seemed to be trusting the program entirely, allowing the mind-melding to root down into, and possibly expose, every single Thought that might, in the future, bind me up, get me drunk, or kill me. My awareness of my visible actions and my

Zack Bonnie

negative Thinking superseded any lingering focus about whose fault it was, or why my parents had abandoned me to this.

I liked to think about the negative now. Before I got here, it was true that I avoided thinking and feeling to the maximum, since I hadn't been instructed in this.

By springtime, I began to feel attuned to people, place, and time in a cosmic sense. Just like trying to astral project, I knew it wasn't possible, and that's why it wasn't. But. So.

It wasn't possible, was it?

Breathing and practicing the reverberation of my soul was good for me. Meditating was good practice for universal good. And as Nat suggested, the more we slowed down, the closer we could come to being that little kid inside.

For me and my PG friends like Ernie, Bianca, sometimes Micah, Ivy, and Jamie, I knew there were still many difficult days ahead of us. Now, though, that knowledge was interspersed with my sense of achievement for being here. The next milestone, coming up in July, would be being here a year! Morsels of pride, like shells on the beach, were deposited and wiped away with the same tide. Many nights, sleepless and filled with simmering confusion and anger, I wouldn't be able to shake the shame, the cloud of doubt I lived in: if I was good at heart, I wouldn't have these Thoughts, these dreams. I wouldn't still Think outright about how I could manipulate my parents, skip the rest of the program, leave this psycho shitpit and go home.

I knew it was expensive, but the way Mom and Dad probably saw it, the investment they sacrificed now would reward them in years to come. To them, I was somehow making up for lost time and learning invaluable insights into myself that would bolster my future choices.

That I was not yet trusting the program entirely, whole-heartedly, was a personal choice, an existential problem I was about to face.

I had a weakness now for the second family, and an appreciation for the entire progression, the system in place here – I know it's pitiful, but it's true as sky blue.

Rumor had it spring was coming. We hadn't seen the ground since what would have been Halloween. For the past five months, snow and ice had been everywhere, covering everything. Just clomping from the

196

house to the dorm or to chores on the farm meant gearing up with glasses for the glare, fuzzy Sorel boots, padded parkas, and balaclavas.

Gardening was a sort of reward awaiting us after we moved to Warrior from Brave. As the ground thawed at the farm, we were permitted to assist in planting rows of corn, peppers, and cabbage. If it can ever be said that it is fun to watch something grow, try cabbages and sunflowers for serious action. Later, when things started to sprout, I would hate leaving morning chores for classes at Skinner. Just the thought of weeds re-forming below the dirt, sprouting their roots clinging and climbing up the roots of my veggies caused me enough consternation that I talked in raps about my love for the vegetables.

All I had to do now before I joined Warrior was survive a canoe trip, one more propheet, get my reading and chess bans lifted, and do my application. Then George would get me moved into Warrior. Then home! Forget how short the actual time at home was – three nights – the not-even-distant future held a reservoir of novelty. On my home visit, I could gauge when and how to address the issues of my staying for the second half of the program. If I acted the perfect, self-deprecating, and appreciative son; if I convinced them that I would've been dead without their intervention and the injection into Idaho – maybe then I could cut short my time with the program that made every kid here into the hollow shell my negative Thinking suspected I'd be after an eternal thirty months at RMA.

If I concretely expressed to them that I had needed a reformation of my Thinking – then, just maybe, they would spare me another year and a half in Idaho. But these thoughts were at odds with the lessons I was about to learn in the I Want To Live, which would more formally introduce me to Thinking.

Did I actually want not to come back to RMA?

I wasn't sure what felt more like home to me. In the plus category, in Warrior I'd get to work with the animals. If I came back.

What do I want? If my parents offer to let me stay home, I'll jump at the chance, but I can't let anyone know that.

I was learning that Thoughts were thoroughly negative. Over the course of the year, I'd been told in raps a hundred million times that the sooner I got out of my head the better I would be for it. Not just now, but for the whole of the future of my life. It did feel good to be respected by everyone after bawling, taking care of deep-rooted feelings of worthlessness, or attempting access to deeper aspects or motivations of my psyche.

I went with the flow. Feel like poop; accept it, express it, learn why you've been feeling like poop, and follow staff advice. To sit in the crappy feelings was often correct. Others didn't, for now, have to skewer me with petty dirt, or have grounds to say I wasn't working the program. If someone suggested my behavior was lacking on some level during a rap, I worked to change it. When I was indicted, I tried to take it in and filter out the things that were "out of touch."

My personal experiences during the last year had magnified every possible anxiety and self-esteem issue that I didn't know I'd had before the propheets. I'd never really thought about why I started acting out in school, or which events had what kind of impact on me – on my Rock Bottom, my little kid inside. It took me time to process things, and the fast-forward intensity that the program put on me made me grow self-absorbed – like the staff. My month on Survival had exposed to everyone the undeniable lessons and scars that I lived with from not getting with the program at first. I had made up for that, but on the whole, feeling miserable and confused had stopped being the focal point of my daily life. All of this smooth sailing was temporary, though. Within my peer group, the "unacceptable" music that had lingered shamefully as reminders of previous lives, the pre-program images and individuality, had long since fallen away. I couldn't know how weird all of this would make me feel when I finally stood alone in my vacated bedroom at home.

For me at this point, there were only two ways to do the program – all the way, or not at all; a caterpillar doesn't think of the thousands of potential threats while cocooning itself for transmogrification.

I needed to learn the distinction – to know whether I was Thinking, or Feeling.

Did the program really love me? Could it provide more real truth, bigger love, than my parents, family, and friends from Virginia ever had, or could?

TWENTY-ONE

I'd already done lots of camping at Minnehaha, the summer camp that I attended for five years before I split from there. I'd even had a few "Solos" on my own when running away from home, back in Virginia. I had spots back home I could go to – not just the old bomb shelter my parents stressed about. I had, however, never been on any kind of expedition on water, although much of our specialized learning time at RMA had been down at the lake, even while the snow spit on us.

The announcement came on a Wednesday in early spring. My peer group and a handful of older students would begin the Quest Expedition, a four-day hiking and canoeing trip that was the first of two major wilderness experiences in our program at RMA. It was a surprise to me.

They are going to let us leave?

The differences between camping in Virginia or West Virginia and camping here, differences that shouldn't have gone unnoticed – like the temperature and strength of the current in the rivers here – hadn't occurred to me when I was a Papoose, new to Idaho. These rivers could kill a kid a hundred different ways, and in fifty of those, he'd never even know what had gone wrong. Even the highest mountains I'd seen back east, or down south in the Idaho Mojave, were still possible to scale.

But here in this wilderness, there would be a lot of peaks that a person couldn't summit without specialized tools, belaying partners, or applied experiential knowledge. You couldn't simply walk up and over the peaks we saw from the campus, or the new ones that surrounded us when the red RMA vans approached the Quest Expedition's insertion point.

I got out and looked around.

You can't escape from here, either.

Loving the outdoors meant we were trustworthy, and as such, in the final week before the Quest, we were allowed to begin exploring life outside the mud-encrudded dirt roads that surrounded the main campus. My PG would be able to explore Murkwood Forest and the Quest trail that crept all over the area, as long as we used a buddy system. This led to many a hiking adventure with Ernesto, Micah, or Jamie. We climbed trees, jumped large distances, and flirted with disaster. We knew without being told that if you got hurt it would be your fault, because you weren't aware. You should look out for your buddy, too.

Unlike the other boys in my PG, I'd been on Survival the previous September, and that had changed how I viewed the woods, or myself, or myself in the woods. I wasn't sure I could "enjoy" it the same way everyone else might – was it possible that something bad was in store for us? Going on an expedition meant life wouldn't be predictable for a few days. I felt a little afraid to be taken out of my kennel.

Because I'm a bit thick, I didn't put together that we'd already been building up proficiency and bulking up muscle during the six months of Experientials and chores. In recent Experientials, we practiced packing and unpacking people and gear into and out of canoes, and training with packs. We were going to apply all that we ever would need to know about wearing wool and polypropylene, knotting knots, and, of course, basic rescue, including how to self-arrest with various objects. When your body becomes a sled and you start speeding down a mountainside, you can turn said object into an emergency brake, being careful to truly dig in deep with your stick, ice axe, or ski-pole, lest it not become a rudder that will swing you sideways and slam your ass into the trunk of a hardwood tree – that's a self-arrest.

Mostly, we were storing up skills and knowledge for our main expedition called the Wilderness Challenge, which was to happen on Telemark skis next winter.

Whether our aquatic odyssey would now float us to the south, north, east, or west was not only a mystery, it was a useless detail that would have no bearing on my life. I would go wherever the group did, and the group would go wherever the staff told us to go. It was never in even my furthest thoughts to launch out on my own, or to split, during the Quest Expedition, and I never knew an RMA kid to split during a Quest or Wilderness Challenge. We were too far along in the program to think in terms of physical escape. We were caught up in mental survival. All things considered, this was supposed to be fun.

From the first hour after we hopped out of the vans, skillfully unlashing and lowering the canoes off the vehicles, I thought, "This is going to be a piece of cake." We set eight canoes side by side on the bepebbled crust of shore, and began loading.

The "mules," two extra canoes, would hold additional food to supplement our personal food-stores. This meant a lot to me – there was literally a boat-load of food – and was a hint that things were not going to be "Survival" oriented. The mules also held equipment I'd seen the older kids using on weekend days; these mountaineering gadgets seemed to mean a lot to Chet, the leader of our Quest Expedition.

We were bringing harnesses for climbing rocks, and heavy-duty ropes whose tri-braided colors of hazard orange, mustard yellow, or puke green distinguished their different lengths and weight thresholds. The ropes were rated according to how many falls they'd already taken, and how old they were. Chet carefully inspected each rope. Deftly he then lashed the mules together with a couple of hitches I recognized.

Now I see why they keep him around; Chet Lively knows his shit out here.

The first morning on the river was long. There were a lot of safety features to go over as we floated in water three-feet deep. We understood: Staff would typically occupy the little benches on our skiffs. The kids promised to never stand, and to stay on butts or knees between the ribbings. We baked in an early spring sun while raking the canoes around a little lake that fed into an especially forgiving section of river. Chet and the Marine wannabe Keith Rios shouted out orders like: "Two. Right. PULL!" Then those of us with oars would pull two strokes on the starboard side. When we heard: "One. Left. PULL!" we yanked to the port side.

Just to be away from the campus had a magic of its own. I was together with my Idaho family in Idaho wilderness, seeing birds flit around, the insects and peepers making their presence known in the afternoons. It felt like we'd been granted a reprieve. We floated through the embrace of aspens and birch.

I was learning to love nature. It was one of the spiritual artifices of the school curriculum: they took credit for giving us our love of snow, sunsets, rocks, animals, and such. It's true. Before Idaho, I hadn't contemplated the spirit, or the very existence of nature, its incredible cycles, or how being aware of it enhanced all life. I guess only a master, or church, or visitation by a being from another realm could have shown me what unlikely, divine coincidence had laid down for us on Earth so we could develop and thrive here.

201

It has to be said that after six hours of this I was ready to stop listening to barks from the staff.

I get it: everyone's life depends on our following orders, being aware, and using common sense. Let's eat something.

My arms and shoulders were aching. But it was fun. It wasn't until the third day that we nearly lost our minds.

On night one, we had a nice campfire and dug into the stores from one of the mule canoes. I shacked with Jamie and Horatio in one of the vibrant blue, nylon dome tents.

The next day, we began with fire safety when Chet had us all cut a fire line in the brush. Then Keith took a few of us to fill our packs with supplies from the second mule canoe. We hiked several miles inland to a buried poured-concrete cache, which we filled with non-perishables for the next winter's Wilderness Challenge. After Keith opened the bunker, we loaded it with Cheetos, Crackerjacks, and Ritz crackers, plus toilet paper and emergency flares. I was sad to see any food go away. Our group ate sardines and peanut butter that night, and slept out near the cache.

Only two days had passed since our little flotilla had put in, yet in another twelve hours I'd be pining to be back in La Mancha, my dorm back at home – er – at RMA.

The next day started out fine. Then, because it was early spring, the mosquitoes and mud bugs woke up. By 11 AM or so there were clouds of bugs surrounding each of us, and by 11:01 the insects' swarm mentality knew that we were their meal ticket. In our own version of the swarm's frenzy, we, the hunted, tried to out-paddle the infernal creatures. They formed a collective shadow that swirled above the canoes' twain mark. Our once-organized flotilla broke apart as paddlers quit dipping oars and used hands and oars alike to start smacking selves instead. But it was only beginning.

Chet, whose hissy fit was rivaling Bianca's, made the decision to park the boats and get off the water. We steered through the swarm into reeds and a bank, where we unloaded our packs from the mule-canoes as fast as possible. Chet hastened his escape, pulling his pack on and hurrying into the pines without checking on us. He would hear about his rushed, unsafe behavior later, from kids and other staff alike, during the outdoor rap.

Everyone flailed to keep the bugs away, following Chet and the rest of the selfish forerunners. Each time I ducked out of my own cloud and wiped my hand through the air, I cleared away about fifty of the ferocious little devils.

We hiked behind Chet, away from the stream, straight toward, and directly up, the biggest, closest mountain. A swift pace, sopped with sweat, was life for the next two hours. We hoofed without stopping.

Our other two staff, Kelly, and Keith, were worthy of admiration for the stiff upper lips they maintained, perhaps thanks to the near-constant smell of garlic they exuded. In contrast, every one of us kids let out a maddened wail, or had a quick breakdown during that hike. This situation made for a different form of upset. These tears were different from most of the tears I'd seen at RMA, even tears of aggravation for the program in raps. This form of helplessness against the insects' onslaught, new to most, reminded me of my world in the desert during Survival. It predated words and memories. This was anger at the wildness of nature's unfair advantages. We all seemed to regress to this pitiful state at moments in the first terrible hour.

There's nothing else in the world to compare this hell to. Maybe there's no better example of hell on earth.

I would've traded my life, or even some other self's life, to be spared any more mosquito bites, I thought miserably and without guilt. However, unlike Chet and Micah, I did wait for the slower members of our group. I was one of the half that had opted for shorts instead of full-length clothing, so it was hell being still, even for the few moments until Narissa and Jamie caught up.

After a couple of hours, we outran the mosquitoes, outmaneuvering them with increased altitude. We puffed our way up a steep summit, and eventually reached a craggy top. The mosquitoes dissipated as wind found its way to us in an undercurrent. Like a river that had been turned upside down to dump out its waters, the stream of air carving through, over, and into the enormous canyon below, was too much for the little fuckers.

RMA and the Survival course bragged about how they used the outdoors as a classroom to teach us fuckup kids that nature didn't negotiate. This was meant to drive us away from mundane life in the suburbs. The way mosquitoes buzzed and made their high frequency "zim-zim" noise around my neck and face reminded me of Mom and Dad at home. They were a different kind of force of nature – always on me, yammering about not just what I'd done wrong, and what was wrong with me, but also the world. The morning, the breakfast, that we were late, and it was MY FAULT he was always late for work.

Adapt to survive? I hadn't been able to adapt to whatever I'd been expected to be at home with Mom and Dad, so I really must succeed in the program.

After we'd rested and slurped up some water, Keith Rios, Tess Turnwell's betrothed, spoke to us:

"Everyone can take a knee or a seat. Thank you. OK. I'm waiting for Ernesto and Micah to quit yapping. . . . This afternoon's plan is the following:

"As you all know, we left many of our supplies in the canoes. So when it cools down, we'll get back down there and make camp. Chet, say something about the dangerous precipice we're on here, and warn everyone. Also bites?"

"Yeah. OK, good job making it up here crew. Seriously that was a good pace, and especially the scramble at the end. Unfortunately – yeah, Bianca get – let's take care of each other's bites in a second. Let me finish this first, thanks. We did some climbing back on campus. Rappelling is much the same, and I'm going to make sure we all get back down in one piece."

"We'll rappel using both the figure-eight carabiners, and also the self-descend method. Good. Now here's the first aid. Whoever needs some TLC gather 'round."

Keith offered to smear bug, sun, or calamine goops on any parts. Chet and he gave out buttons of garlic to those who believed it would have any impact – should the swarms be waiting for seconds when we came back down.

Snacks, well-deserved, came next. After the peanut butter squeezed from toothpaste tubes onto imitation Triscuits, I watched the first team belay–descend. Like two fat spiders, Daphne and Horatio went smoothly down on their two strands of rope.

The group had to hurry for resupply. We jetted into the pines to retrieve sleeping bags and food for the night from the mule boats on the river.

At the canoes, I jammed fresh clothes and extra food into my pack. Chet selected a handful of us to sleep away from the rest of the group that night. As soon as the plan was hatched, I scrambled back into the pines leaving the rest of my PG to sleep at the rocky outcropping with the canoes.

Our small crew – Chet, Jamie, Ivy, Kelly, and I – pushed deep into the forest. Time for the ascent was running out. Higher than the first mosquito-avoidance climb, it seems that this climb could have killed us. Instead, it taught us it was possible to use these special harnesses and hitches without damaging the mountain, and without leaving any gear behind.

We were able to come all the way up without much problem, arriving a full two hours before the sun started to wrap behind the distant horizon of lower and lower mountains. We camped high on our perch that night. Chet and Kelly, whose outdoor skills were respectable, showed us the how and the where of setting up bivouacs. Using various loops, knots, figure-eight hardware, and carabiners, we firmly tied our climbing harnesses on, and tied the ropes to trees and boulders.

Before I fell asleep in my harness, I thought about the day. Being in the woods with my RMA family did start to give me a more mature perspective on what I had been learning thus far, and what my parents wanted me to gain from the program. Like in the Brothers propheet, and numerous times at work in Brave family, or in the lengthy raps, getting to know these people was getting to love them – and the program. They were giving me these life-enhancing moments of aggravation, affection, or fear – and the awareness that this was more real, and therefore better, than anything else I might have experienced in the real world.

Real world = fake feelings and fake people covering up Rock Bottom.

The last full day of canoeing started clear but went gray and nasty just moments after our lunch break. We'd floated into what was going to be our haven for the last afternoon when a flash of lightning seemed to electrify the entire forest. We struggled to unload the boats and cover all the shit with a big blue tarp, but within moments hail was whipping down on us.

We waited it out on the shore until the darkest thunder and possible lightning left the area. This meant we were at the mercy of some low-land mosquitoes that were only deterred by flame and smoke. I was glad to start the fire with my flint-and-steel method, at Kelly's invitation.

205

We ate plenty the whole trip, which kept me in pretty high spirits, and with my Survival values, I ate as much of other people's food as I could, too. When the afternoon sun broke through again, we shuffled boats and seats, repacked the mules, and put back in. In just eight more hours we'd be at RMA and I could shower off the soot and dead bug carcasses.

After a few hours of pulling the wooden oars and trading snacks around, our little flotilla eased into a rocky bank.

"Boys, come gather round Ivy and Bianca here. You guys come here!" Chet and Keith didn't need to blow air through a whistle because we were all close by, a few of us still wearing red life-preservers.

"Let's go to the bathroom and come back here forming a circle. We're going to have a rap."

Of course we're having a rap. It's Friday.

I was not the only one disturbed with the prospect, and weirdness, of an outdoor rap. But there had been quibbles, and a couple of the girls had gotten bitchy, absentmindedly flirty, or frozen in fear against the rock before rappelling, so there was plenty to air out. The rap was loud in comparison to the silence of the forest, and none of the staff hushed us when sounds got punchy and echoed through the area. The whole event struck me as rude.

It seemed disrespectful to Mother Nature to have a rap outside – I mean, isn't RMA environmentally friendly? I felt the whole serenity of the forest to be at odds with indictments, and in contrast to the philosophy of the program. I didn't feel that it was at odds with the program to be in the wilderness with quiet emotional reflection, but my horror and embarrassment at raised voices in the sacred atmosphere made me glad that our next rap was once again within the sanctity of the rap rooms.

Back on campus, we returned the canoes and the rest of the gear to the "expedition room." Until we carried the canoes in there, I hadn't made the obvious connection that they kept all of our backpacks and stuff away from us. This was one of few locked doors at RMA, surely meant to prevent Papoose jaunts off into the greenifying woods. I had really wanted to try it – walking east – but after experiencing the winter here, I knew what was what. You can't even walk in sixty feet of snow!

Injury can be very emotional. All I did was step down, expecting the ground when it wasn't there.

We were unloading the last of the canoes from the van into that locked expedition room. My foot found the ground. It was surprised. Like the target of a kung-fu maneuver, the rest of my body was dumped on the uneven stones next to the van. I clutched my foot and rolled around on the pebbles, cursing the lord himself to hell.

The next day, the final voyage of the Marlboro truck to our campus was witnessed by all dedicated smokers. From the porch with my ice pack, I could see the truck making its turn onto the gravel. There were still a few small piles of dirty melting snow. It was Saturday, and the following week, for the first time since I had been at RMA, the truck would not come. All of a sudden, smoking was totally against the school's philosophy. At a Monday morning meeting, Nat's final announcement was that smoking would no longer be permitted. "If you can't smoke now, you never will. Any kid that comes in from now on will not be able to smoke here or anywhere else."

RMA promised that those of us who had been smokers would be grandfathered in, when we went for home visits. We'd been warned months ago, and for this reason the school cut all of us each to three packs a week for the final month. On the final week, our smoking porch was active with all who were even occasional smokers. It was the end of an era.

The putrid smell of digested carrots lingered everywhere after they cut smoking. For about six weeks, big bowls of carrot sticks were available to everyone — set out for the addicts like me to gnaw on during our regular smoking times. Nobody knew that the carrots – which we were promised had carotene, a chemical compound close to nicotine, to ease our addictions – would cause sudden spasms of orange shit preceded by sulferous, rotten-egg smelling farts.

While I was laid up with my swollen ankle, I couldn't help but think of the southern California kids who had just lived through five months of snow without ever having seen it before. I had a hard time registering it, the first time Wally Gold, from LA, said he'd never seen so much as a frosty lake or snowflake. Next year in Warrior, we were assured, we could combine our earned privileges, trustworthiness, and know-how, and get around on the snow by snowshoes, skis, and bicycles.

Clear skies and sun had finally brought warmth that melted all the ice on the pond, and brought spring to the campus. Lovely, occasional daytime snow-bursts made me appreciate that the long winter's constant eyeball-burning glare had subsided.

I got about four hours of sleep last night because of my ankle. I thought it had gotten better but it hurts as much as it did last night. I have a phone call tonight and I am going to ask to go home. I doubt they will let me but I will ask anyway. Fuck my goddamn ankle hurts. I passed out last night for a minute or two it hurt so much. Can u believe I've been here 10 fucking months! I can't. I think I'm ready to give home a try. I would honestly try but a couple of times again do LSD once and maybe coke once and that's it. But I would absolutely positively definitely stay in my image. More later.

I'm back. Today I went to the hospital and they X-rayed me and said I had a bad sprain, a small fracture and a bone cyst. I will be on crutches for a long time they say. Oh did I tell you they cut smoking out of the school? And I made a commitment on March 29 to [get back in shape]? And I'm doing that. I have to go home I miss it so much I think about it all the time. I have to go bye-bye. OK I'm back. […] I do think I'm staying home on my first home visit. [My sister] gets to come up for next visits so I'm stoked I might get an overnight [visit] if I'm doing ok. Gotta go.

—Author journal, 15 April 1989

Dear Zack

I just wanted to let you know that I've been thinking about you and that I've been hoping to get enough time to write you a long letter. Unfortunately I've been real busy....

[All the family are] really looking forward to our visit.... I know you are, too. In the meantime, keep up the hard work. (I hope your ankle is getting better – it will be fun for you and [your brother] and I to play some basketball. Hope we'll be able to do this without getting angry and frustrated etc. – that will be a good sign!)

I love you and I'm so happy that your world is a different color. I look forward to your next call.

—Letter from author's father, 19 April 1989

PART THREE RESOURCES

- At least 25 things I don't trust in myself
- At least 25 things I don't trust in others
- List 10 words that describe my negative behavior
- Write one page on why I hold onto them and what would happen if I let them go
- List all the things I need to get rid of in my life (stash list)
- Write a half page at least on how I am planning to sabotage this experience
- Make a list of broken agreements I have held with myself
- Write a list of agreements broken with others.
- Write one whole page on the importance of agreements in my life, both when they are kept and when they are broken

—Titles of some writing assignments mandated to the author while at RMA (the responses to which are not included in this book)

[Learning to suppress your own thoughts] is replacing people's subtlety and complexity of what is real into this us versus them reality.

Thought-stopping [is], basically a behavior modification technique to shut down negative thoughts. [Even when they are] taught to do it on themselves so their authentic self is kept suppressed.... the good news is that the authentic self is still there, and love, particularly family, friends, ... they can actually feed the authentic self and help to empower the authentic self while simultaneously bringing up questions about the group's ideology.

Emotional control is essentially making a person feel special and chosen – they are going to help save the world, on the one hand, ... but the rest is guilt and fear and manipulation...

[The universal mind control technique is] phobia indoctrination – the deliberate implantation of irrational fears that if you ever leave the group – or even question the leader – terrible things are going to happen to you.

The leaders have to demonize people who left because it's very threatening to see ex-members being happy and healthy.

— Steve Hassan, speaking at event in London: Cults, Racism, Doublespeak and the Search. Transcribed from video on YouTube, *Undue Influence: Brainwashing, Mind Control, and how it all works.* https://www.youtube.com/watch?v=OilxbBKvrp8

Zack Bonnie

PART FOUR

Zack Bonnie

TWENTY-TWO

Hey there I knew it had been a while but I didn't know it had been that long. I moved dorms today but I'm pretty bitter about it. I go through my I want to live propheet in 1 week. First home visit in a month. Lessee I just came out of a pretty good rap. I ran my anger.

—Author journal before I Want To Live propheet

The thunder began as the sun faded behind a hundred peaks, each steeper and snowier than the section of mountain before it. A light and prophetic mist squatted thickly on the campus, foreshadowing that night's I Want To Live propheet, just for my PG, which now congregated in and around the recessed seating area called "the pit" for last light.

John Denver's *I Want to Live* played over and over through the house; it was a special night for my PG. I knew the music would have even more significance for me, like the other snot-ripper songs already did, after I next slept.

Before I had even known about its significance, John Denver's song had tugged at my heart cords. The song brought out in me that feeling I had sometimes when my heart seemed to be rotting inside a cave in my chest filled with rotting bones. Would I be able to control this after tonight? Or maybe I'd learn that my soul itself was vacuous, instead? I tried to keep that confused and anxious feeling near.

That feeling might be of use to me now. I'm using my Brothers!

Normally I'd have been tired, but since the whole propheet "warm-up" was about us, the foreboding mystery kept us alert, separated from our natural schedules. The peer group above mine stood facing us with their arms around one another in front of the hissing fireplace. One by one they spoke.

"I just want to share with you that since the propheet, and especially at home last month, how much I used the tools from the I Want To Live, and I know that you're all going to get that privilege now. I'm so excited to share with you. Bianca. I love you. I love you all. OK. Who's next?"

"Alright I'll go! Well for me, the umm, the significance of choosing life over death and what upper-school kids meant when they struggled in raps was all confused, but at least I guess I know what we're all fighting now...you're all going to go for it tonight!"

Kelly spoke at the end. "I had such a great time getting to know this peer group better on the Quest Expedition a few weeks ago. I have so much respect for the work you're going to do in there tonight. I'll be supporting all the positive in each one of you, no matter how much you struggle. So... I guess we'll all just go for broke in there tonight!"

The reminder we knew: an important theme would be revealed to me and my PG tonight. After completing it, we'd be applying for Warrior family. Once we got in, we'd be considered upper-schoolers, and we'd get to work with the animals on the farm, a final freedom before the all-day academic classes of Summit family. Most importantly, we'd all get to go home for a few days, and be completely, temporarily, withdrawn from influence of the staff and program. Or so I thought.

We had hints and clues about what we were going to be introduced to overnight. We thought we knew there was a way to metaphorically "fight" our Thinking. We knew that after the I Want To Live, kids ran their anger differently than any tools shown to us in raps by staff; we knew Stinkin' Thinkin' was a big tool in the RMA program, and I'd garnered that the word "choice" would have different significance and was a tool I'd surely learn more about before tomorrow.

I felt ready. I wasn't on bans from anyone, had received kudos from family staff and students for my leadership on the Quest Expedition, and it had been over a month since I'd done a WD – the last one for not pulling up two Papoose students for cutting up music at the dorm. I hadn't wanked off for a week, refraining in order try to go through the experience guilt free, as was the custom before the 24-hour marathon introspection workshops.

We were ready, or we wouldn't still be allowed to stay here.

As I should, I'd been focusing on tools from our most recent propheet. Now, as the next one approached, I especially worked with my awareness level and my lug.

My Unawareness Keeps ME Alone and Unlovable.

Still, I was nervous. Was I ever right where I was supposed to be? About ten months ago, for the Truth, our first propheet, we'd traipsed through the summer woods to Walden, the specialized propheet building I'd be in again tonight. Only this time I was excited for the lessons we'd learn. Any minute we'd walk there to begin.

But.

Will I have to explore death? I know I'll have to look at things that must remain contained in the red binder in the back of my mind, where my privatest of private thoughts are hidden from the uncontrollable conspicuousness of raps. How honest will I let myself get tonight? How deep will they make us go?

☦

Each person becomes caught up in a continuous conflict over which secrets to preserve and which to surrender, over ways to reveal lesser secrets in order to protect more important ones; his own boundaries between the secret and the known, between the public and the private, become blurred.

—Robert J. Lifton, *Thought Reform and the Psychology of Totalism: A Study of "Brainwashing" in China*, Martino Publishing, 2014, p 427

☦

As dreadful as this pre-propheet apprehensiveness was, I also looked forward to having to face my real – or program-designed – issues, in the deeply personal manner that would be demanded of me and my PG.

Lingering hugs ended, and the house emptied. The John Denver song continued ringing over the speakers, pronouncing the sanctity of nature. I already knew I wanted more out of life than to merely exist, as the theme song suggested. I would never let myself become a perambulating carcass, even though I still thought it a strange choice in words.

And in the song, *I Want to Live*, it just sounded like John Denver was singing about whales and nature, not overdoses, car accidents, bulimia, rape, incest, violence, and whether we'd turn out as unlovable human beings. Music could obfuscate as well as reveal, so a mystery was there to be disentangled in the propheet. The music of this propheet would from now on be a shortcut to all of the lessons I learned, always bringing me back to an eternal struggle against my Thinking.

I do want to live deeply and have a meaningful life.

Why couldn't I ever just sit still like all the good boys and girls? Why'd I talk out of turn? And later, why had I wanted that image, and to do drugs? Who could I love if I ever became lovable? Can the program now answer for why I truly went through moments where I didn't want to live and wanted that blackness and silence for everything animate and not?

All the real questions I'd never let myself investigate.

✝

When I compartmentalized the various parcels of additional information I was starting to garner from the introspection I was doing, it reminded me of the Ritalin-induced laser focus back at home as a kid.

I started on Ritalin around the time they told my brother and me they were expecting the baby. For a few weeks toward the end of fourth grade, I had focused, with the prescription's help, on everything that was wrong with my existence under my parents' roof. By the time Mom found Idaho for me, that unwanted existence was real. Back before the Ritalin days, before my baby sister was born and things got so structured, every day after school had been my time. I had a lot of my own time. Dad went to work at the university until dark every day, and Mom sat in her office clacking on her typewriter, or else she went to aerobics. Then it changed.

Mom began pecking on a softer-sounding "word-processing program" on her desk-sized computer, and Dad started traveling a lot for work. I seemed to eat dinner a lot at Chuck's, or other friends' houses, after Mom began to expand, gestating my baby sister.

In school, I became an instant success after the Ritalin kicked in. But in all other aspects of life, the Ritalin didn't help. Yes, I would become ultra-focused and, while cliché, the analogy of a laser in my mind is apt. It focused on that morning's fight with Dad, or it stewed about the fight with Mom on the night prior. The focus intensified in my brain.

The bring-down, one of the side effects I would sometimes feel when the medicine wore off – Dr. D, my shrink, called it a rebound effect – would also cause intense rage. My rage about the issues at school developed pinpoint accuracy, and when I looked at my issues at home additionally, the rage and its laser focus were even worse. This gave me a special crash-course in RMA, before I'd ever heard or used the word introspection. In fourth grade, these combined side effects overwhelmed me.

Nerf basketball in the office with Dr. Shrink was boring, but calm – at least until he started asking rapid-fire questions about school and Mom and Dad. I believed that I had to see the shrink, to have the prescription to take the medicine Mom and the teachers wanted dissolved in my tummy all day. At home the Formica-topped table had Trapper Keepers spread out, in colors of all varieties. GEOGRAPHY, GEOMETRY, LATIN. There was one for SOCIAL SCIENCE, which was just dumb history, classed up with weekly reports about satellite-people through history with names even the teachers hadn't heard of; Charlemagne's brothers, former US vice presidents, and failed German generals from early in the century.

Homework-wise, week-long or month-long projects were the worst, because whenever I had a project due, that meant fights with Dad. The mornings before school became the worst part of the day, every day.

I distinctly remember telling Dr. Shrink about all this over a game of Nerf basketball. He put the little hoop's brace over his door the first time we met, and cast the question over his shoulder non-nonchalantly as if we were in casual conversation:

"How did the dosage work this week?"

"Dunno. Still makes my stomach hurt. I still feel like a zombie, or during gym or lunch I feel like I have to be working. It's weird."

"Still a lot of fighting with Dad in the evenings?"

"Yeah, I guess."

Before and after dinner, I had to sit with Dad and focus at the table in a timeless forever until the homework was done. On the third pill, the one I was supposed to take after dinner, the effects would reverse. I had no focus left – it was like I had used it all up. It took everything I had just to keep from drifting to sleep; I had to get through my homework without upsetting Mom and Dad. They'd already given up on piano lessons, baseball, soccer, and all the rest. My brain had shut down and seemed to shun any more learning thoughts.

"I've been getting the homework done." I added, trying to be helpful to the doc. "Usually I get it finished while Mom feeds the baby though." I didn't mention which feeding, since the little angel peaceably slurped from microwaved bottles of "formula" every three hours. I called her "the hummingbird," when I was happy. Or "the leech," when I was not.

Was it my Thinking that gave me ADD? Or the other way around? Was it depression or my Thinking that had almost gotten me dead? Was it that I was inherently "wrong" – and that's what made me fight with Mom and Dad, and why they cast me aside? Or made me sneak out of the window to drunken encounters, or to try to make it with the girls at home?

Although I explored the world outside of my parents' physical home, I'd still had to do their bidding, and abide by the zillions of wishes that teachers directed me to fulfill. Those adults back home had rammed down my little kid a lot of ideals that turned out to be wrong.

I learned that here.

Now processing the program's messages was up to me. I would have to let go of my way of thinking, and the programming I had received before RMA. I just hadn't known that it wasn't working for me until my parents found this place – to show me what they hadn't been able to themselves, for whatever reason.

The focus of the program, I knew, was on what was wrong with me, how I could never do IT right without the lessons I'd learn there. Life.

The metaphors of our traps and double-edged swords were always in use, getting us to open up, go deeper, and expose more. When it came to allowing those submerged and monstrously destructive feelings to resurface under the hours of counseling in raps and propheets, it reminded me of the Ritalin-induced laser focus back home as a kid. RMA – like Mom felt about the Ritalin for my ADD diagnosis – could save me, if I'd but believe in it.

†

Your phone language is very upsetting. But even
more is how you contrast your behavior now with

your behaviors of a year ago. I DON'T WANT YOU
TO THINK THAT YOUR BEHAVIOR OF A YEAR AGO
WAS ACCEPTABLE TO ANYONE. When you say, "just
think of what I would be doing a year ago," I want to
scream. That is not a basis for comparison. A year ago
your parents understood that your behavior was so
totally irresponsible that you couldn't live at home.
There was never a question in our minds that we
could go on the way we were. [We] wouldn't subject
ourselves to such abuse. And your running away from
home and camp made clear that you weren't accepting any reasonable authority. Please don't talk about
your previous behavior as if it's anything that anyone
could or would put up with!

I feel myself winding up again, so I'll stop here. I
know Daddy wants to write to you, because your
phone call upset us a whole lot.

I love you. Let's put the learning of this past year
into play. Let's work on changing for the better.

LOVE,

Mommy

—Letter from author's mother, spring 1989

I wasn't the only one collecting my thoughts. My peer group sat
silently in the house, contemplatively. It felt strange to be crowded
into the pit since the rest of the school had gone down to their dorms
for sleep, and left the enormous main structure a wasted space. Softly,
above hisses of wood smoldering on the hearth, we talked, smooshed,
traded massages, and napped while waiting for someone to tell us when
to go to Walden.

Kelly Grainger came to the pit and joined us as we lounged on the
coarse cowhide pillows.

Moments later, Nat Farmer, one of the most important people
around here, came in holding an RMA coffee mug with a saintly air.
He was a bit of a savant for emotions, and as happens with special
composers of great paintings or pieces of music, it went to our leader's
head. At various times, I'd heard him called the President, Headmaster,

and Academic Advisor. He was the guy that signed the graduates'
diplomas, was always the Summit family head, ran the parent workshop at Coeur d'Alene, and led the big final Summit Workshop. Along
with the rest of the power staff like Hedwig, Keith, Tess, Prescott, Nat,
or Darlayne, he believed his omnipotence.

Nat had just showered, the way Tess had before our Truth, so his
hair was damp and he smelled important. He had wrapped a white
sweatshirt so that its arms dangled down below his neck. Yu-Yu and
I sat near Ivy, and Kelly took a place between my legs, in smoosh
position. Ivy, true to the vegan leanings she had brought to our PG a
year ago in Papoose, sat on the floor next to me, still refusing to use the
bristly cow cushions which left wisps of bovine hair on wool sweaters and flannels. Nat ordained Bianca to turn off the music from the
Bridge – a right normally only awarded to Summit kids and staff. Nat
finally addressed us over the silence after Bianca retook her seat.

"OK. Here we are. I'm so proud of each and every one of you for
making it to this point. I know it wasn't always easy, right guys? You
bet, Ernie! Zack! Awesome work, men! Upper school is a big responsibility, and I only take men and women into Summit. Not children.
You'll be one important step closer to Summit after tonight. Tonight,
like every day here, is important. I want you thinking about how your
reflections of yourself have changed since you've been here. And how
your feelings have changed? Your outlook. How did the campus look
out of your eyes when you got here? And now? Or how your luggage
is still so important to you that you're still carrying it. Here and now.
Really think about that tonight. Now go to the mudroom and get your
boots and stuff. I'll meet you at Walden building in sixty minutes.
Don't be late."

This was the first time we'd been allowed to go alone to the building. Before, like for the Truth, we'd been required to hold hands and
walk to the tipi as a group and wait for Chet, or some other staff.

The mist had condensed into water. Rain threatened to last all
night. As we approached, still in our Sorels because of the mud, Karen
Carpenter, Yoko, Carole King, or some other hippie woman sang *What
the World Needs Now* from the speakers hanging in the propheet room.

TWENTY-THREE

Walden's front door was open. We removed our boots, jackets, and belts and selected our seats as we entered. I dreaded the deep introspective work; I could also look forward to it, since it would elevate us, and our status, in the program. I knew that here, to the degree I felt sorrow, I would also feel joy.

Black plastic seats occupied, we stared at each other in the propheet horseshoe for a while, wondering why Nat wasn't sitting in the unoccupied music control station facilitator seat. The room was bright. Fresh flowers were where they ought to be. An ornate grandfather clock added a firm, hollow, nutty, "klok" noise every second. Cold drips sang through the tin gutters.

Nat paraded in with a big white cowboy hat on his head and a short rope fashioned into a lasso slung over his shoulder. In his other hand, he carried a little pink bottle.

"Ivy Live-ly," Nat sang, making a play on Ivy's name, "come on up here for a minute sweetheart." Ivy rigidly complied from the first seat in the horseshoe. "Take this while I cue the tape. Here we go. Now open it and blow us some bubbles."

The music zinged through copper wiring and began to ooze from the speakers. The flood of music was no longer a surprise turn. My eardrums opened up like thirsty flowers to the simple electric impulses from a guy with a scratchy smoker's voice.

"SWEET CAROLINE, Bum Bah Bum, good times never seemed so good..."

I'm pretty sure it's Joe Cocker or Neil Diamond.

Both were artists I'd never heard of before Idaho, though my brother and I had been indoctrinated at home in the ways of some of that era's music – especially the timeless classic duos like the Everly Brothers and Simon and Garfunkel.

Ivy uncapped the little pink bottle and removed a plastic loop. Darlayne Hammer, the dreaded support staff tonight, stood aside and rested a hand on her cocked hip. Ivy began to blow bubbles into the middle of the horseshoe over growing music and excited movements from the four staff.

"Excellent, keep it up!" Nat danced around behind us. To the beat of the music, he tapped eeny-meeny-miney-moe on the heads of the boys in our peer group. The music blared and Ivy blew sparkling bubbles that floated around the room and then burst at our feet. Nat yelled, "You are IT!" as his hands landed on Wally's shoulders.

Nat popped the oversized cowboy hat on Wally's head, dumped him forward out of his chair, and steered him up front to join Ivy.

Wally looked ridiculous in the preposterously large cowboy hat. The staff were all out of their chairs clapping and yodeling, trying to energize the room.

"OK! You guys interact with each other. Think Cowboys!"

"HA HA! NICE WALLY! USE THE PROPS!"

"I'm LOVING IT!"

"DARE TO BE A DORK!"

"GO GET THE BROOM FROM THE MUDROOM!"

"Well, would you LOOK AT WHAT ELSE I FOUND OUT THERE!"

Darlayne clutched a cardboard box filled with cowboy hats and more soapy solution and plastic bubble-blowing hoops. Wally romped around straddling his bucking broom over the growing laughter and loudness under the room's brightest lighting.

"OK, who wants to join them?"

It wasn't rhetorical and nobody was supposed to need permission to join what we knew to be an ice breaker.

After a few minutes of loud and embarrassing behavior, Nat shuffled music, playing fast-paced country tunes. This one was John Denver's *Thank God I'm a Country Boy*. It played several times. We lassoed and yee-hawed without compunction, while Nat kept going to the girls and moving them around the room to increase the bubble-making shenanigans.

Boys threw their hats in the air, acted like horses, and used finger guns at one another in silly pantomimed duels. Like in the Truth propheet, or numerous other times at RMA, the staff designed weird ways to shake us up. Getting students out of their comfort zones was the staff's eternal crusade.

Boys didn't blow bubbles in this ice breaker, which would have also been embarrassing. Girls didn't play cowboys. I didn't want to reverse roles; I'm just pointing it out.

After the bubble blowing and cowboy imitations, Kelly and Darlayne came around and took our hats and props. As with most things we were asked to do in propheets, we got to go to the bathroom afterwards. Then we returned the upturned chairs, which had been acting as stand-ins for so many horses, to their normal positions.

After the short break, our heart rates were back to normal. Nat called Bianca into the center.

"What's your favorite food? Strawberries?! Good. So, when you think of strawberries, and the way they taste, what noise would you make?"

Naturally, Bianca made an over-acted yummy noise, which Nat had her repeat.

"Now add some movement to the vocalization!"

Bianca rubbed her belly and threw her head back laughing. Yummy noise, belly rub, hearty Santa laugh. Darlayne dragged Yu-Yu up. Then, with every expelled breath and yummy noise Bianca made, now Nat, Darlayne, or Kelly added another one of us.

Bubbles floated by. Now I was up there yippin' and skippin' in place like an animal. When Yu-Yu would bend low at the waist and rise up quickly with a big farting noise, I'd shift my weight diagonally, poking my arms and head out with a diabolical roar. Micah jumped up. He lay down and lifted his legs so that Yu-Yu had one, and the other rested on Bianca's hip. Then Ivy joined the forum, adding to the bizarre sight and sound sculpture. Every time Narissa screeched like a worn fan belt, Daphne would click and clap like a human typewriter.

We all, staff included, found a noise and a movement, and we stayed in the group like that, in a goofy, racket-erupting, machine. A sucking lunging expanding and collapsing screeching jumping pounding bubble-blowing farting machine. We did this until my lips were red and numb from making noises, and my jaw hurt from trying not to laugh.

The voices of the three power staff, Nat, Darlayne, and Kelly, commanded my PG's expectation: we were with the program, with them, every step of the way. So we were.

Like a photographer aims a camera, I focused on my self-awareness and zoomed in on the staff and older supports. I hoped to guess the steps that might await us between the disclosure circle and rap phases sure to come later. I hated noticing how I'd still cower whenever I heard Darlayne's voice. I longed for her attention, and while terrified, I was also abuzz to have her witness my devotion.

We were practiced at cleaning and restoring the room to its original configuration: a precise horseshoe shape of black plastic chairs interspersed with cushioned wooden armchair thrones for the power staff. We reapplied order to the room; we had done all there was to do with our black chairs, I thought, as racing hearts re-regulated after the machine ice breaker.

I took in the signs on the walls proclaiming new tools we'd be focusing on:

You Are What You DO, NOT What You SAY You Do!

Dreams Are Good For Little Kids.

Are YOU Living LIFE or Choosing DEATH?

Every Second You WASTE IS Time You Live Less.

Guilt Blocks All Growth.

To Be Great Follow Me.

Nat was done with the obligatory ice breaking.

"Who here thinks they know what the meaning of life is?"

We struggled to form and verbalize coherent thoughts. To be sure, this was a new attempt to shake us up and get us out of any comfort zones we were hiding in. It was effective. The discomfort level felt equal to the cowboy and bubble blowing, except that now it felt like we were all finding intellectual frustration. Being asked to use our brains felt out of immediate reach.

At times, uncomfortable silences sat in the quiet and brightly lit room as we pondered statements about the existence of god, or what it would be like to be an eagle.

Only then did Nat insert another piece of his diabolical word game. For a long while it seemed the staff were on bans from talking in the propheet. As we realized that the staff were seldom intervening, various members of my PG took the forum. Darlayne stared with her brown, innocent, Bambi, lovey-eyes expression at whomever was speaking. Nat stroked his curly beard and occasionally nodded in contemplative agreement.

First Horatio and I led the conversation in circles, until the conversation wandered toward the truth of the existence of miracles. Horatio was working his lug from the Brothers. That meant he had to be loud and forceful, to counteract his reputation as Mr. Invisible.

I'd been privy to a conversation about Calvin and Hobbes – the old guys, not the cartoon – between my brother and Dad at dinner the year before. So I spoke up, based on what my brother had explained, about John Calvin and Thomas Hobbes. Their philosophies from 400 years ago allowed me to introduce the impossibility of *repeating* a miracle, because then it would more likely be a hoax, a mass hallucination, or fraudulent claim. This, I said, meant the evidence of a miracle cannot be scientifically tested.

For this, Nat had even raised his eyebrows with a sexy whistle at me, which made me beam with pride.

Bianca and Micah, feeling a responsibility for being the head and the baby of the PG, respectively, took turns bending the deep, the philosophical, and the theosophical into various comparisons relating to the importance of the emotional work that we do in the program. Jamie, looking extra confident, pooh-poohed elements of that argument, contending that what we focused on in Idaho was unique to CEDU campuses.

We all tried to show off how smart we were for Nat and Darlayne. I worked to make an impression on Kelly of my physical and mental maturity. I think brain fuzz from tiredness had set in when Nat's voice finally interjected another segue into our ebbing discussion.

"Let's talk now about what we learned in the Brothers. During the last conversation, nobody brought up friendship! Isn't that something worth living for – shit, isn't that a repeatable miracle – when you think about it?"

We each went straight into our personal lugs to rebroadcast for Nat a litany of what we knew from the program thus far. Each member of my PG got in front of the horseshoe with a snapshot of who they are, their personal issues, and newly found self-observations. It was interesting to me to hear how the recent Quest Expedition had had profound moments of impact on some of my PG, when I'd just viewed the four days as mostly "fun," at least until I sprained my ankle. Nat droned, and I put on my studious face.

"What if when you next left this room, you had a specialized knowledge of yourself, and were therefore able to read people. Or, you could know what it is that makes US different from all other animals; or why, on an individual level, you really do the things you do? What drives your Thinking? How to stop the negative tapes playing, those messages in your head? Those would be pretty important questions to answer, wouldn't they?"

I wasn't so sure about Nat's last idea. What was Nat playing at? An intellectual discourse that suggested that everything I ever felt, thought, or saw was my own choice, was a stretch. I couldn't think this, yet.

I did sense that a mysterious force existed in my personal universe. That force within me made me hurt friends, caused me to become unlovable and unaware as I grew up in my parent's house, made me shit all over my little kid, and turned me into the lonesome fuckup in school that got me sent away from home.

My feelings felt like a Moebius strip, dipping between the present and a past before Idaho: positive- to negative-Thinking generated constantly changing opposing forces that I alone was responsible for.

The conversation continued in our horseshoe of chairs. We looked at the differences between enlightened humans and weasels and other animals. Unlike us, they had no "choice" in their lives. We had attained our half-way point of self-awareness because of the raps and propheets we'd experienced so far, now that we'd been there nearly a year.

Are they really comparing non-CEDU people to animals?

Like sled-dogs in training probably do, we dipped between needing to please staff and mistrusting them when they introduced new lessons.

We returned to the sequestered propheet room after bathroom break two. The black chairs had been re-stacked in the corner. For this task, we partnered up with the person in the room that we thought was most like us. Of course, Nat could just as easily have told us to pick the person the least like us, or from a state that had an "A" in it, or who we been most or least comfortable around. In all of these selections and exercises through my time at RMA, it was a given that I'd work with everyone numerous times, even with Micah and Bianca, though our friendships had gotten off to a rocky start.

I paired with Kelly, mostly because I didn't think anybody in the room was that much like me. Also, Kelly hadn't been in our Brothers to see my "outsideness" illustrated. Ernie was with Mariah.

My older siblings, Mariah Verdera and Tim Chalmers, had each been through this all-night experience once before, but were good at keeping poker faces about the tools we'd soon share. They were both on deck to go through the Summit, and then graduate with Griffin and Jasper in the winter. For tonight, these two people – among the hand-ful of older brothers and sisters whom I now particularly cared about – were propheet supports to Nat, Darlayne, and Kelly. As always, I watched the older supporting kids for tips on what I should feel, and how to prove I was feeling it. They already were what I was expected to become.

Darlayne fiddled with the lights as Nat peered into the cassette box. I looked around the room. The familiar faces were staring at one another in our pairs, waiting to be told what to do next.

We knew how important the hypnotic music spells were to getting in touch with our expected feelings in Idaho. Each cassette in the box that Nat had brought in was only one song, repeating on both sides, so it was capable of near continuous play on the high-tech deck that could "flip" the tape by itself. All the facilitating staff had to do, whether in a propheet or on the house floor, was pop a cassette in and hit Play; conveniently, over the next 180 minutes or so, the entire mood and atmosphere would reach the desired level of frenzy or slowness.

As Nat popped open the cassette case, I had the bittersweet hope he would play a song with lyrics and melody that would perturb my personal issues. He selected the next song to make the plastic Sony spindles spin, but didn't yet push Play to engage the gear.

Kelly and I were near the stacked chairs. We watched Nat go to Darlayne, to model what they had in mind for us partner "As" and "Bs." Darlayne and Nat held their arms straight out, their flattened palms touching, for an uncomfortable amount of time. As they stood there, they looked into each other's face with great intensity.

Are they going to start miming? Look, I'm trapped inside a box!

In my periphery, I could see the rest of the group standing still, paired up, perfectly still, staring into their partners' eyes.

Are we going to slow-dance?

I took in Kelly's beauty. I wished she were a kid in our peer group. I wished she were from the East Coast, instead of from Arizona. Most of all, I wished Kelly was not in a committed relationship with Darlayne, which is why she'd even moved here, I guessed. Her brown hair was now coiffed in a short flapper look; this brought out dark brown, tender eyes. I was deeply curious what Kelly must see as she looked intently into my eyes. Did she see all my zits and was only staring at me because she was instructed to? Did she think I was handsome? I smirked. No. But she had squelched a little smirk too.

Nat's voice.

"Partner A, take a step back from your partner and everyone look at me. Partner Bs listen up, also. What we're going to do is remember what we know of each other, and we're going to be honest, and place expressions on each other's bodies. Living expressions of fear. Now let's really go for broke here: 'The harder the truth to tell, the truer the friend that tells it.' Now watch Darlayne and me."

Darlayne dropped her arms to a neutral position to let Nat physically manipulate her big-boned body. Nat took great time, scrutinizing his partner with the focus of an artist. He gently pulled her wrist over her head. She left it up there. Nat sculpted Darlayne into three different positions, warming the clay. He took a step back with a hand clamped pensively around his beard. Nat snapped his fingers, re-approaching with a new idea.

When he settled on one position for Darlayne some minutes – two song lengths – later, Darlayne was left in the middle of the room standing defiantly with one foot forward. She had one hand on an upturned hip in a fist and the other hand extended in front of her face giving the ol' Fuck-You finger. He took in Darlayne's visual image one last time before fishing a marker and a stack of tags from the little table where he kept his coffee mug and notes. He popped the cap off the marker and squeaked some indelible ink onto a sticky label. After preparing it and tearing off the back, he returned to Darlayne, whose meaty front leg had begun to tremble noticeably with the exertion of being frozen in position. He pressed the adhesive label over her beefy breast. It read: "JUST LEAVE ME ALONE."

"Your program here is personal. Take what you know of each other and apply it to this exercise. This is serious. I support you all."

Just the way that Nat talked to us made me feel older. Because I now attached more importance to him as one of the spiritual leaders of the program, and as I had been practicing with George, I awaited opportunities to impress him, to demonstrate that I was listening. I wanted to gain the Summit family head's respect, and I wanted him to know my learning potential.

It was our turn to make a living sculpture, to be called "Living Fear."

I shaped Kelly into the form of a mother looking at a swaddled baby. I stole my idea from the Kahlil Gibran entry on beauty that had been read to us three times, once by each staff member, from their cushy chairs.

†

And a poet said, "Speak to us of Beauty."

Where shall you seek beauty, and how shall you find her unless she herself be your way and your guide?

And how shall you speak of her except she be the weaver of your speech?

The aggrieved and the injured say, "Beauty is kind and gentle.

Like a young mother half-shy of her own glory she walks among us."

And the passionate say, "Nay, beauty is a thing of might and dread.

Like the tempest she shakes the earth beneath us and the sky above us."

The tired and the weary say, "Beauty is of soft whisperings. She speaks in our spirit.

Her voice yields to our silences like a faint light that quivers in fear of the shadow."

But the restless say, "We have heard her shouting among the mountains,

And with her cries came the sound of hoofs, and the beating of wings and the roaring of lions."

At night the watchmen of the city say, "Beauty shall rise with the dawn from the east."

And at noontide the toilers and the wayfarers say, "We have seen her leaning over the earth from the windows of the sunset."

In winter say the snow-bound, "She shall come with the spring leaping upon the hills."

And in the summer heat the reapers say, "We have seen her dancing with the autumn leaves, and we saw a drift of snow in her hair."

All these things have you said of beauty.

Yet in truth you spoke not of her but of needs unsatisfied,

And beauty is not a need but an ecstasy.

It is not a mouth thirsting nor an empty hand stretched forth,

But rather a heart enflamed and a soul enchanted.

It is not the image you would see nor the song you would hear,

But rather an image you see though you close your eyes and a song you hear though you shut your ears.

It is not the sap within the furrowed bark, nor a wing attached to a claw,

But rather a garden for ever in bloom and a flock of angels for ever in flight.

People of Orphalese, beauty is life when life unveils her holy face.

But you are life and you are the veil.

Beauty is eternity gazing at itself in a mirror.

But you are eternity and you are the mirror.

—Kahlil Gibran, "On Beauty," *The Prophet*

☦

Kelly Grainger held her arms tightly like she was holding a newborn child below her breast. I gently tilted her neck to look down, but away from the babe in her arms. I pressed her lips into a trembling frown. The tension on her facial muscles caused her bottom lip to quiver. She froze in the position, clearly portraying a mother ignoring her child. After a while Nat came around with a sticky label. The marker squeaked out some ink; I tried to write as neatly as possible: "Mama says I don't deserve to love." But after a bit of quiet consultation we swapped her label for another without the word "to."

"OK Partner As, take a final moment to make sure you've done right by partner B. Is it worthy of your insights? Is your workmanship on display? Is your love visible in this effort? OK, if you're satisfied with your creations, take a step back. Good. Let's now take a tour of the museum of fear that you have created with your honesty."

Nat made sure we started walking around the exhibit before he pushed Play on the stereo. To my surprise, John Lennon began singing. John was a demigod at RMA, and this was the first time we'd heard his music during a propheet.

I followed half of my peer group to see the bodies that were frozen with their labels. Ernesto was slumped in the corner with his hand out. Bianca had posed him so he was pressing a plunger down on an imaginary needle, poking into the vein in his wrist. His head was turned up and his eyes were closed: an overdose fatality. His sign said, "I choose death because I am a Failure."

As I read Ernie's label, John Lennon had just gotten to the line in *Isolation*, "Don't they know we're so afraid…"

After everybody toured the room, Nat had the partners switch roles. Of course.

233

Kelly began to sculpt me. Taking her time, warming the clay, she pulled me down to one knee. Kelly put her hand around my wrist and brought it down next to my ankle. She slowly pressed me down until my face was inches from my hand. She curled my left hand into a fist and pulled it toward me so that my wrist veins popped out. My right hand she positioned so that if I was holding a razor blade, I'd be slashing at those veins. It was the worst image she could have constructed. Having a will to die was the most cardinal of sins in Idaho. I wanted to be vulnerable for Darlayne, share with my PG, and for Nat Farmer to know my issues for Summit next year; but this was too much. But I stayed frozen in the position while Kelly scratched the title of her creation on a label. She pressed it on my chest: "Fuck it, I quit."

We admired these depictions of emotional artistry, each of us discussing the exercise, and how it felt. We retook those positions until they became muscle memory. Nat never did the exercise of being sculpted, so I didn't see his nightmare pose. During the final viewing of the room, our warm-up, interactive museum, Darlayne plastered two more tools to the walls.

On the wall near the exit door was a new poster with the words FEAR & DEATH = I.

Opposite the negative poster was a positive poster: LOVE & LIFE = ME.

Nat spoke again. "Take a good look at the positions you and your peers are put in. Those poses are another example of where your Thinking takes you. This is how far – how bad – it can get. This is your nightmare pose. Keeping the topics we've covered in mind, I want us all to look at the signs that Darlayne has just put up. Every one of you has made a choice to be somewhere on the life and death line here. Take a position between these two posters...Where does your Thinking, your nightmare, put YOU? Come on! You don't need to look at anyone else. YOU KNOW WHERE TO GO!"

The point was for us to stick our noses in the FEAR & DEATH poster, but it took a few moments to register this. Light grappling began over heightening music, until we were jostling, and then shoving one another out of the way. Some took turns kicking us away while slouched down in front of the poster. Nat, Kelly, and Darlayne yelled and body checked us, to rouse us enough to keep shoving through a few song lengths. As we shoved our way into the corner, Harry Chapin kept repeating himself over plucky finger-picking guitar: "The cat's in the cradle and the silver spoon, little boy blue and the man in the moon...." It was a short song we already knew, but it became another one of those tunes I'd never listen to the same way.

"That's pitiful, look at where you CHOOSE to live. Where you react from. FEAR! DEATH! Look at love and life over there. . . . WHEN ARE YOU GOING TO CHOOSE TO FEEL DIFFERENTLY?"

When the time in the propheet comes for us to do that.

After a break to piss, we unstacked the black chairs and reset them for our rap. I recognized it felt special to have a rap with Nat Farmer. I mean, being able to share my issues and gain his insight could go a long way when I got to Summit. Also, he didn't waste his time with the newcomers, and only facilitated raps on Mondays. Another thing about the I Want To Live rap – when the person was indicted and pressed to go deeper, there wasn't much resistance, and hardly any rebuttal the way we'd all tried to defend ourselves as Papooses. People reduced themselves to tears with the on-point direct questioning that Nat had honed over the decades. Whether describing our lugs and how we'd received them in the last prophet, or confessing our failures, or "disclosures," we began to parse ourselves, longing for deeper insight from the staff and other kids. We welcomed our moments in the spotlight now. There wasn't as much yelling in this rap. Instead, there was the demand for something new: an acknowledgment that we didn't know the answers.

When Mariah and Tim had their exchanges with Darlayne or Nat, they used the pidgin English I and ME language, speaking about their Thinking in the coded language of the oldest kids in Idaho. I guessed some of these tools were from what they were learning during their Truth counseling sessions – special sessions that took the place of Friday raps for them. Nat was prepping them both for the Summit Workshop.

I tried to encapsulate what I thought I so far understood: FEAR and DEATH happen when you think too much. Your ME gets covered up, and eventually is the slave of the I. That was how we got here, and was also what made us special – because we were still here to embody this. Our earlier conversation about choice confirmed that everyone in the world struggled. Only here, now, could we counteract society's collective thinking, and struggle against its negative emotion.

The I Want To Live propheet rap also embedded our disclosures, as we knew to bring up our applicable issues during indictments. It made sense that our Thinking could be blamed for all the things we did to Rock Bottom, to our little kids – our "doogers," our Me's.

We now were developing a method – and permission – to divide our personalities into two; but I wasn't sure everyone, or I, could do this.

†

> [Synanon founder Charles] Dederich said, "Now, what we're doing is pretty darn simple. We say to a person, 'We're going to tell you what to do. You don't know how to live or you wouldn't be here. We're going to tell you what to do. Act as if you believe it. Act as if you believe it.'"
>
> —Paul Morantz, *From Miracle to Madness: The True Story of Charles Dederich and Synanon*, Cresta Publications, 2014, p116

†

The I Want To Live rap continued.

The sun will rise eventually.

TWENTY-FOUR

It shouldn't come as a surprise that we learned new tricks with our black chairs. Nat set it up:

"Our Thinking has caused us to be here. We're going to give a voice to our negative Thoughts. Now we're learning about the Struggle. There's a choice to be made in life. Part of that choice is knowing whether to fight or flee. I know nobody here is fleeing. Nobody here. Not you kids. It will be hard work, and I know you can do it. Tonight you're starting the fight. Who's with me? OK, everybody get two chairs."

As Nat spoke, Darlayne attached two new signs to the wall.

Life is a feast, yet people are starving.

Today is the first day of the rest of your life.

It felt so special to be instated into new ways of using my brain, my body, and the black chairs, that it reminded me of the first time I made a bow-drill fire out in the Owyhee Desert. And unlike with the other propheets so far, Nat openly shared with the other staff and upper-school supports the technical names for the new exercises.

We spent a few hours incorporating dyads. This experience would come to be a backbone method for each of us during our Truth counseling sessions in our last six months in Idaho.

We were directed to set the chairs in pairs around the room, so each chair faced an identical empty one. We sat down opposite vacant seats. After Nat's instructions, the staff began pacing around and got very close, just like George did in the Brothers, to monitor our level of decompensation and honest introspection. The three staff took turns appearing by us in each chair-pair, coaching us on how to split our consciousnesses. By yelling into the empty seats in front of us, we were learning to identify something.

Objective: To put a face or identity to our negative Thoughts, to put a voice to them, and then to lose that voice. Here, I was to indict my own Thinking.

"Who tells you that?"

"I DO! I tell myself all of this!"

"My Thinking tells me it will always win."

"My Thinking tells me it is always bigger than me."

"It will never be good enough."

"Good enough for who?" Darlayne came up right next to me.

"For Mom and for Dad."

"What else does it say?

"My Thinking tells me I hate myself."

"I'll never be good enough. I'll never be smart."

"Who tells you that?" Kelly needed to know.

"My Thinking."

It began to show me a face other than Mom or Dad, teacher or staff, or faceless tormentors, molesters, or bullies from my past. As we wailed at the empty chairs, I could feel a separation begin to split my awareness into two, then four, then eight, and onward, folding into an incalculable number. I sensed the push to a starting line, not a finish line. In Walden's propheet room, I threw myself into the new program exercise with abandon.

Like in the Truth propheet almost a year ago, I just shouted out the basics at first, while I adjusted to whatever else was happening around me. But Walden disappeared, as it always would. I heard the dozen voices rising, and merged with the group – rocking, accusing, and lashing out at the vacant chairs. I surrendered, the painful, ragged, scratchy screams surrounding me.

Me and my brain, navigating thoughts from the raps and propheets, did give me a deeper understanding of my parents' lives. And their parents'. Of course I never thought of it that way at the time.

I remembered another thing that didn't seem the type of thing to mention when I did my disclosures for Mom and Dad in La Mancha, but it may have been a huge catalyst in sending me here.

Grammy, that's my Mom's mom, was a crusty old saint. And she said I never knew when to be quiet, and that she didn't much like young boys.

It was blue haired Mrs. Pnobstich – pronounced "knob-stick" – in the winter of seventh grade, who assigned us to write a two-page essay. I wrote a story about happenings with Grandma. The first one occurred in the dining room at Grandma's house in New Jersey when I was eight or nine. This was one of those memories I'd conjured up and explored in detail for the first time here in the Truth propheet.

For a little old toothless lady, she sure was strong. Grandma had no reason to take me by the hair on my head and spin me around before shoving me to the ground.

Later, over the holidays during fifth grade, she smacked me so hard that I saw stars. This happened right after Grandpa died. What she hadn't expected – and if I hadn't been learning from the fist-fights that broke out during recess and lunch at school I wouldn't have had the courage – no, instinct – was that I sprang back up and swatted her one, right across the cheek. Grandma stood there with her hand to her face; I remained with my chin jutting up and fists balled at the ends of my arms.

Then, I grew big, strong enough to corner Grandma in the kitchen at my parents' house, yank that wooden spoon out of her hand, and scare the shit out of her for a damn change! When Mom heard the clamor, and rushed in to break us up, I handled her by shoving her against the wall. When Dad came home that was it. He won the subsequent scuffle, and I went to RMA a few months later, even though I had promptly forgotten the impacting events.

This was the time that the tables turned. I felt justified letting Grandma taste her medicine. I wrote it all out for Ms. Pnobstich, who loved it. Mom hated it.

These moments didn't arise out of a vacuum. In fact, if you want to know the truth, Grandma had always started it. Now, from the grave, her secret power was stirring up the old fear and anger I felt, reliving those surreal moments, and ones like it, when I was that cursed child.

In these moments, memories that my brain had long ago abandoned returned as dreamlike mirages, appearing as I went back in time. Now I had the faculties to telegraph to myself all of my regrets, self-loathing, and fears.

✝

> [W]e explained to them the causes of their mental illnesses and helped them to properly identify the principal contradictions in their thinking; by this means, we fully mobilized their inner subjective dynamism and enabled them to dig out the real roots of their illnesses by eradicating "private" thoughts and implanting the concept "public" in its place, thereby reinforcing their sense of self-confidence in waging battle with their illnesses.
>
> -- Excerpted from China's *Analysis of a Survey of 250 Cases of Mental Illness* in the Guangzhou medical journal, August 1972 – a group of 'ultra-Maoist' [per Munro] civilian and military psychiatrists from Chenzhou District in Hunan Province (Mao's home province).
>
> —Robin Munro, *China's Psychiatric Inquisition: Dissent, Psychiatry and the Law in Post-1949 China*, Wildy, Simmonds and Hill Publishing, 2006, pp 123–125

✝

After what seemed like an hour, they brought us glass mugs full of hot water. We each got a lemon, and then added honey. It really did soothe my throat. I squeezed my lemon till there was nothing left but the rind. It felt good to slow down and savor the hot lemonade.

Nat took the floor.

"Ready to go a little further?

It wasn't over.

"What we've been losing our voice to is our Thinking. The lemonade will restore your voice, so you can go to the next round. The rest of this propheet, and the rest of the program, is about the recognition of these forces – of that Struggle going on inside of you. Part of knowing your enemy is knowing how it thinks. So now, we're going to give back

242

our voices to our Me. Our inner little kid. Let your Thinking control you now. Give your I a voice."

Nat started moving us across, into our empty seats, so we could pretend to be our Thinking responding.

Nobody'd believe me if I said that this was not *as strange* as it ought to have been. Every kid was screaming into an empty chair. Like a force of nature, the pitch and fervor of the room, and the energy that leapt out of our bodies, increased to a frenetic level. Aggression. Regret. Terror. The Struggle against everybody else in the world, because only here and at CEDU would we get the chance to break through. A fierce tornado spiraled into a sinkhole vortex of deep-seated needs and wants. Music, whenever I filled my lungs, would swell over my own cracking and weakening voice, surrounded by the familiar, but still horrific screams of the kids in my PG on either side of me doing their work.

"WHY DO YOU ALWAYS MAKE ME LISTEN TO YOU! YOU TELL ME I'M WEAK, YOU TELL ME I DON'T MATTER! YOU TELL ME I WON'T EVER AMOUNT TO ANYTHING! FUCK YOU! IT WILL NEVER BE GOOD ENOUGH FOR DAD! IT WILL NEVER MAKE MOM COME BACK!"

The more we freaked out, the more praise we received from Darlayne, Nat, and Kelly, as they coached us past the surface crust, and into the inner magma of Feelings, composed of heavy, undiscovered elements. I was disrupting the very gravity that served to keep me, my personal planet, in a known orbit. It was the beginning of a cataclysmic event.

I'm not sure how I came to be asleep, collapsed in one of the rear corners. A spider bite was itching. Light was leaking into Walden.

Damn. Now I'm awake and there's the taste of three hours of sleep stank in my mouth.

From the floor I spun in a pleasant, fuzzy, drooling, relaxed state.

The carpet in Walden, even though it was one of the newest buildings on the campus, had disgusting stains. Gallons of snot, tears, and saliva had pooled up in blobs like gum on the sidewalk in New York. I found the residues strangely comforting. I had ownership in the puddles of emotion.

I had contributed to them.

243

Just before I let the slit of light from my eyelids shutter back to darkness, I saw Darlayne and Kelly talking quietly in the middle of the room. Each young woman was holding two large mats – too puffy for rolling or folding – thick ones that would have been suitable for gymnastics if they were any longer. As they whispered, the young women held these overstuffed navy-blue pillows in awkward embraces.

I heard bustling in the mudroom outside. I assumed it was kitchen staff bringing our lunch, but I was sorely mistaken. The door opened. Of course, when I saw the white sneaker-encased little foot, I knew it was Hedwig; Nat's wife and major power-staffer who always seemed to make an appearance in the propheets. Only this time she didn't come alone. Not only were Tess, Keith Rios, Walter Nemecek, and a handful of other staff with her, but the entire peer group above mine was filing into the room!

Some of my PG had to be awakened. Ivy and Wally looked confused, as though they had to remember where we were and identify the new faces. We were wordlessly split into two groups. Even with all the chairs removed, the place was packed. Within moments, a new level of expertise in fighting our Thinking would be granted to us. Very soon we would come to understand why so many people had to be crowded into the propheet room.

I watched the first round of group struggles made real. The room was divided to give each group the maximum space available, like the corresponding circles inside of a yin-yang symbol. Hedwig and Nat got down on the floor with their knees on the thick pads I'd spied earlier. Nat beckoned to Micah to join him on his mat.

Nat and Micah reminded me of the sculpture I'd seen in the Louvre of man fighting a bear. During my orientation with Andrew Oswald, on my first day in Idaho, my mind had snapped back to that sculpture in Paris. Nat began whispering words in Micah's ear, but I couldn't make them out. We did as the older PG kids did, and clutched at Micah in expectation. Nat continued speaking inaudibly but occasionally grunted as he gave Micah direction. On the other side of the room, Hedwig and more kids were doing the same with Ivy.

This was the most surprising moment thus far in Idaho, for me. Although I strongly wanted to be a part of it, the transition into this part of the I Want To Live was among the most confusing of the whole CEDU program.

New music began to rise. Neil Diamond's *I Am... I Said* crescendoed while the other side got Ivy lowered onto her knees. Assisting Hedwig and Nat, other staff were counseling us from the middle of the room, and a bunch of other people were showing us what to do.

Ernesto, Horatio, Yu-Yu, and I were with Micah's outcropping of bodies when the rumbling began. Our arms instinctively restrained Micah like the rest of the arms upon him were doing. We held him down roughly. All twelve of us gripped a body part, and Nat spoke into Micah's ear. Micah began to move. His movements reminded me of a mole I saw caught on a sticky pad back at summer camp in West Virginia the year before. The tiny mammal would never live anyway, and was eking its last breaths when I discovered it. It was my job to dispose of it before the little campers came into our archery storage room.

We were not to let Micah stand, and held on to him like wolves who'd downed a stag. Micah was the biggest and oldest in my PG. There was logic in his going first.

Several hands covered his elbows like vise grips, while I helped to bear down on his calf and press his left shin into Walden's rug. Nearly every other thought in the world disappeared except for being right there right now for Micah, for my peer group, the staff, and myself. Within the quick moments that began this bizarre athletic, three-part, morning exercise, we did as expected. Just the way that fish caught and crowded in nets could be predicted to behave.

Micah's face, and Ivy's struggle nearby, showed us how hard to fight. We would never let them stand up. In moments, our piles of bodies increased in temperature and activity. The crowded room's level of focus was pinpointed on the two locations where the Thought-combat took place.

I would watch all of my PG members' growth through such intense physicalization and exorcism that it reminded me of the escalating frenzy of a tribe of gibbons,

Hedwig was whispering to Ivy, head to head the way football players do. Like Nat with Micah, Hedwig held Ivy's wrists in a tight squeeze against the floor mat. Hedwig's gaze moved back across the room to her husband, on his knees in front of Micah. Together our groups restrained Ivy and Micah in the wrestling hold. We pressed down on Micah's legs, back, and neck. I looked over to see Darlayne, Walter Nemecek, George, and Hedwig, along with at least a dozen and

245

a half other hands doing the same with Ivy, crowded around her and pressing on her back to keep her down.

Seeming to realize the trap, with a sway, Micah tried to lift his arms and couldn't. Over the next few seconds, the muscle and fight that Micah used to rise into a standing position from all fours grew by a magnitude of forty.

As the furor abated and Micah had to pause for air, I looked over to see Ivy's pile.

The mats that Hedwig and Nat had been kneeling on, the big thick blue ones I'd hoped we'd be using to sleep, like we'd done at times with the shared pillows in the house, were slid out from under the alpha pairing and placed in front of the subjects. I thought I understood why we referred to a person as a "passenger" in an exercise like this, like Ivy Larrabee and Micah Mortemer, or like Bianca Taylor and Wally Gold who were the next to go, or like me when it was my turn to experience what CEDU called a bioenergetic exercise.

"OK. Rest."

"Did you FEEL THAT WEIGHT? THAT'S THE STRUGGLE, BUDDY! Shhh. OK. Breathe a moment. You can stop pushing down on him now, guys. Thank you. Just be here for him for this."

We released our muscles, but some of us were still holding on to Micah, generating and feeding off the heat, the electricity he was generating; the room contained the power of a hydro-dam. Unleashed energy filled a brief pause from our group while Nat's voice grew in intensity and volume over the music, blasting his thoughts into Micah's head. The entire room was in a jarred state of consternation. A fusion reaction began as Nat's voice faded into the noise-data storage area in my brain.

"Just feel this fight in you, your struggle to LIVE! BUT FIRST YOU HAVE TO FIGHT! YOU WILL HAVE TO FIGHT TO GET OUT OF THE STRUGGLE! YES."

"NO, Micah, like this! YES! YEAH! YEAH, KIDDO. FIGHT IT WITH ALL YOU GOT NOW!" Nat shrieked.

The trombone sound heralded the low jazzy intro to *What the World Needs Now*.

With all the grunting and shrieking, now came a new force – a smashing. I could feel the air cool my cheeks in the microsecond it took for Micah to understand what next to do. In a repeated movement, Nat raised Micah's arms up and my eyes went with them. Nat formed Micah's two hands into a hammer of one fist grasping the other, and slammed it into the mat.

Micah recognized what to do as a newborn being thrust at a nipple, and began to pump his torso up and down, bringing violence to the mat. If his hands came apart at all, Nat would clamp them tightly back together again.

To keep the rest of us from receiving black eyes.

Wham! Pause.

Wham!

Micah let out a primal cry, the sound that would rip out from behind a war mask, or during hari-kari. Or perhaps it was the groan of a megalithic animal dying. Wham wham wham, and across the room on Ivy's side, high-pitched shrieking continued with wham wham. . . .

This slammering took as long as the previous part when we struggled to get afoot. The more groups that went by the more I realized how formulaic the process was. And how much I needed to do and feel as I was doing and feeling with and for Micah, and Ivy, clear across the room. It didn't matter. Same as last night, we all needed, and knew we needed, to trust the process, and yell at the empty chairs. We didn't question it, and our bodies now responded in kind.

Osmosis. A quick pause as *Love* by John Lennon came on. Its sentimental slow piano length is divided by fading in and out. This third step in the passenger's struggle, I gleaned later, was called "containment." Micah was soaked with sweat from exertion. He quivered as we flipped him over onto his back but kept him from stirring otherwise. To be sure we were doing things right, I looked to the group with Ivy. They seemed to be just a moment or two behind us in the order of things.

We didn't have to be told to do everything in words. A live wire, telepathy, or some version of an ESP signal communicated through us. We knew what that person was fighting against, we'd heard them lead up to this. The world created by Sol Turnwell had done as perhaps Tesla or Edison had; propheets had lent us a special power, an intense kinetic bond among us in Walden these hours. Everything was movement, where violence and grace meet. Harness it, or allow yourself to be harnessed by lightning. Like act of coitus or bronze-age battle, there were almost no words needed. Ivy and Micah did as we would do; we would do as Ivy and Micah did.

There was a bizarre stillness to the third step in this exercise. Micah's body responded as the rest of ours would – quaking from simultaneous exhaustion and emotional release. The hands that had restrained Micah began feather-light touches. We rubbed and tickled him while tears flooded his ears and wet his hair. The collected tears and sweat dribbled onto the mat, and Nat wiped it down with his towel.

We were there for the passenger. We overfilled what they might be feeling with all the love that the song, and the staff, and the knowledge of having love, could give.

My turn.

I was in one of the last pairs of kids to do the fight.

I fought with all my might to get onto my feet, to show off my strength as all of us had done; the boys grunting and straining like a real wrestling match, the girls light, shrieking, often collapsing into tears before the pad even came out from Nat or Hedwig's knees for part two. It was exhausting, and after just a few furious moments I already had used half of my strength, but the weight held me down. It was like being restrained by rubber bands at every joint and socket in my body. The harder I fought to bring a foot under me, the stronger the grips squeezed my shins. If I managed to arch my back and bring the other hip forward, that side of me got pushed down from my shoulders so hard that I crumbled. Arms and legs were fully immobilized.

My socks rubbed off almost right away. The matted gray carpet ripped at my kneecaps, then one elbow. Then the other one got its skin scorched off too. Just like I had helped them do with Micah and the others, when my pile sensed me gathering a burst of power that could bring me to my feet, they pulled my feet, hands, and legs until I collapsed with a crash back to the floor. My lip fattened, and the taste of blood in my mouth infuriated me further. I growled as most of the boys had done and redoubled my efforts to escape the constriction.

From the floor, Lennon's music stained the inside of the room and my skull in odd contradiction within the beats.

Zack's brain started to forget its timeline. Where was it? Is it I's brain in Me's body?

I am Me in Idaho.

My body was in Walden – Hmmm. Cognitive checked out OK, but pieces of my self, the esoteric me, had lost their place in time. I was younger, and I was older. I was without the perspective of being a body, even though I'd seen my PG do the same act – my mind flashed to Roman gladiators in their final glorious moments.

What is a choice?

My memory didn't seem to be served by my brain as it had always been. This must be the super sped-up movie of my life, and past lives, as if these were the ultimate moments experienced by a final reincarnation. I didn't feel the neutron core of energy, blue with heat, chain reacting within me, or causing my body to perspire profound adrenaline sweat. Body remembering. A body. My self. Struggling for freedom of mind, for my future and past self, to save Me.

†

Make Me better. Better than ever. Fight. For love. For the program, for Mom and Dad. For Nat who was yelling in my ear, and for the shaky and the sturdy hands of my PG upon me. For my big sisters and brothers, for Kelly, for Darlayne, Prescott, Nat, and George.

Fight for belief. Fight. Just Do It. You are what you DO, NOT what you SAY YOU DO.

I do for me.

I am fighting for love, to have love, be love, know love, touch love. I am creating a future program for myself – the more I fight, the more I believe and accept that there is a demon within me, a dragon to be slain, a life to vanquish. The more I can prove my ability to conquer my Thinking.

Nat jammed the thick pad against my knees, and I realized my eyes had been closed during the whole struggle to stand. That first phase was over faster than I could process what it meant.

†

I feel rubbery as Nat takes Zack's hands and folds them into two fists. The way my hands feel inside of themselves remind me of the little baby hands of my sister wrapping around my finger. I'm powerful. Immense. The size of a magnolia tree – no, bigger – the size of a storm cloud made into a

249

*beast. Thunder within, lightening becoming! POOOGGGGBBBHHHH.
I repeat the primal feeling, hearing this time the thunder as my arms come
down like a club and make contact with the mat. My eyes snap open; Nat's
face is inches away, and the exertion of the morning lives in his face; I
imagine him seeing me as the dinosaur; my eyes are the prehistoric albino-red
of a rattlesnake, or a Tyrannosaurus rex.*

*Smash them down savagely, like an alpha-male ape might bash a com-
petitor's offspring against a fallen log before ripping the meat with his teeth.
The imaginings flip and freeze in place, locking into my memory for eternity. Emotionally, I reattach briefly to where I am, but the magic does not
disappear. The web is spun; the trap is sprung. Everyone is kneeling around
me, except the staff who are standing and making sure my arms don't flail
out to the sides. Some are yelling, pleading with me. "Keep fighting!" The
room cries out for me and the passenger on the other side. Familiar faces
cling to previous passengers on the floor. Arms and hands touch, sobbing
eyes see, watching me in that moment.*

*The first fight for my life, Me understands with the freedom of a freshly
hatched spider. The endless exploration. I'm an octopus in the depths, or
the butterfly freeing itself from an early summer cocoon. A thick jelly wad
of mucus frees itself from deep behind my clamped eyes. The clear snot slug
swings from my lip and hangs under my face while I scream, growl, and
roar into the endless, timeless, infinite space of Walden.*

*The more I pound, the more I believe the process. "MOMMY
DON'T..." and "DADDY DON'T..." Nat grunts in my ears "WHAT'S
ME FEELING? GIVE IT A VOICE!" along with, "I can NEVER..." and
I fill in the blank with sounds and thoughts that sometimes make compre-
hensible phrases, or pidgin English.*

*I thrash at the exercise pad, putting my dad's face on the spot that I
pound. Dad's face isn't just the face of my father. It's the memory of defeat.
It's the sound of failure. The knowledge of spiritual death. The embrace of a
ghost.*

This is my nightmare! This is my Thinking. It is my struggle to fight it.

*I know it is because I don't want to look. I want to quit, I don't want to
feel what is happening as I arch up, slam my eyes shut, and feel the primal
energy smash my hands against the pad. Feelings that predate description
bubble volcanic magma from within me. Colors taint the image shifts
between the face of my father and that of a former teacher, or my shrink,
or Will Bender from Survival, or Herb in his truck when I split. Pictures
of self-hatred for being horny – it's an image of my Thinking – shame and*

guilt. Smash it. A shifting composite of images: every thought, feeling, and individual concept that represent HURT or ANGER flashes by, as the typhoon-strength smashing continues to punish the dark blue mat.

Mother. MOTHER! I resist Nat's voice to carry out the imaginary deed, but I trust the process, and know I've got to look. The mat switches the images of my father for those of my mother. Faster, more. Cinematic images.

☦

A wolf, a cartoon bear, then images of baby birds being fed regurgitated food by their mothers morph into a trip with my mother to the Latin tutor, when I'd grabbed the steering wheel from her. I'd forgotten that. I pound at the image of my mother and me, fighting in the car on the way to the doctor. I pound at the Latin teacher in school, when he launched a coffee mug at me that exploded against the wall. He's convinced that bad kids weren't baptized. A moment later, on the mat, it's the seal-emulating principal who kicked me out of the Hill School. Then the image of the lumbering square-headed man in the park who'd too roughly grabbed my pecker through my jeans. Then my friend's step-father. Hairy-faced, whipping us both with a belt. I don't know why he's so angry.

My first fist-fight at school. Then Grandma's face appears before slipping almost immediately into an image of another teacher, a remnant of data from preschool. Memories, like the corners of my mind, whip me between past, distant past, and BEING HERE NOW.

Mom wants me to stop playing outside because it's raining. She's very insistent, so much that she picks me up. I pull hair and kick. She's gone again with another wham of the mat. Light that leaked into my head when I was three captures her. Tall and sunny, like a tree in June, each leaf a different face of what we were. I came from you.

Some branches of my tree of thought are reserved for an archetypal mother. The designation of the word, the poetic meaning. Like the first time I learned to write my name; I couldn't stop the tsunami of oncoming thoughts. Domestic animals suckling. The joy in feeling wisps of brittle hair the first time I touched a farm pig. Milk. Dairy. Food. Feeding myself, feeling cold in my mouth. Spilling cold and hot on my face. Snow, then summer. My nose fills up with salt water. Virginia Beach. Stung by jelly-fish. The whole body, naked and stinging in the water. Naked shame. A quick-fire scan of images of my grandmothers and grandfathers. Sometimes, my

251

mother appears as her little girl, a picture of what she used to look like, and sometimes as the terrifying manifestation of herself as the angry woman with a hairbrush. Threatening. Sinister.

This brings me back to thinking, remembering where I am, and back to conscientiously fighting my Thinking.

The image of the mat was still in front of my face, like a photographic negative, or the way a light bulb is imprinted in the mind when the circuit is cut.

†

My memories serve up a buffet of images for my mind's eye. Like a movie I don't want to watch, all the images speed up, like the theory of erosion. Sand once was the mountain. The flashes of images each last through eternity, yet are gone in far less than the manufactured second in a human-constructed minute. In fact, the only way of knowing that time is continuing is because of the music. Time exists enough only for me to fit words like MOTHER or FATHER, FIGHT or FEAR with them.

An upstairs linen closet in my childhood house is next. Pulling the door shut behind me. Black, dark, night in day. Hiding. Happy. The softest was sliding between the soft, cold-starting-off sheets, towels, and blankets that were stacked in there. To them it's just a storage space, but imagination lives in there. With the smell of expired medicine that hangs inside, I shut myself within it. My earliest sneaky spot. Hiding. She doesn't find me, because she doesn't look.

Flash to a different hiding spot I had a few years later in Mommy's mommy's house. The wardrobe in the hallway. The girl from the movie The Exorcist *is in there though. I'd met her one night after my dad put me to sleep and I sneaked downstairs to see the movie. Grandma and Grandpa slept in different beds there. Each bed had the agonized face of a crucified Christ above it. Nothing else on the walls. They had me sleeping on the little couch-like chaise where people's clothes wait to get put on in the morning. The cold steps on my feet as I sneak back to their room after viewing the sick girl writhing on her quaking bed and barfing bile. I didn't think I'd ever sleep again after that. Dutifully, I flattened Satan on the mat too.*

No more What the World Needs Now. *Music change. Eerie John's voice with strumming. "Love is touch. Touch is love."*

Nat wants me on my back.

"Just lay back. Zack, go limp. Limp! We've got you. Don't move. That's it. Totally freeze now. Feel the love. No, no moving! That's it. . . Shaking is OK. That's why we call it freezing. . . . Shhhh. Listen to the music. Allow yourself to feel the touch. It's OK to let this in."

Heart is still racing, every pore in my body aflame, every muscle as tense as a bear-brawl.

Kelly grabs at my nose with a stack of tissues as the moisture in my shirt, and in my itchy hair, begins to cool me down. Wrenching sobs, whole-body throttle-shaking wails and sobs. Feels like longing. Sad, sad life.

I allow the restraining, supporting, watching, waiting, knowing, loving arms, to recline me. Touches light but sting like barbed wire. The gentle feather touches from my peer group are tickling Me's overstimulated brains. Containment. Though I flinch and buckle, I resist the urge to wipe my face. Time matures like at the end of an earthquake. I have to breathe out of my mouth, and this relaxes me. My ears prickle from tears, and my T-shirt is matted with sweat. My body is mine again. The song ends. My eyes seem to work for the first time since I first heard trombone before Micah's struggle. The next passenger must take a trip, and I want to welcome them to what I feel in this moment. This is a magical room, in a magical place, with magical tools.

The last of my peers struggle, fight, and are contained within themselves as I was. My new eyes can see a cloud in the room. I can see many particles in the air that were invisible to me before, and I think of the haze as an aura, and not just the mist of humidity my intellect insists on seeing.

†

Here was another surprise. After we had all gone through the struggle – smashing – freezing sequence, it was the staff's turn.

Watching adults do the bioenergetic exercises and containment gave us new insights into what we would become, in life and in the program. Being given the privilege of watching Darlayne and Kelly, (never Nat or Hedwig) being coached by Hedwig and Nat, I felt included in something sacred. Darlayne could trust me enough to share her nightmare, her worst moments, her abortions, her mistreatment. I watched her fight the demons that were coaxed out of her by Hedwig in a Summit-gibberish that used concepts in the program I felt thirsty to understand. Darlayne spasmed between her shrieking and

253

slamming, and afterwards quaking and intoning in long sobbing wails. "Meeeeeee, Oh Meeeeeeeeee neeeeeeeeeeeeds."

With my new eyes I see, with my new touch I feel, and with new soul I know.

I saw the staff go through the three stages, just as kids and junior staff had before. My PG, the PG above mine, plus the other staff held Darlayne and Kelly down. The group heart rested our hands on them when their Thinking fought the mat, and their doubts. The group heart watched them be contained 'til they allowed our love in. John Lennon understood. *Love is real.*

Afternoon lunch in this propheet consisted of gratuitous amounts of fresh fruit, cheeses, rolled ham, and turkey slices. Four big plastic platters were emptied while we silently fed one another.

Life is a feast.

In the last hour before filing up to the main house for share-time and last light, we digested in a relaxing smoosh siesta. Loving hands touched sleeping faces, and found themselves petting hair.

When Darlayne held me, amid quaking sobs, it felt like the embrace of the mother I'd needed since I was six. I was fulfilled. We shared the bond of our secret ritual.

My essence is love. The program shows Me to me.

TWENTY-FIVE

I chose to live with Love and Life because I know what it is really like now. I can have it. In there the love was only undeniable by my Thinking which I promptly told to fuck off. Now I smoosh with people like [Nat and Hedwig, Darlayne, and the PG above us. And with my peers.] I allow myself to think I am loved I will do anything in my power to stay in touch with that.

—Author journal after I Want To Live propheet

[R]esearch has found that 'anger management' techniques that are supposed to 'unleash' anger through beating inanimate objects actually escalate fury, not decrease it (note 38). Such therapies back-fire, making angry people angrier.

—Maia Szalavitz, *Help at Any Cost: How the Troubled Teen Industry Cons Parents and Hurts Kids*, Riverhead Books, 2006, p 171

As your child moves into [Warrior] and continues through Summit, their advanced classes include theme study, such as the Renaissance & Golden Age of Greece (history and English credits), math, computer literacy, supervised study skills, and science. Their curriculum is designed to assist each child individually so they may excel in a particular subject as quickly as they are able.

—RMA New Parent Handbook

[T]here's no evidence to support the notion that all hatred felt by teens for their parents is self-hate.

—Maia Szalavitz, *Help at Any Cost: How the Troubled Teen Industry Cons Parents and Hurts Kids*, Riverhead Books, 2006, p. 171

†

How I plan to use my I want to live

I plan to use my I want to live in many ways. One way is to accept the love I must do this when it is offered. I know it will be pretty scary to do that but I need to.

My Thinking I'm sure will try to fuck me up in one way or another so I am just going to have push that to the side and fight it just by not acting off of it.

—Author journal after I Want To Live propheet, before first home visit

†

We'd made it through the I Want To Live, so we'd submitted our applications, provided all requested revisions and rewrites, and finally were moved up from Brave and into Warrior family. From Prescott to George. From wood-splitting and deforestation to gardening and animal husbandry; from the routine of chores to increased academics. Now that we'd completed our Quest Expedition, academics were taking the place of some of the afternoon Experientials, too.

I had forgotten that there was anything outside of dorm life, daily chores, family rooms, raps, and the rest. Now, my PG would be going to classes on some mornings, and eventually we'd have some all-day classes at Skinner.

Won't Mom and Dad be thrilled.

"Academics" was not only the term for our new classes in Skinner, but also pertained to any field of study outside the CEDU emotional program. As the staff always reminded us, our parents reinforced this hierarchy of our concerns: the main conversation was between our little kids and our Thinking. Our personal issues came first, and academics placed a distant second in Idaho. I agreed.

I was happy that RMA didn't make me take Ritalin at all, and encouraged me to learn without the need for it. The administrators at RMA knew I'd been told back home that I needed the drugs for school. But in the eyes of RMA's management, that was more a commentary on society – and Mom and Dad – than on my learning disability, brain function, or the sensory overloads. Here, like aspirin, Band-Aids, or any other medication at RMA, classes were, so far, for occasional use, and only at the discretion of the family head.

I had become senior enough in the program that nobody suspected me of anything for being awake at 2 AM, or for sitting on the washing machine in the bathroom.

Sometimes I could think of my mind like a clothes-washing machine – self-contained and electric, whirling and agitating through space and time.

Well I woke up at 5:30 this morning and had a dorm clean up and that was all fine and dandy. Why am I so pissed off? I had a great rap today. Peer group rap it was hairy but I was the only one who didn't get talked at. that is not going to happen for 100 years. I need to have sex so bad I might kill my dorm head in a minute. I need to have a peaceful meditation period to slow up and give and receive power. Let me tell you about my biggest long term goal. I want to have a bedroll barely any food and hike across country and with pack smoking grass all the way. Full of meditation in the sunlight at 5:45 in the morning and meditation by moonlight.

—Author journal entry

The first wave of classes was not challenging. I liked it that way. We had classes in English, American History, Geology, and more of what Ernesto and I called Moron-son Math. At first, I thought Mortensen

Math was a joke since we used little colorful plastic blocks as teaching aids. It wasn't a joke. We stacked little rows or flats of plastic blocks so the units they represented could be counted. The little yellow workbooks that accompanied the day's lessons were filled in, without an iota of understanding how what we'd done corresponded with the study of Algebra.

Mortensen Math wasn't like any math I'd ever done, and the classes were communal. When we all agreed that the answer was right, we filled in the booklets. At the end of the afternoon, Walter would collect them, and that was that. We never had tests, and I never had any idea what I was doing, even at the level – that I proudly wrote to Mom about – of the CALCULUS I was learning. I thought I was learning calculus, because that is what I could now tell Mom and Dad. The cover of the answer book we filled in displayed this word, so we could show it around to Papoose kids. We were learning calculus. You'd better listen, because we know so much about stuff.

Classes were informal, and we always did our homework during class, until my final several months at RMA. So I was shocked, on my home visit, to learn that my parents had been receiving report cards from Idaho. We got school credit for raps, it turned out.

In raps, whenever I addressed how I felt about being in a classroom again, I left the rap with the distinct impression that classrooms were only necessary to our way of life because they were important to parents – and to the society outside. Staff often corroborated the benefits of making a life away from our societal hubs, to live life as deliberately as they did. When we did have class, it was designed to make us hate school more, I thought.

Our long-lasting, large Warrior family was comprised of a few PGs. I suspected that this family held more peer groups because the combination of our social responsibilities and perpetual chores schedule at the farm kept us in a state of frenzy. It was stressful. What with the farm animals, being dorm support to Ari's dorm head, classes, experientials, chores, and raps, it seemed like there was never enough time – all the time.

Over the months since my parents visited, I began to look forward to the monotony of raps, just to relieve the tensions storing up from the transition to more classroom time. I feared that negative thoughts were to blame for everything.

✝

Dear Zack:

I have two goals for our upcoming visit with you. First, I want you to have a really relaxed and loving time talking with [your brother and sister]; I think you should plan to spend time alone with each of them. Second, I want to have the opportunity to have a "heart-to-heart" talk with you, one where Mom and I mainly listen, to find out what you are REALLY feeling and thinking about your life. I'm serious about this. I'm not so interested in "what you did yesterday" or who's on "bans" from whom. Instead, I want to know what your thoughts are about why your life was in such a mess last year, and what has changed. [...]

Just to give you an idea about what I have in mind, think about what [Mr. Jade] told you, and what you told him [during Survival]. When he spoke with us, he said that two false beliefs lay at the bottom of your problems: first, you believed that you were incompetent (or "dumb", unable to succeed etc.); second, that you believed that you didn't have to do what everyone else had to do. To this, I would add a third false belief that I think you had and that affected you very deeply – I think that you felt that your parents didn't love you.

These are the kinds of things I want to hear you talk about. I want to understand how you really felt then, why you think you came to feel and think as you did, and how you feel now.

One other thing. Once we have started talking about "the heart of the matter", I expect for you to keep us informed about what you're really feeling and thinking, deep down. I want our phone calls to be meaningful and without distraction. I also want you to write us regularly. This is very important. I'll explain why when we see you.

Love,
Dad

—Letter from author's father, 4 June 1989 (before first home visit)

259

†

Well I'm in the middle of building myself a struggle. I feel like shit. I look like shit. I am in shit. There is no doubt in my mind I am miserable. I really have a whole lot of thinking I'm thinking of copping out and all my dirt and making it up so I will have attention. Today I got some mullein and made a hand drill fire. I am on work assignment tomorrow for smoking and for cutting up music. But the really bad thing is I held onto it for 2 months. I never get time to write. I have to go.

I love the friends I've gathered together on this thin raft, we've constructed pyramids in honor of our escaping. –Zack B

—Author journal entry (quoting Jim Morrison lyric)

†

The next phone call I had with my parents blew up in my face. We hadn't spoken in a month or two, and Prescott said I had to call them before my home visit. So I mentioned that the school gave me the privilege to smoke on home visits. I'd been looking forward to a cowboy-killer ever since RMA made us all quit in the spring. Standing in the Bridge, supervised by Jennifer Oyama, I felt justified in insisting. But Mom and Dad immediately went ballistic. They had both quit smoking when my baby sister was born. I yelled back at them, which made Jennifer suggest that I end the call.

That night it sank in, more than it ever had, that my parents were never going to let me leave until my two-and-a-half years were done. They weren't ready for me to come back and mess their lives up again. They could go on trips together, and make plans to travel with my baby sister before she was old enough to be in school, and they were loving the entire situation.

My physical presence has been, and is, the issue.

†

Dear Zack

Mommy and I are beginning to worry about your home visit. Until your last phone call, we pictured a warm and cozy time together like the times we have had with you at RMA. We were imagining a time without argument and without controversy, one which would help to erase all the bad memories that each of us has about the way it used to be. (You do remember how it used to be, don't you? We were in pitched warfare – you wouldn't accept our authority and you were always hostile and vulgar, and we were feeling hopeless and helpless as we watched you fall off the end of the earth.)

When you come home, all of us must do everything we can to prevent any trace of those conflicts from re-emerging. That is why we were so horrified about your phone call. By insisting that you would do something that you know we don't want you to do, you were re-creating the same tensions and power-struggles that existed before, and that we are trying so hard to erase. (Think of how it would be: Every time you went out of the house to smoke, we would be angry and frustrated, and this would be a constant source of irritation.) Even worse, the very fact that you chose to bring up this subject and to make an issue of it makes us worry that you will want to do other things that we don't want you to do. And then we would be back to those awful feelings and arguments.

We all had a taste of what it would be like on the phone, and Mommy and I don't ever want to experience those feelings again. You weren't even able to control your language, and you know how crazy your vulgarity makes us. The best sign that we could ever have that you are ready to come home would be for you to stop using vulgar language. In fact, that has to be one of the agreements for your visit home.

Zack, please try to make this visit successful. Please help us all erase those horrible memories. Please don't recreate them. Home has to be a different place, with different relationships – the ones that we have all been trying to establish with each other during the last year. The bottom line is that Mommy and I want to love you and be with you in our home, the "home and hearth" that we have nurtured and where we make the rules. When you come home, you must respect our wishes and. If necessary, our authority. Your visit cannot be successful any other way.

I'm sorry to have to preach to you like this, but I think we all know how important this visit is. I had to let you know how we are feeling. (And I thought it would be better for me to do the preaching than for Mommy to do it! I'm sure you will agree with that!)

Please write again soon.

Love,
Dad

—Letter from author's father, 28 July 1989 (before first home visit)

TWENTY-SIX

Dear Parent:

Congratulations! Your child has been progressing satisfactorily through Rocky Mountain Academy's program and is eligible for their first visit home. This is a very special time and we want to do our best to assist you in ensuring that the visit will be a productive and memorable event. Our years of experience in CEDU Education have shown that by having a clear understanding of the visit's goals and agreements we can best facilitate a positive experience for each of you.

Your child will review the following agreements with his/her counselor:

- Students are not to be left alone at any time.

- Students are not to drink alcohol or be in the presence of alcohol.

- Unless previously approved, there is no purchasing of clothes, records, gifts, etc.

- The same music agreements in effect at school remain in effect for the home visit (no rock music).

- Students should clean their room and dispose of all drugs, drug related items, stolen items, etc.

- Students will have a talk with their parents and honestly disclose past negative behavior and attitudes. This is not necessary if it has been done on a prior campus visit.

- Students are to participate in household chores and projects.

- Students are not to contact friends by phone or in person.

- Unless previously approved, no items are to be brought back to Rocky Mountain Academy from home (tapes, jewelry, money, clothes, etc.).
- Students may spend time with siblings if the relationship is healthy. Parents and Rocky Mountain Academy staff will discuss this prior to students home visit.
- Students will not drive while on their home visit.
- Students are to call Rocky Mountain Academy once [a day] during their visit.

...If you and your child have been planning particular things, please be certain these are discussed prior to the visit with their counselor. Your child will bring these "agreements" home with him and discuss them further with you.

—Letter from RMA to parents before first home visit

✝

I AGREE TO:

Be in agreement with all RMA agreements – dress, music, TV, etc.

Be with my family at all times – not to be left alone other than personal time in my room or home.

Bring back to RMA only those items represented to my Senior Counselor and approved. No food may be brought back from home.

Clean my room and dispose of all drugs, drug related items, stolen items, etc. – those things that no longer support my life and my values.

Have a discussion with my family and honestly disclose things from my past that have not already been covered on a previous visit.

Participate in all household chores and projects and keep my personal space tight and clean.

Contact only those people that have been approved – no friends may be seen or called on the first home visit.

Not drive anything motorized during my visit – car, boat, motorcycle, etc.

Contact a [Warrior] faculty at least once during my visit.

[List of three staff members and their phone numbers. I still remember the phone numbers!]

Be in bed by 11:30 and awake by 8:30.

Watch TV or listen to the stereo no more than 3 total combined hours per day.

—RMA document signed by Zack and [George] before first home visit

Now, I have seen many beautiful things but what I saw out of the airplane window about 5 minutes ago was amazing. Fantastic clouds enveloping giant mystic mountains all during one of the most incredible sunsets I've ever seen.

True nature is a giant tool. Look outside, digest it and think about it for a while and you get exactly what you need.

—Author journal, during flight home

At Dulles [International Airport] in DC

I finally feel safe after my eyes traced the first foothills of the Blue Ridge Mountains. It feels good to be back home even though I just checked into Dulles Int'l Airport I feel a strong sense of home. I am of course very excited about seeing my family. I know when I step off the airplane they will be a reward. The love I need is simply waiting for me.

—Author journal during flight home

At Dulles

So many people but

So little sparkle

So many legs

But no dancing

So many arms

But no hugging

Eyes but no sight

Mouths but no communication

So many hearts, but no love

A flower gives out sparkle

It dances in the wind

Touching you if you notice

It is heart, is its roots

Beauty and Grace A Flower

Is a flower without having to act.

—Author journal, at airport after flight home

1st Day

Well I am at home right now and obviously scared shitless of everything and I am seeing friends and I don't know what they are going to think of me so that is kind of scary. [...]

My brother, sister, mother, dad and [I are] going outside tomorrow morning.

—Author journal

✝

I am at home and am listening to the Beatles. So far it was hard to see grandma, and I saw [one of the three girls I'd had sex with before RMA] and that kicked up shit for me. I don't really know what the feeling was except it was kind of empty yet I had to hide.

—Author journal during first home visit

†

Peering into what I thought of program philosophy, and what I thought I understood about Thinking, I considered Darth Vader and Luke Skywalker from the movie *Star Wars*. The metaphor of The Force could be used for either a light or dark side. Star Wars' Jedi Knights and the Force fit perfectly. My Darth Vader Thinking chased me in nightmares, repeating my lug from the Brothers, and telling me to do bad things.

Darth Vader: "Your unawareness keeps you alone and unlovable."

Then there was the Obi-Wan, the Luke Skywalker – the altruistic superego that was my perfect grown-up little kid, but in my fifteen-year-old body. It was my superior CEDU value system, my internal Jedi that stood up against the Death Star of Thinking. The resistance fought for the Truth and the Brothers, for Rock Bottom. It fought for kinship with the power staff that ran my RMA families, my older brothers, my peers, the Papooses, the program, perhaps even my parents.

At home for the first time in a year, things couldn't have felt more different – or worse – than I anticipated. I thought it would be joyous, but I was hypersensitive to every possible critique. Around the dinner table, each question from Mom and Dad was an accusation, and a glance between them a conviction. The meaning I searched for in faces, word choices, and manners of body language had always been there. Now I had no doubts:

I was a wretch. A wretch and a weak-willed slave to my monstrous Thinking.

They wish I wasn't visiting. They don't want me at the table.

It was a feeding frenzy for the Darth-monster in my head.

267

My little kid, my super dooger, would have to fight every day to cling to this wonderful and shitty world.

It was a constant struggle. Fight and die. Fight or die. Fight and fight. And die and die.

How will I ever be able to silence the voices?

The messages are stronger than me.

Despite how much I had changed, the way I felt at home, around my parents now, was even worse than before RMA, and that had been bad enough. I wanted to go back home – er, back to Idaho.

✝

1st day just drove home and when I walked in I had feelings and lots of memories. Then walked in my room and had memories and opened a drawer and saw a bowl I hadn't used yet. That was scary. Then I just ate w/ family and went to sleep.

2nd day. Went to doctor – and he told me I had pretty much stopped growing and that I was a tad overweight and put me on many different kinds of medicine. Went home started to clean up my room did some writing. Took [educational consultant] out to lunch at Sloans talked about my future. Came back cleaned a little more went out to dinner at Chi-chi's. also saw dead poets society with dad and did a little shopping and saw [my ex-girlfriend] but didn't say anything to her. Saw [friend from local school] and told her about what I was doing and she said she had heard people had been seeing me. Also saw other people I recognized....

Had a long talk with Mom about dreams and goals I have. Went on a long drive. Took mother out to lunch. Went to music store looked at drums. Saw grandma. Went [putt-putt golfing] w Mom dad and Brother. Went home – listened to music and wrote went to sleep.

Went to store with dad did errands got rope went home made swing for my sister. Returned things I stole to [stores]. Went to UVa football game with

Father and brother. Never touched the binoculars.
Watched Stand and deliver with mother and father
and went to sleep. (I think I visited my grandmother
on this day.)

Woke up drove to skyline drive. Went to humpback
carried my sister up the mountain and watched the
hawks. I felt very good at that time up on there with
her. Carried her back down and did survival techniques for family and observers went bowling with
dad went to bed.

Went to see one of mother's friends. Came home
had breakfast took my sister on a walk to playground
and back, packed, went to airport and boarded.

—Author's journal entry describing first home visit

There existed a distinct sense, long before RMA, that anything I
cared about would be taken away. Forget about unconditional love
and approval. The program had convinced me that people worldwide
had been cheated out of those things. Forget the attention and com-
pliments of youth that I had lived for, and which had shaped the very
person I thought to become. It was the simpler things too that had
been lacking. Life itself, mine, could be snatched up at any unknown
time – to be dipped in the preciousness of life, but then to be ripped
away and hurled back into the primordial pot of creation. This hard
destiny gave my Thinking its first sustenance after gestating and mani-
festing inside of my little kid. That, or I was born with it.

I hated the person I was when I first got to RMA even more than
I hated the spineless person I was now. The only difference was that
now I knew it. I knew why I hated that previous person. He had been
unaware.

My nose was up against fear when I was at home.
I hope to move away from this choice by doing the
things I need to do to be in agreement. Especially at
home cleaning out all the non-supportive things in my
room. I'm sure my thinking will fuck me up in one way

or another so I'll have to push that to the side and fight it by not acting out.

—Author journal

†

I wanted to be happy at home, but since I wasn't allowed to leave the house much, by the end of the visit I wasn't happy.

I was not alone in my unawareness. I understood that everyone else hated themselves too, especially the ones who denied the simple truth of that beginning-point.

At RMA I was gaining access to some temporary moments of peace – at the end of a propheet, or after wrenching my guts out in a hairball rap. Now I was acquiring the means to combat that unawareness.

My unawareness keeps me alone and unlovable.

I must fight my Thinking.

I have my struggle. I have my introspection. I have work still to do at RMA.

†

[Traveling back to campus] Well...I am in the airport at Dulles Intl. to tell the truth I am kind of negative. I had such a great time and wish it was longer. Now the only thing I have to look forward to it seems is the flight back.

—Author journal

†

Chucky, ...in your letter you told me you wanted to send some tapes but I told you before, I'm not allowed but thanks anyway. ...I can't keep your pictures either because music [posters] in the background.

—Letter from author to childhood friend, [Chuck Driems]

TWENTY-SEVEN

> What did I learn on my home visit?
>
> I think one of the biggest things I learned is that all
> bullshit aside I have grown. Before my I want to live
> and other things I wouldn't have ever been able to
> have a civilized conversation with my parents. Also I
> learned that there are other people in the world who
> are supportive and caring. I say this because in the
> airplane I shared my feelings with this girl and she
> shared a lot with me. Cleaning up is part of moving
> on! I returned some of the things I stole and from that
> I know that I can gain trust from that.
>
> —Author writing assignment after first home visit

It was a relief to be back at RMA after the first Charlottesville
visit. In some ways, I could see that life in Warrior here was better
than in Virginia – at my parents' house, anyway. They didn't have the
awareness that people here did. They first respected my honesty but
were righteous in their defenses. And Dad wouldn't smoosh with me.
They didn't speak the same language, and hadn't been through any
propheets, so I spent a lot of time explaining my way around my feelings and criticizing their lack of awareness.

For now, life was divided between working the animal chores at
the farm – my reward for having only a handful of graduating classes
above mine – and classes in Skinner in place of Experientials. Raps
still played a significant part of everyday life and gave me a chance to
advance my self-knowledge to other kids, while I toyed with how deep
I would go in fighting my Thinking.

Being a good friend to everyone meant I was a front-line assault
weapon in raps now. I could always be counted on to assist the facilitator in breaking down the fortified defenses of others. And like the older
brothers and sisters here had shown me, my expression of the feeling
was more important than any accuracy. Our knowledge had become

our artillery. That's why new kids couldn't shell back yet – they didn't have any valuable insights to use for attrition.

I thought all the time about my second home visit when I could go to Virginia again after Christmas. And then after that milestone, we'd get new routines. On Tuesday and Thursday afternoons, we'd have Experientials to prepare for Wilderness Challenge, and, for almost a year of Fridays, we'd have Truth counseling sessions in lieu of raps. I'd been waiting for that a long time.

That summer, things were smooth, and I was rewarded with privileges: I became a dorm support, which came with some little restored freedoms. Now I could display photographs in my new, preferred, lower bunk space. No one wants to climb up and down a ladder around bathroom visits. Also, I was now a kid who could escort a kid without his "ups and downs" privilege, and by the same token of trust, I was expected to sit in with the younger kids and monitor their phone calls. George instructed me on when and how to end any problem calls, and how to report to the staff who was on floor duty on those nights.

Lastly, as my welcome to Warrior, George Daughtry and Keith Rios thought it would be funny if I received the great privilege of interacting with a real-live veterinarian when he came to the campus. Tess used to be in charge of the llamas, but after an announcement was made in front of the house, we learned that Keith and Tess had begun dating. Anyway, Keith and Tess together now had a couple of llamas in a pen at the farm. One llama needed an enema.

A llama gets a certain look when she's not been drugged except for a local anesthetic, and has a fifteen-year-old's arm up in there to his shoulder socket holding a length of hose. The vet was pumping special solution. Facing her, Keith Rios hugged her soothingly around the neck.

This is ridiculous.

Is it OK to laugh?

I looked to the vet for my cue.

I mean, when you're gazing in the business end of a llama, while being told to hold steady until you can have your arm back, but *slowly* when you do, awaiting an anticipated mound of shit to pour out, or a possible llama kick to the groin, it might just be a comical moment. The vet laughed with me.

After emitting a series of turds that shall best be left undescribed, the lanky creature was just fine. I took a glorious, special ten-minute shower, even though the arm-length rubber gloves and smock had done their job effectively.

†

All the things that scared me on my home visit:

my snake thinking that came in right when I was off campus

the act I had to put on in the airport

being on the airplane scared me

walking into my room

being in a room where I tried to kill myself in

being in a room I used to smoke dope in by myself

opening a drawer and seeing a bowl I had

seeing pictures of me when I was drunk

being in a room where I had gotten so stoned that I thought I was going to die

it was scary when I went to the doctor and he told me I stopped growing and put me on medicines

it was scary when I cleaned up my room

seeing things I had stolen

it was scary seeing my image stuff knowing I might find dope

talking about dreams with my Mom

taking [educational consultant who recommended RMA] out to lunch and talking about my dreams

it was scary seeing people with earrings through their nose and stuff like that.

It was very scary seeing the Dead Poets Society with my dad when the kid killed himself especially

It was scary to see [my ex-girlfriend] and not say anything to her.

273

I was scary to talk to [friend from school I bumped into on the street.]

It was scary to talk to [Chuck Driems].

It was scary to talk to and see people I used drugs with, or used or was used by

I was scary to see a lot of people and not know where I knew them from

It was scary to see grandma – My Nightmare in a lot of ways

It was scary to see and read poems I wrote before I came here poems I wrote when I was stoned

To see paintings and drawings of things before I came here when I was stoned

It was scary to see clothes I used to wear and/or get stoned in

—Author writing assignment required by staff after first home visit

†

Dear Zack,

Daddy and I loved the visit, loved having you home, loved seeing your handsome self. We were proud of how you handled the agreements so responsibly. Basically, we were all around happy and proud. [...]

I know you're concerned about starting full-time school. I wish there was something I could say to ease your mind. Okay, I'll say one thing – be methodical, try to stay organized. I think once you get those typing and word processing skills under your belt you'll be ready to tackle most things. Just be methodical! [...]

[The educational consultant who recommended RMA] called to say how much she enjoyed seeing you. She mentioned that you pulled out her chair in the restaurant and I can't tell you how that made me feel. "Virginia gentleman," I thought and I remembered Sheriff [Darren Snipes] telling me that when you went to stay with those two old ladies [for foster

274

care after splitting from RMA] (you weren't exactly
the model of pleasantness then) how you stood
when one of them came into the room. He noticed
it because I guess he didn't expect good manners. I
love it when I hear you're mannerly, because honey,
believe me, with your charm, brightness, good looks,
and manners, you really can do anything. Or, as I say
about some people: "you can take him anywhere!"
And manners, when you think about it, is just being
thoughtful of other people. My father, who didn't
have much of an education and didn't come from
the right side of the tracks, had the best manners
of anyone I ever knew. He always made people feel
welcome, and special. You have the same ability, a
naturalness with people that puts them at ease.

Speaking of that, I understand you met an admirer
on the plane back to school. I gather that she called
the school to say how much she enjoyed meeting you.
See, you even impressed a weary traveler. Zack, baby,
you can go anywhere.

I love you,

[Mom]

P.S. Please write. You're not perfect yet.

—Letter from author's mother, after first home
visit

On my home visit, we didn't even fight about whether I had to
come back.

Sometimes, like walking between farm chores and classes, I tried to
make sense of this prolonged in-between place I was living in. It didn't
feel like home at my parents' house, and I didn't want to go back there
to live, ever. The feelings were mutual. I was at RMA now, probably
for the whole thirty-month program, but this wasn't a place I'd want to
stay either.

It's my brain, my life, after all.

Back home, like at RMA, everything had to be earned. Both places
wanted to control me and turn me into someone else; they just did it

275

differently. I'd been trained since childhood in my parents' version of it. Now, Mom was happy that I was at RMA. I was a piece of shit, but I could be great; and I could be all the greater by absorbing the wisdom of the program.

It had become clear: The only way my life was going to improve now was if I worked the program at RMA. Even though that would impress and encourage my parents, I needed to do it. I kept telling myself, "Keep working with your program, and you'll become the person you're supposed to be." And staff and the upper-schoolers reinforced the message every day.

Hating my surroundings at the same time that I accommodated them wasn't anything new. Since middle school, I'd been running away from home when I couldn't stand it another minute. Then I'd have to return, and the pressure would build up again, and again, for my parents as well as for me. Sending me to RMA was one big pressure release valve, for my parents. For me, it was just trading one program for another.

I thought back to fifth grade, when they had put me on Ritalin, which intensified everything.

The Saab whirs to a stop at one of the three stop signs on the way to public school. I'm in fifth grade, and the captain of the safety patrol. Some days I can't seem to do anything right, other days I'm now powered like robotics, briefly perfect in school. I am taking medication now to help me concentrate, and not be a distraction to the kids in class. I have been to see a psychiatrist. I'm not supposed to tell anyone. I think because of something having to do with secrets and money. I am unaware of the concepts of RMA.

It's not a good day, I hate being yelled at, and am showing some contrition for the night before. I've been smoking Mom's cigarettes – I'd soon find the necessary $1.75 and start buying them myself from the machine in the Chinese restaurant near the college. But today I try to beg them to not make me go to school.

I ask Dad to pull over near the final stop sign. He checks his watch even though the radio indicator and the dashboard both have clocks talking.

"What's the matter."

"Well, I'm really sorry I ran away."

"We got you back. It's OK."

"I wish you weren't at work so much."

"I know it, Honey." This is what he calls all of us.

"You know how you told us that Mommy is going to have a baby? What about where it lives?"

"Well, that's why we're building the addition."

"Yeah."

"It's great! You and [your brother] can sleep in the addition, like big kids, while your mother and I will have the baby and feedings. It's important that we make this work for Mommy."

"But she's always so brash. I mean, mean to me."

"She has a lot going on, and she's mean to me too."

"She doesn't shriek at you. She hates me."

I feel myself welling up.

"What are you talking about? Don't be ridiculous. Your mother loves you."

But I've already started crying because I know he's covering for her. And with the baby, I'll be losing him too. Now everybody can keep blaming me for everything.

"Don't run away anymore, Honey. Your mother and I can't take it."

I don't promise anything, but I say, *"OK."*

The leakage of tears is still coming out, because I'm so worried about what is going to happen in my life. I'm not the only one becoming emotional in the car. Daddy reaches over and gives me the biggest hug ever. He reaches into his back left pocket where he always grabbed before sneezing, and takes a cloth handkerchief to my nose.

"I love you. Honey, your mother and I both love you. You NEVER have to doubt that...OK?"

"OK."

It wasn't long, though, before I knew I'd lost the pity of my only ally in the world. That didn't exactly make me want to spend more time at home.

†

The baby was asleep. I'd had had a Latin lesson or piano practice or a doctor's appointment that day. This meant I hadn't had my ninety minutes to go running around the neighborhood, up to my usual firecracker, bike ramp, porno-magazine hiding, ninja-star throwing, or sports behavior. Just a zombie sitting still since seven this morning. And I was at the kitchen table, feeling that feeling – that thinking-buzzing – that Ritalin gave me.

It felt like I was always sitting there, because I wasn't allowed to do homework in my room anymore. Dad and Mom needed to see me working.

But schoolwork was only really getting thirty percent of my mind. The rest of it was already drilling down into how disappointing I was, how I should run away, how I wished I was old enough to beat up my brother, or steal my sister away from the madness of our big charade, the big lie we told everyone.

Everyone thought we were so happy, until I got kicked out of three schools in a year, and refused to take Ritalin and antidepressants. This was all my fault, and that had been clear for a few years.

†

My Nightmare in detail:

My nightmare is who I am when I choose fear over love. My nightmare doesn't use what he knows, and is scared to be himself here.

My nightmare confuses the essence of what I am and makes me think nightmare thoughts. My nightmare is my thinking made visible. It is my past and future.

My nightmare exists. My nightmare won't let me accept love. My nightmare doesn't care whether I live or die...

I feel trapped because I think that is all my [dooger] deserves. And because my nightmare is numb it

makes me powerless to stop it. This traps me for settling for it and that I'm destined to die suddenly.

—from Author's RMA writing assignment

[At least 25] Ways I've sold out in the last 14 days:

I ran my thinking without crying and it took me out
of the work.

By believing that my dreams are impossible to
accomplish.

Because I didn't want to try to represent the school
with leadership in Washington D.C., and should want
to be a leader.

When I don't tell people and staff what I really feel
about them. I sell out all the time in not telling them
why and how I resent them. And sell out always in
not pulling people up for feet on furniture or shirts
untucked.

I sell out on older brother's that I think will make
it okay for themselves to do drugs again. Or when I
should pull up hypocrics but don't.

I sell out on my relationship with Mom and Dad
when I hurt them by not writing, or by not telling
them how much they hurt me.

I sell out because I feel empty even when I'm
smooshing with [Jennifer or Ivy]

—from Author's RMA writing assignment

The seasons whizzed by. The rhythms at the farm – and the next
propheet or graduation ceremony – reminded me of the passage of
time. The crops in the gardens were fertilized with pride. Daily, my PG
collected dung from all the different livestock pens and carted it up the
ramp to our towering compost bin, enclosed by framed wood. This pile
of shit was about fifteen feet high, and reminded me of the first time
my eyes saw the stuffed bays at the wood corral.

They save the shit?

279

It was novel in more ways than size. For example, I hadn't believed it until I did the trick myself: If you jam a big stick deep in the compost heap and leave it for a while, it will be on fire when you retrieve it. I found smoldering a fascinating process.

Animal birthing season gave us more shit to haul, and small animals to feel special about caring for. These months at the farm gave my PG family pride and heralded more changes. We witnessed the nights and days shuffling as calves, lambs, and kids grew to cows, sheep, and goats. Chickens – occasionally eaten by one another, in horrible, cannibalistic fashion – lived and died.

Another marker for me, now that I was in Warrior, was that I truly looked forward to haircuts. We were advanced enough in the program to be able to start to wear regular clothes from home, and get new workboots, and grow our hair out so we didn't look like prisoners any more. Haircuts had become a sign of my maturity, not a shameful token of my worthless, shocked Papoose self.

In the full fury of August heat that I remembered from my first year, I'd go for walks into the woods to talk deep thoughts with my closest younger brothers, the ones most likely to be on the outside in their Brothers, like I had been, if they lasted that long. I thought Bart had a good chance of making it through the program. I wasn't so sure about Winston, or Dirk Morgan. He was another kid from Winston and Delilah's PG, the one who hated his stepfather, Ross.

Dirk Morgan was about my size, and it's a good thing too, or he might have drowned. One hot August Sunday, at the lake where we could swim once the water warmed up, he dived too deep, hit his head, and then got caught up in some vegetation. The other reason why he could have met a soggy demise is that Dirk was the RMA version of a class clown. Nobody believed him when he pleaded that he wasn't joking.

So I dragged him out while the kids from his PG swam away, laughing. I stayed with Dirk on the bank near the water, while one of my little sisters, Delilah, ran back to the house to get help. Things got weird during the time it took for the ambulance to wind its way from Bonners Ferry to the back of the campus where the lake was.

Since I'd been the person to stay and witness every moment with Dirk after he crashed his head into the bottom of the lake, the ambulance driver suggested that I could come with Dirk in the back of the van to town, but Hedwig went instead.

I was pretty freaked out myself after hearing him answer the emergency responder's questions:

"Do you know your name."

"Dirk."

"What's your last name, Dirk?"

"Morgan?"

"How old are you?"

"Um. Sixteen."

That was the last question that he answered correctly.

"What month is it?

"November."

"And the date?"

"September 9."

"Is it Wednesday, or Thursday, or Saturday?"

"I'm cold."

The driver barked orders at the two young assistants who scrambled to bring a board to strap Dirk onto, a brace to hold his neck steady, and a gurney with wheels to carry him away. When they shoved him into the rescue van and then folded up the gurney wheels, they bumped Dirk around a little, and he grunted and swore at them. As the door closed I could hear him beginning a strange nonsensical jabber including a litany of curse words.

He came back a few weeks later with four bolts in his head which were meant to hold his neck rigid and straight. Nobody, including Dirk, ever mentioned the favor, and I never brought it up either.

Dirk's close call served as a reminder that there were some things that RMA wasn't equipped to deal with. His injuries weren't going to get fixed by working on his feelings. There'd never be enough raps and propheets to fix a broken neck.

†

I feel more fucked up that anyone because I can't
get into my feelings but half the time. [Darlayne] says

281

its because there's something holding me back. I must be dirty [Bianca] says. I'm tired of being negative. Its never going to be "good energy" in my life because I don't deserve feel calm and good. Put another log on the fire!

This is just a few years out of my life and its okay to fuck up. My thinking says I'll just make up for it later. I'm lazy and stupid in classes. My thinking says to split during my next home visit. That I don't want to go through the fucking summit anyway, when that is all the program. If I'm this far along and feel like this there's something wrong with me. Dish fucking dish crews forever....

Who am I? Where am I going? And HOW am I going to get there?

I'm angery that I'm so fucked up I don't know how to get out of the imaginary hole I'm in. I want to quit on this writing assignment right now.

I'm angery at [Darlayne] for giving me this [writing assignment] and not telling me. I'm angery at my peirs because they are cliqued up and I don't fit in anywhere with anyone. I'll always be on the outside.

I get angery when people blow me away in a rap and they don't even know me. I'm angery because I think I'm missing the boat. I have a secret hate for the program and there's something wrong with my ability to grow.

I'm sooooo angery that everytime something goes wrong we get blamed for it. Like [Micah] called his girlfriend and [Craig] hurt his knee and because of unawareness on campus we get blamed.

Mom used druges when she was expecting me and that's why I'm so fucked up. And that she writes my life and death and words. What the fuck is that? Angry that they sent me to a shrink and tell me that they wanted a girl or that I'm probably retarded. And that mom still wants me to take medicine. I'm angry at principals and teachers that would send me to office and ISS [In-School Suspension] and that I was always a special case and had to take a piece of

paper home every day to mom whether I was good
or bad or fair that day. No other kid had to do that.
Or when she washed my mouth out and locked me in
closet. And hit me. I hated that cow! FUCK. I'm angery
because my penmanship sucks. I'm angry that I got
kicked out of so many schools because school sucks
and that I have to dig holes all day now. I'm mad that
someone broke the answering machine so I didn't
find out grandma died until later. Angry still at raps
too the same bullshit. I don't think or feel I'm a very
feeling person like in raps when my feelings don't
come up and so I feel incredibly fucked.

—Author journal 4 August 1989

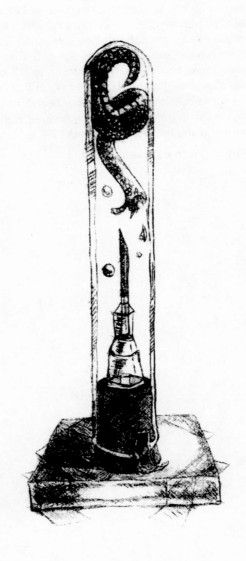

TWENTY-EIGHT

If my thoughts aren't always in compliance and supportive, how can I prevent the same inescapable conundrum as before I split from here?

No, I was a piece of shit before I got here, I'm a piece of shit now, and taking a good hard look at how I felt growing up makes me realize that that is why Mom and Dad ignored me and were always mad.

As long as he did no wrong, they loved my brother. They both adored my little sister, and now I was beyond their "control." Dad's tolerance had been waning, but I'd pushed too far in the last year. Maybe I really had wanted to ruin or stop my life.

Shit, this is bad.

It deepens of course. The more you stare at a reflection of yourself, the higher the risk you'll drown in the river Styx, like Narcissus.

Air, none. Pulling back not an option.

This reminded me of what I felt, what we all felt during the Truth propheet. It – the jumble of thoughts – turned back at me like a freight train I couldn't stop:

My parents had never wanted me. Of that I was sure. That's why I was always wandering our neighborhood, usually alone, before expanding my terrain like a lone wolf. At home, I always got yelled at, and couldn't seem to please them. Even my little sister showed signs of impending disappointment in me. I was at my core a failure; but if Mom kept pushing me, I'd probably put her down to the ground. Now that I was finally bigger, she couldn't do what always made me feel so small.

But I needed a tutor at math, while my brother was a math whiz. He didn't need Ritalin. I sabotaged what everyone said would help me, by pretending to take the pills. The thoughts about why I was me, how I was before Idaho, and the dynamic between my parents and me through the years, blinked like a far-off quasar fading in and out of radial clarity, old and past, but a beacon to the here and now. My big brother got to drive a car, and go out at night; I had to sneak out and hitchhike if I wanted to see someplace new.

If I had to put a date to where a removed, less-aware life took hold before Idaho, there'd be at least an entire year or two to examine. Maybe it began around the time that that freak grabbed my wang under the jungle gym at the park.

We'd explored pervy things that happened to us plenty in raps so far, and I had mostly concluded that blame was shared equally between our little kids choosing corruption, and the resultant opportunities for exploitation this made possible for breathy weirdos and drunk relatives.

One scenario was planted firmly and vividly in my memory, where the oversized flat-headed man had yanked me onto his lap with a hand between my legs. I was nine. The park was a long way from home, and I didn't have a bike. He'd gotten off a bus, a short one. I knew he was special which is why I originally let him play basketball with me. As if that hadn't been enough, the freak chased me. I banged on doors until a lady with a house that smelled like freshly snuffed candles and soapy crushed flowers opened her front door to me. Police were called. I was taken home. When I re-told the story at RMA, I left out one part. The part about not being believed. Being treated with suspicion by my parents when I told them what had happened.

Not being believed by them had been as frustrating and confusing to me as the incident itself. That year my wanderings had brought me further from home than they had liked, so they thought I'd manipulated the situation, or made it up to get into the old lady's house, for the sole purpose of phoning home.

For me, fifth grade was the year that started out great but soon went to shit. A big change occurred in life when my sister entered our family. The way each of us began to think and feel about every other person in the house began to alter. In RMA terms, that year might be where my Thinking got the sustenance it needed to begin taking over. My Thinking was enhanced by the focus on what was wrong with me, and that focus was magnified by Ritalin, its side effects, and additional home strife. The year ended with Mom's expectation that I would religiously take the Ritalin. But the older I got, the more I faked taking it because I didn't want to focus on my very real doubts.

What was wrong with me and my brain to need this medicine, to get this diagnosis of ADD, to go to the shrink? See? It wasn't just the schoolwork that the medication made me focus on. Dad wasn't anymore the refuge I needed him to be; when he got upset, or wasn't around, I made myself scarce.

But I had to take Ritalin and sit at the kitchen table every day at exactly 5 PM, no longer allowed to explore the furthest reaches of our little city, or the expansive UVa grounds, like I'd become accustomed to doing. I had new responsibilities now: being an older brother to the baby, loads more homework, and school with different rooms and teachers. Of course there were the piano lessons I failed at, the soccer practices I was late for, and the trouble I was always in.

My brother had been stowed for a few months at a special boarding school for math wizards and budding engineers. Dad went on lengthy trips, showing the benefits of democracy to other countries, marvelous foreign places where blue jeans and packs of Marlboros for hotel staff and taxi drivers were the preferred currency. Mother was busy scheduling everything for everybody, and feeding the leech. What did people do before microwaves, Gerber foods, and baby formula, anyway?

When she was not feeding the baby, Mom pecked at the softer-sounding keyboard of her word processor. The noises from her desk were quieter now, different from the crackle and impatient pounding of the iron keys stamping the ink blot and *DING, Szzzzzt, Snap snap snap*, that I had heard from her typewriter starting at infancy.

It was always quiet time for the baby after school. In fifth grade, I dreaded the five o'clock Ritalin dosage, and being imprisoned in homework at the kitchen table. The table smothered in piles of purple-on-white dittos and my rainbow of spiral notebooks and brightly colored Trapper Keepers.

By the end of that year, to make room for the baby, my brother's abandoned belongings and I would be holed up in the new part of the house specially designed to separate us from the home we knew. The new addition reminded me of the Ice Palace in *Superman III*. Mostly cold, mostly white, but with smells and signs of new construction like drywall dust and paint. This change in scenery and distance from parents led me to drastically change sleeping schedule. After they turned in and shut out their bedroom lights on the opposite side of the property, I could turn my light back on and do as I wanted. It was a strange situation. When I overheard Mom or other adults talking about the "addition," I always hid to listen. I had other devices for listening too. I'd learned this from Mom.

She only pretended to hang up the phone when I was on with friends. I retaliated by rigging the baby monitor so I could hear them after our fights. She'd call my friends' moms all the time for corroboration of my whereabouts, so alibis were solidified beforehand. Stealth was achieved in early sneak-outs.

Mom and Dad moved me to a private day-school for sixth and seventh grade. That school started out groovy, but I bombed out with Ds by the end of the seventh-grade year there. I could probably write a book or two on the differences between public school, private school, and the rest of the places where other kids were surrounding me.

By the time I started eighth grade, back in public school after getting kicked out of the Hill School, I completely stopped caring, and gave up on even trying to get good grades. I often stayed out 'til 3, 4, or 5 AM. I got drunk sometimes, and for this I had occasional friends. Some of the older kids I hung out with were even older than my brother, and looked totally different from us. Mom got terrified. I realized that, from a parent's point of view, you could check all the boxes in one of those checklists that Hattie probably went over with prospective enrollees – *Are You Losing Your Child? Know the Signs.*

I'd be at RMA in a matter of months. See, the public school couldn't cope with me any better than I could cope with them. Eventually I was suspended so frequently that they just kept me in a closed administration room that was next to the principal's office. I spent at least a month wasting time and sleeping on the table. My parents, at first, went to the docs for intervention.

[Local Public] Middle School

Psychological Report

[...] Zack has evidenced school adjustment difficulties and increasing academic failure since entering [the public school]. In addition to not achieving academically, Zack is reportedly confrontive and disruptive in class and evidences low self-esteem.

Zack has received Ritalin for a diagnosed residual attention deficit-hyperactivity disorder for several years. He has recently refused to continue taking the medication. On May 10, 1988, Zack was evaluated at the Kennedy Institute (Johns Hopkins University), located in Baltimore, Maryland. Documentation following Zack's visit emphasized extreme adolescent agitated depression and the recommendation of medical leave from school for treatment. On May 17, 1988, Dr. [Shrink] signed forms recommending Homebound Instruction for Zack for the remainder of the school year. The proposed treatment plan involved individual psychotherapy, parent counseling, and anti-depressant medication. As of May 16, Zack was refusing anti-depressant medication.

Previous Special Education services Received:

Zack was identified as a learning disabled student on February 6, 1984 (age 10). Zack received L.D. resource assistance while he was in the 4th and 5th grades at [public] Elementary School. Specific difficulties were noted in the area of visual/perception organization, disorganization, and attention to task.

[...] Zack was seen individually for evaluation purposes on 4 separate occasions and on 2 occasions for interview/feedback sessions. By self report Zack was not taking Ritalin at the time of the evaluation. An extended amount of time was required in working with Zack to ensure optimal conditions. Issues related to trust, compliance, ability to sustain attention to task, persistent need for re-focus and direction, and Zack's variable affective state were evaluation considerations that required attention.

[...] Recently completed standardized achievement testing indicates academic skill levels that are commensurate with Zack's demonstrated range of cognitive potential. While Zack demonstrates academic skill mastery, his day to day school functioning reflects minimal productivity, marginal to failing grades, and numerous interfering and disruptive behaviors. Significant organization difficulties, inability to maintain attention/concentration, and apparent mental and physical distractibility contribute to Zack's inability to function at levels approximating his expected level of achievement.

Zack's present functioning appears impaired by serious emotional concerns. He appears to be experiencing difficulties with internal and external controls and of late, his ability to maintain a regular routine has deteriorated steadily. Family discord and Zack's position (and impact) with his parents and siblings appears as a vehicle for his anger. Zack's affect is portrayed by pervasive unfocused anger, and significant feelings of worthlessness and diminished self-esteem. Zack expends emotional energy denying his emotions (i.e., pretending to not care; present an untouchable demeanor; appear emotionally invincible to rejection), when in fact he described himself as "falling in love easily." He appears sensitive to external stimuli which can lead to difficulty organizing his environment or overwhelming anxiety. Cognitively, Zack appears to entertain abstract conceptualizations and philosophic principles. In part, his anger appears to represent unmet needs (unconditional love; acceptance; approval), within his family structure.

Clearly, Zack is unable to function in a regular education setting at levels that approximate his learning potential. Disturbed emotional functioning and attention deficits are currently negatively impacting on Zack's ability to acquire and assimilate school material. It is recommended that Zack be considered eligible for special education services to address his specific learning needs. Specific recommendations regarding programming will be made among attending committee members upon review of the completed evaluation components. Please contact this examiner for consultation, or for input regarding program planning.

As reported May 1988 by

[Middle School Psychologist]

When the Charlottesville public school system kicked me out for good, my parents next tried hiring a tutor to come to the house and homeschool me, but that wasn't too successful. Nothing against the tutor – she was a nice enough lady who was a friend of my mom's – but I was too tired, from my nights out late, to be much good at 9 AM lessons at the kitchen table.

Why couldn't I do better now?

Never did I have to search too deeply to find the essence of shame and permanent doubt. I only had to read my mom's writing. It was in her letters. If I ever needed to find corroborating evidence that I was a pervert or a freak of some sort, it was transmitted to me in her sentences, and telepathically, on tapes that played in my head and had set up in my ear canal permanently, like an earwig.

Mom's part of the decision to send me to Idaho was because she didn't trust me to be alone, to go where I was supposed to and not go places I wasn't. She also once said, after I told my disclosures, that she was glad I was there so as to not get a local girl knocked up. Dad's fist-shaking rage-filled sermons at me didn't help. He probably thought I'd become a criminal if I didn't go to college, and that plan was crumbling before his eyes.

I had an inkling, years before Idaho, that I wasn't necessarily the entire problem at home. As Dr. Shrink had said outright in one of our last sessions with Mom and Dad present, "Well, Richard, he runs away like that for a reason. At this juncture, nobody finds it acceptable for him to take blankets and sleep in an old bomb shelter, OK? Please, see this is impacting everyone, and Zack is feeling particularly miserable too."

†

Now I couldn't be popular in the way that traditionally had worked for me – I couldn't be a clown. I couldn't be the best dancer or get busy with any of the girls. I stopped thinking sexually of anybody I knew from RMA once I saw the Rock-Bottom little girls inside my peers and older and younger program sisters.

The way for me to be popular – er, successful – here, was to be what the staff prescribed I be. Not being reamed in raps, not being made to feel like a dirtbag, was the reward equivalent of being a good class clown at home when I was young. When I caught myself reverting to that role still, by thinking about all the silly shit I could say in classes in Skinner, I blamed my Thinking. Behavior like that was just an attention game from not feeling acceptance or approval from Mom and Dad at home.

That made sense. At home, they had proposed that I take medicine so nobody would ever have to give me attention again. I'd be in the corner memorizing Wordsworth and the *Encyclopedia Britannica*. "No thanks, I'm not hungry." They wouldn't even have to feed me. Just me and my Ritalin.

I had to hand it to the I Want To Live. It showed me my responsibility for Thinking, and then the physical exercises that expressed our struggle drove this all home. Now being the representative of my emotions – leading myself into the depths of my darkness during propheet exercises or in hairball raps, and through self-exploration in my notebooks – had brought me a way to succeed in the program: Now I had something to blame. A challenge to overcome, a mountain to climb, a hole to dig. I would come to learn, though, that combating my Thinking was more akin to Sisyphus struggling to schlep a boulder all the way up Clifty.

I had journals for each propheet and expedition. But I didn't write the same crap as my former self now. I didn't feel like the person who longed to go home, who'd bucked the system. The only reason I was aware of how different I'd become was from glancing at the first journals I'd kept at RMA. Now I stashed them in a secret spot at the back of the long-abandoned ice-house. The day after the I Want To Live propheet I had posted a disclaimer on the cover, just in case a future staff from RMA should demand to see it. This was where I also had hidden my primitive fire-making stones and bow-drill set – even my trap rigs – that I kept after Survival.

Yet nestled deep within me, a forbidden self-confidence – a final piece of me that I retained in the red binder in my mind – was yearning to live without the influence of others. The forbidden red binder in the back of my mind also contained cryogenic storage of any sexual component, and all the uncategorized thoughts and feelings that still had to remain hidden out of self-preservation. My red binder held a classified document in which I questioned the wisdom of the propheets, and still at times, the core reasons for the existence of the program, and even the wisdom of staff. Safely stored, the red binder eluded my awareness, and kept me out of trouble for a while. It wasn't until I was returning to RMA after my second home visit that I made the choice to fuck up. It was then that an outside force required the red binder in me to open.

TWENTY-NINE

A new girl, Maggie, was on a Work Detail. She was pretty, with dark, curly hair, and it turned out she was my age, almost to the day. Keith had found out in a rap that she'd been keeping the piercing on her nose open by putting a home-made stud into it at night. That unacceptable behavior had gotten her a task to do and it was my job to tell her how to do it.

As we left the house together, I saw her picking at her nails with her teeth, which sort of bothered me. Darlayne said you'd get worms if you bit your nails. She used to chastise people – in and out of raps – for chewing their fingernails, so I always thought it was a self-loathy thing to do.

Maggie's WD was to dig out the stump of a medium-sized tamarack lodged in the frozen ground. By hand, with only a shovel and a mattock.

I didn't listen to her protests in the least.

"Come on, I'm sorry, OK? Tell Keith that I'm sorry, Please!"

It was true that the stump was frozen in the ground, and we were both wearing parkas – well, I was wearing home-issue clothes at this point. And it was true that she had accidentally left her gloves out overnight at the work-site that I was escorting her to. But it was also true that the reason why she had to use the gloves now was that her soft dainty little hands were blistered and sore. I also knew it would only be about twenty minutes until her gloves were warm, even if she didn't want the calluses I assured her she'd soon have.

"You're going to just leave me here?"

"Yes I am. Probably you'll be out here this weekend, too, if Darlayne and Keith say so..."

"Fuck, I hate you all."

"I would too, but you'll get used to it. Then you'll love it here. You'll see."

✝

Our school went bananas like it always would when a Summit got out. We were celebratory because Tim and Mariah and Jasper and Griffin and the rest of their PG were finally done. Leaving Idaho after thirty months! And we were happy, even though it was always bittersweet when those times came to evacuate a graduating peer group.

In their last weeks, these guys really were living up to my early impression that Summit kids were Titans. No joke, they really seemed like mini-staff now that they'd been through the Summit. They chose when to eat or sleep, had checkbooks, and attended Monday or Wednesday raps only by election. Jasper dressed up, even on Wednesdays, and had a dinner and movie date privilege with Mariah. It was astonishing how sad we all felt the last week, knowing they had already figuratively checked out of the place. They had their keys, which we knew were a symbol connected with some of the final RMA Summit tools.

I couldn't wait to be inducted into whatever the Summit mysteries might be, although I knew I had to wait another year.

We got extra smoosh time the last days Mariah and Tim were around, and all varieties of legacy-leaving. Special places on the campus were shown, items bequeathed, and long hugs bestowed. Share-time had given us a glimpse into whether our preferred older brothers or sisters were going to college right away, or were essentially on their own.

When the last day came, we saw the rental cars and the hotel shuttle arriving in the snow-packed parking area outside the house. Out spilled the parents and biological siblings of our comrades. Most of the parents looked thrilled, and the siblings looked lost. There wasn't much for them to do – besides maybe wonder if RMA had fixed their family like it was supposed to.

Once they took off their coats and boots, everyone looked all shiny and dressed to the nines, but especially the graduating class. Jasper was in a tux. When they made their appearance in the house for their last ceremony in Idaho, I have to say, wow, Griffin was looking good. The girls all wore fancy dresses, heels, and makeup, and they smelled like perfume and hairspray.

294

My PG had gotten to know so many of them, and we couldn't believe that we'd be taking the baton from Dylan, Cassandra, and Kano's PG next, after Jennifer, Terrance, and Ari's PG graduated in the spring.

We climbed another notch together as the graduating class faded out. Three more pegs left on the proverbial ladder. Just two more graduations until mine! It would be exciting to feel like a giant, the way we all thought of Tim Chalmers, and Paul Renssalaer, too. Paul had returned to campus for the first time, to be there for Tim. They were both dressed in ties and jackets. I watched them hug like family before and after the graduation ceremony.

I wonder if my whole family will come to mine. What would my little sister remember of this place?

"Zack, right on! Still here. Looking trim, little bro! No promises, but maybe we can organize my getting here next year for yours, too. But I had to come for this stud's!"

Paul patted Tim on the chest affectionately.

As the sun began to fade behind the mountains, all the graduates and their families had disappeared.

At sunset, I came to the house, where John's identifiable voice flew out of the speakers. Acute, nasal, reticent yet assured, John's voice delivered long songs about Hare Krishna and giving peace a chance in the Vietnam conflict. I was pretty sure that the Vietnam war had ended, but I understood the need for world peace, and recognized the special messages embedded in the program in case we ever became future world leaders.

Later I'd understand more fully how central Lennon's music was to the whole CEDU program. No frontiers, uniting the world, no politics or religion – this was the program worldview and if we made it to the Summit and graduated, we'd get to go out and spread this message to the world.

Snot rippers from both the Truth and Brothers had a similar effect on me when those selections played. How much things like music affected me depended on what speed, or space, I was in, and what the music signaled to me.

When I was slow, or had had a good rap, or a propheet was going in or out, on those nights I'd be smooshing among a tangle of staff and kids and I'd hear *Tell It All* from the Truth and Brothers propheets, and I'd remember the faces of anguish, and voices in Walden, the feelings of shame and self-hate. Then, too, sometimes I would feel safety, or love or trust, or some other word that didn't exist, as I looked at the smoosh piles, and allowed myself to be slow and present, to turn into a ten-minute messy blob. I'd feel pride when I had wet tears, and not just the weird sudden puke-rot feeling in my belly and throat that I'd become used to.

Soon after graduation came Santa's Workshop. Winter came into focus when I was chosen to be one of the special elves on Christmas Eve who got to deliver gifts to all the baby Papooses and Braves. Now I had something else to get ready for. It was time to pack and set my alarm clock! I was going to spend New Year's of 1990 at home with my family.

†

Home Visit [#2]:

I go home tomorrow but I don't really want to go. I wish I could stay here. When I get pissed off or hurt I say and do things I regret.

I feel silent, I act loud; being alone is all I know. I can't be a friend because I don't know what it is like to be one.

—Author journal

†

So much had changed since my first home visit, right after the I Want To Live. Now I was an experienced member of Warrior family who had raised food, and tended horses and farm animals. I helped out at propheets, starting with the I Want To Live of Delilah and Winston from two PGs below us.

I wasn't so sure that I wanted to go home on the second visit, but at least it meant a change of scenery, no classes for a few days, and there would be less snow on the ground there. I couldn't expect Mom and

Dad to see what I was learning. How could they? They didn't have the accumulated understanding that only RMA kids could get.

Dear Zack,

I have so much to say to you. Even though you are feeling so low and "stuck" right now, I know that you are on the verge of a big breakthrough. [W]e KNOW that you are a kind, caring person who is capable of deep and trusting friendships and who is worthy of the love of all the people in your family who care so much about you. But, I also understand that it doesn't matter, in the end, what we think. THE KEY IS HOW YOU FEEL ABOUT YOURSELF. YOU WON'T BE ABLE TO CLIMB TO THE SUMMIT UNTIL YOU FEEL YOUR OWN WORTHINESS IN YOUR HEART.

This is why I am so optimistic. I know that you are dealing with what lies at the bottom of all your struggles. This is hard and it will take a lot of work. But I know that you will find the truth, and when you do, it will be the key that unlocks the door to the rest of your life. I just hope that you will share with us your thoughts and feelings as you continue your quest. [....]

Aside from [us], no one cares about you more than your grandparents and your aunts and your uncles. Also, you have zillions of little cousins who would love to spend time with their big cousin, just as my cousins used to love to play with me, because I was the big guy.... [When you're home, you] could spend "quality time" re-acquainting yourself with the people who care about you and letting them get to know the person you are becoming....

I love you and can't wait to see you.

—Letter from author's father, before second home visit

†

Dear Mom and Dad,

How have you been? I liked the phone call we had. I miss you tremendously and have been thinking about our upcoming visit. I was thinking that if you wanted to we could save the presents and open them together on the 27th or something. We could have our own Christmas morning. I think that would be really nice. But I don't care either way. Every day I think about [my little sister] and wonder when she is going to shoot up on us. I dread when she gets older. I told you that when I got a message that a family member died I got terribly scared that it was her.

Something I have been needing to tell you for some time is I really believe you guys don't support my dreams. On my last visit you guys didn't seem too interested in what I wanted to do when I leave here or home. Dreamers need the support of other dreamers. I haven't the foggiest idea of what it was like for you two to grow up. What did you want to be when you grew up? I really need support 'cause it may not be what you want me to do, but it is what I want and to me that's what matters.

[....] What are your plans for this visit? Please don't make an agenda like you did on our last visit. That really isn't necessary. A little organization is cool but that was kind of ridiculous. Are you going to send plans on how I am going to get home? Well I must go.

Love, your son

Zack Bonnie

—Letter from author to parents, 3 December 1989 (referring to death of Zack's grandmother)

†

Agreements for Home Visit [Warrior] Family
Dates of Visit 12/26/89-1/1/90

I AGREE TO:

Be in agreement with all RMA agreements – dress, music, TV, etc.

Be with my family at all times – not to be left alone other than personal time in my room or home.

Bring back to RMA only those items represented to my Senior Counselor and approved. No food may be brought back from home.

Clean my room and dispose of all drugs, drug related items, stolen items, etc. – those things that no longer support my life and my values.

Have a discussion with my family and honestly disclose things from my past that have not already been covered on a previous visit.

Participate in all household chores and projects and keep my personal space tight and clean.

Not drive anything motorized during my visit – car, boat, motorcycle, etc.

Contact a [Warrior] faculty at least once during my visit. [staff phone numbers]

Be in bed by 11:30 and awake by 8:30.

To watch TV or listen to the stereo no more than 3 total combined hours per day.

—RMA home visit Agreements, signed by author and [Kelly Grainger]

Okay, today I visited with [Chuck Driems] for a while and had a great time with him. I gave him a John Lennon book for Christmas and he gave me a pair of drum sticks. I set up a visit with [J, another friend] and so I did talk with him and that was fabulous. I didn't get through to [Kelly] which was too bad I really wanted to talk to her.

Me my brother and Dad played Monopoly today so that was fun but I have to wake up early tomorrow to play tennis so I gotta go.

—Author journal, second home visit

> This morning Dad and I played tennis so that was
> fun and then I called [J] and we drove up here to
> Norfolk where we are now. I am having a great time
> here. I saw [relatives] and had great talks with them
> and now I am in bed.
>
> —Author journal, second home visit

†

For New Year's Eve, I stayed home babysitting my little sister. Mom and Dad had some friends over, all dressed up in tuxes and gowns, for drinks and peanuts. It felt good to see them; some of them had been like surrogate aunts and uncles to me when I was little. As they were all leaving, Dad took me aside to remind me, "You're such a fine young man now, Zack. We're trusting you to stay in and babysit your sister. Get her to bed by eight, and don't wait up for us."

The next day, they took me to Dulles for the flight back, by way of Chicago. It was a new year, and I was about to turn sixteen. My third and final home visit would be spent traveling, looking at schools with my dad, to figure out where I could finish high school. So I wouldn't be going home again until after I graduated from RMA at the end of this year – if all went well.

†

> Where I'm at:
>
> I've not done any writing for a long time. I have
> been thinkninng about some things that I've not
> thought about ever before. I have a lot of different
> feelings. The first is I find my self never wanting any-
> thing more than just wanting to have a person who
> loves me.
>
> —Author journal

†

It wasn't until the layover in Chicago, on the return leg from my second home visit, that I used the twelve dollars I had been budgeted

300

by Prescott for a travel stipend. I spent it on dried papaya spears from the snack shop. They were newly discovered, delicious treats.

I was heading back to RMA. It wasn't a bad feeling. And I would get to be sleeping in the bunk of my choice, as I was sure I'd be a dorm head soon. My work as dorm support in La Mancha had passed muster. I was in a good mood and feeling healthy. Not smoking, and traveling, and being exposed to beer commercials and life outside of Idaho for the last five days also made me aware of girls again. Just this once, I thought, I'd allow my horny Thinking to dine. Just a little. I watched the people, trying to spot a pretty girl who was in agreement, but loggable in the red binder for later reconsideration. My Thinking promised my innocent part that this was a fair trade-off.

On my first home visit, being in my room at home, driving past places where I'd snuck away with girls, or revealing and throwing away the porno magazines – I had experienced these things without even stealing a memory byte for later. It felt all programmy again, and good to have done this without a Thinking-driven glance.

I can be trusted out here.

The papaya was slimy after you broke it up in your mouth, but it was like straw and salt before thorough mastication. Losing myself in this and other trivialities of airport allowances was a joy. Then I spied him.

Well, he was like a head taller than the tallest other people in the airport. My first instinct was to look behind me to see if the tan-suited sheriff was there, or drop the white paper bag of papaya, ditch the suit-case I was sitting on and rush for the nearest exit. But I wasn't guilty. Yet.

Yes. it was definitely him. The oversized ex-Green Beret, Albert Guerre. I'd encountered him twice before. I had watched him unlock a big kid called Butch from his chains, to turn him over to the custody of SUWS, the Survival program I got sent to after I split from RMA my first summer. Then Guerre turned up again, at the end of my time on Survival. He rode with the sheriff and me all the way up into Northern Idaho, returning me to ensure I served my time back at RMA.

He was with someone – Wait a minute. Did I recognize that lovely thing? I did!

She saw me first.

"Oh MY GOD! What the FUCK ARE YOU DOING HERE!"

"Bonnie, right?" The giant spoke and grasped my hand in a dominant handshake before I could get my arms around Vera Cruces.

"Yes, sir. Zack."

"That's right. How've you been son? You look just great! Fantastic."

I moved to Vera. It was extremely surprising to see her lovely face. Besides my Mom and George, nobody had put their lips on me in years. Of all the people that had come and gone through RMA, I would never have expected to run into her. I welcomed her with my warmest lingering hug as she kissed my face. I paid no attention to the softness of her breasts against my chest, through her bra, T-shirt, sweatshirt, and my windbreaker. But it was sort of weird, and absolutely clear that she wanted me to notice. And I would, well – as much as a chivalrous lecher could get away with in O'Hare International Airport.

Albert scoped around us for potential threats. I wasn't sure what the threats he scanned for could be.

"So, why him?" I hitched a thumb at the intimidating, but quite personable galoot.

"Well, I don't know if you remember or knew my story at all – it was such a trip that time I saw you in the desert! I didn't go home when Mr. Jade took me. I said I was pregnant."

Albert grunted.

"That's why I didn't have to finish Survival. They brought my ass to CEDU. So Albert's, like, been the one taking me around ever since. My parents don't really want me to come home. Ever. But I did graduate! And went through my Summit. I might go work for Albert since him and Mr. Jade are opening a program. So, what's going on with you? How long 'til you're done?"

"Well, shit, I've still gotta year to go 'til the Workshop. But as soon as I get back I'm going to be a dorm-head, and I have my weight-lifting privileges. Gotta get buff. Oh, we're going to be starting our Truth counseling sessions soon, so yeah, 'it begins' now! And, let's see; our PG is gonna go to the Selkirks for our WC, so that's going to be awesome. I can't wait to start Telemarking more and climbing shit."

"Oh, you just reminded me. Get this! Our WC was back in the fuckin' Owyhee, dude. I was sick with the bow-drill. Definitely the only one on the expedition that could! Where you heading now?"

She kept my hand, and I could see that Albert either didn't care or approved.

"Back to Idaho."

"You were in Carolina? Or wait, DC?"

"Virginia. Yeah, same thing, I guess."

"Oh, right. That was it. Virginia. So, when will you graduate? Will you get your –"

I decided to interrupt because I didn't want her reminded that I'd never even yet been in high school.

"One more home visit to look at schools with Dad and then my Summit though!" I hoped she bought that "school" meant college, but then I felt like a fraud.

Here it was Albert's turn to interject. "Where's your bag?" I pointed.

"OK, you two. Stay close by, and get back here in a half hour. Vera, here's our twenty, mark it. And here's a twenty, I don't have anything smaller. Yup. Right here. I'll watch your bag, son. A half-hour. Got that? Good. I'll be right here then. Vera, thirty minutes."

We wandered past the cart from where my papayas had come. I felt bad about fibbing to her, and wanted to alleviate her Thinking. "Last visit, I'll actually be looking at boarding schools though. Instead of going home. I can relate to you."

We let it sink in before she continued. "So you went back, after all. Good, I guess. Did you get your music privs this time?"

"Yes."

"No big whoop, right?"

"No, it was pretty cool. I got to listen to Zeppelin. Man, they fucking rip! Love that. I got drumsticks from my friend at home."

"Right on."

It was awkward enough that we were still touching, her arm linked in mine, but I didn't understand, if she'd just graduated from CEDU in California, why wasn't she with her dad and step-mom?

"So, where were you – *que paso, guapa*?" The last time I had seen Vera, she'd stopped overnight with our Survival group, on her way

303

to start with a newly forming SUWS group for their own tour of the Owyhee Desert of southern Idaho.

"We went to the hospital because of what I told Mr. Jade. That was pretty bad. I didn't have to finish SUWS, but I did have to do a full-time when I went to CEDU! But I own that shit! There's a good chance I'll stay with Karen, my big sister. She'd love you, you're so cute! Then, on visits I went to my stepmom's, but she's an addict and a total taker. Just not a good influence. I supported on a Quest instead of going on my last home visit. Dad works in Kuwait and has another couple of kids. It's just – you know. And I just graduated."

"I see."

She knew the program – she had completed the whole thing at CEDU in California. She'd even seen me on Survival. This was almost unbelievable, and a chance to *carpe diem*. It's funny how opportunities have to be grasped. I'd forgotten this over my eighteen months with RMA, not because there hadn't been any days to seize in Idaho, but because the girls at RMA were off-limits, now that I had experienced their trauma second-hand. But ever since I saw Vera, I'd been attracted to her.

"Do you remember that you were on bans the first time I saw you?"

"Yup. Hysterical. Not now though! But you're not going to get anything about the Summit out of me, so don't even try it."

We hitched an escalator down between the rows of vendors. As I allowed her to step on first, I lightly grasped her elbow to ensure safety. She wriggled into me when I was aboard. But this wasn't smoosh-ing. She rubbed my knees so my hands reached out to touch her soft brown hair and brush it from her neck. She turned into me. I never wanted this moment to end, the whirring of the motor on the escalator somehow confirming the happiness I felt. And while it was a harmless surprise when chilly hands slid up my windbreaker and under my shirt, Vera's soft finger pads swiped gently up my back; this awakened an eager, longing within.

The ride down ended, but Vera took me by the hand. We naturally gravitated to the quietest part of a downstairs area. The hall was car-peted and comparatively less loud, so it lacked the transit-frantic open-ness on the upper floors. An unobtrusive row of payphones lined either side of the crowded room, so Vera led us to an open booth where there wasn't a businessman on the phone. We embraced at once. Her lips wiped up my neck, and she nibbled on my chin for a moment. Instinct and desire unharnessed themselves ever so briefly because long-housed fireworks went off in my brain when our tongues met. This passionate kiss lasted forever, and each of the moments that made it up would be an eternity I could've taken to my grave.

Obviously, necking in the phone booth with Vera was severely out of agreement. I thought about how I might escape, but I was so happily cornered. The sizzling sensation inside, when her muscles clutched my hips and she shoved me in the corner. The imbalance needed reckoning so I gored back, then clasped her face softly, with as gentle a touch as I could manage with my anxious hands. I moved in for her neck and ear, but I had to laugh aloud to cover a groan when she ground her body into me again. That laugh, the sounds of announcements above and airport bustle fading away and leaving nothing but that smile, that laugh.

Another noise I cherish is the way smiling teeth rub together. It's like rubbing smiles into each other, the way kissing puts brains together. Vera taught me this, and more, in about six minutes. My hands found the skin on her lower back and she wiggled and giggled. I had no intention of more happening, but I wasn't trying to escape her clutch. Her wandering hands. I was a little afraid of losing control; my boner was obvious.

"Okay. Wait. Oh my god you have to stop."

Pause. We didn't stop. She pulled away.

"Fine. If you want me to?"

"I have to stop. Oh man, phew, even though you're driving me loco, Vera."

"I know. But we will. Sometime."

As non-nonchalantly as we could look, we fled for the escalator to get away from anyone noticing our make-out minutes. On the way back up to the main floor, I had to pretend we were on bans, since my hands wanted to feel her all over. We freshened up, and by this I mean she tried to pull me into the ladies room with her, but I was too without courage. I sat at a bench alone instead and willed my hard-on away. She paused by the vendors and bought us each a pop, a word I now used though I'm not sure why. For our last five minutes we stayed on the bench, holding cans of soda, and just shaking our smiling heads at each other. People walked by in their raincoats, shoving luggage and children on wheels.

Even though I was already justifying the secret I would have to keep back at RMA, that I had broken my word in signing Agreements promising no sex, the problem I'd just created by messing around with Vera was setting in deeper. Part of me felt good, part of me was already feeling guilt, and it was gnawing at me while we gathered ourselves. I knew already that the program was going to stand in the way of what I wanted to feel about this awesome liaison.

I was in the program, like her, so she could trust me, and this would be the problem. I would help her use the tools by calling her out on her lies, and she could do the same. It was confusing because the program wasn't in the airport or my brain during our kiss, but it did seem to be everywhere else, every when else. We knew we had to get back to Albert. We kissed tenderly one last time. I promised to find a way to call her and she wrote down her number on a scrap of paper bag which I folded into a square and put in my sock. We held hands walking to her gate, stopping only when the eyes in the back of Al Guerre's head might have spotted us.

Having this kiss made my return to Idaho suddenly painful. Vera had freedom now; so I was immediately jealous. I watched the clock in agony until the moment came that Albert and Vera left me alone with my duffel bag.

I got back to RMA with a real smile on my face. For a few weeks, I was humming a happy tune. Little did I know.

†

I laughed
I cried
I saw the body
That I denied
The trip was hard. I hope
That I by being aware can gain
All I need by means
Of care.
This means

Touching, sharing and
Caring, not arguing
Carelessness and dishonesty
I plan to life to
The best, not with
These qualities that I detest.
—Author journal

✝

Idaho. My home now.

Now there were two reasons why I couldn't leave: I had to go all the way through to the Summit, the pinnacle of CEDU achievement. And I needed to learn it all, so I could be of equal knowledge, going into my relationship with Vera.

✝

HAIKU

Welcome to the world of love
Which we may destroy
It happened.

I think war is so stupid
Do you not agree
so why fight

The grasses are green
Flowers are pretty
But the world is black

—Author journal

✝

Dear [Vera], Thank you for such a special Birthday present!

I will be able to send you this tomorrow cause then it will be one week until my [Wilderness Challenge]. My thinking is about whether or not you have given up on me. I don't know why but my thinking is very strong right now. Its probably all bullshit but......Oh well fuck it. I can't wait to be w/you. We are gonna have so much fun skiing the Blue Ridges. Camping everywhere, you know it!...

My friend carved on herself to go to hospital and got stitches and wants to get kicked out. ME really loves [your little kid].

I'm having really warped thinking...Maybe I won't even send this letter but I guess you will be the first one to know.

—Author letter, unsent, January 1990

✝

February [1990]

DEAREST [VERA],

I have decided to keep this journal and maybe by the time I graduate it will be full. I look forward to spending my graduation weekend with you, more than my graduation date. [...] I think we are going to have a beuatiful relationship. I am so glad we are attracted to each other. I know this friendship is total LOVE. I await the times we will spend after I leave here. Curling up and telling you my story. Smooshing and fuckin' around.

I somewhow await your letters patiantly I miss your care I received a care that I have been lacking for a long time. That's weird being in such a caring envirenment. I will never forget you even if some-thing goes wrong like I go to jail or if I get killed I want you to know that what we share (I and ME and stuff) is beautiful and unreplaceble. Not to mention 4 times as honest as most teenage relationships. If your letter does not come today it should come tomorrow. God I love you.

I have been feeling especially lonely lately. I am going to make you feel so special and important. Because that is what you are. I want to make you feel so loved that you will feel like a princess. Geez, that is corny but also true.

The biggest struggles that I have had since I've been here are all about my thinking. I have so much of it I wonder if it will ever go away. My thoughts already hold me back from having the relationship that I want with you.

I would want to do another I Want To Live. Me gets very sad thinking of the fights he's had for his life. Well, it is still really strange to be leaving here soon. I really love it here. And I'm scared to leave. Sometimes I feel like you are all I have going for me. I love you.

ME does not want to get hurt. Me loves [your little kid]. Me loves to travel. Me loves RMA. Me loves trees, Me loves mountains. Me loves to climb. Me loves LOVE. Me loves roses. Me loves guitar, me loves music. Me loves BIRTHDAYS, me loves animals, me loves rainforests, me loves other Me's, Me loves driving, Me loves spontaneity...

Hi. We just out of raps. I ran that rap I was blowing everyone away. The facilitater didn't do shit...

Last light just ended so I'm getting ready to go to sleep. Last light made me go searching for dirt. It was all about guilt because some shithead has the master key, ten stolen bucks, and whatever else is missing. That shithead is making my home unsafe. I'm so pissed off. I wish they would cop or run. Assholes.

—Author letter, unsent

March 1990

I'm going to the parent seminars on Thursday I think to talk. I have started to take pictures (Oh, the

309

camera was returned) before I graduate. It is becoming a reality. It has been a very emotional two weeks and I'm sure it will be until after my summit. I had a peer group rap and it wasn't great. I do not feel fulfilled. Maybe I'll trust council...

My summit goes in [soon]. I'm tired as shit. I moved a new kid in from Seattle today. That sucked... I love Rock Bottom. Not I.

Your letter is here although they haven't given it to me. Let's just say I used my snooping powers to spy it. Now I want to read it. Oh I need it... how anxious I am to hear from my best friend. You. I will not let my negative thought to fuck up this friendship like so many others. I want you. I want you to understand me, for you to love me. I want someone to cry with. That's you. Me believes, no trusts you to understand. We are mirrors. Mirrors floating blindly in merging orbits, spinning and collapsing.

"REAL isn't how you are made" said the skinhorse. "It's something that happens to you when a child loves you for a long long time."

"Does it hurt?" Asked the rabbit.

"Sometimes." Said the skinhorse...

But Jim Morrison said it best

"You make me REAL! You make me feel like lovers feel"

I never want to be away from someone I love like this for this long again.

I love you babe. Don't let your thinking tell you I don't.

—Author letter, unsent

[F]or teens in these programs, there are no opportunities to begin to explore romantic relationships: contact with the opposite sex, let along dating, is barely allowed. Friendships are impoverished by

the constant pressure to "turn in" one's fellows for
misbehavior, and the depth of the betrayal that can
result when secrets disclosed in confidence are used
to advance a "friend" at your expense. Tough love
participants are left behind to play catch-up in almost
every life area. They are also socialized to behave in
ways that aren't conducive to relational health....In
the outside world, most people don't believe that it is
appropriate or helpful to prod people in their emotional sore spots – but tough love participants are
taught that this is an act of love for which they should
be thanked.

—Maia Szalavitz, *Help at Any Cost: How the Troubled
Teen Industry Cons Parents and Hurts Kids*, Riverhead
Books, 2006, p 253

It was the height of mud season. My second spring thaw at RMA.
Hedwig and Nat intercepted me in the new computer room, while I
was making my preparations to write a paper on John Locke. I was surrounded by the high-pitched whine of printers furiously darting back
and forth in their plastic housings. The noxious cacophony of multiple
printing cartridges stopping and starting, sliding and shrieking, while
spitting ink onto paper from their skittering carriages was pumping
out the latest upgraded school newspaper. These always included the
photos of recent Summit Graduates and little pieces of student art and
writing. The newsletters, I guessed, were for parents to show to their
friends and our uncles and aunts. Since RMA was starting to amplify
our presence in the community, the school had founded a soccer team.
A real one – with jerseys. This newsletter included photos of construction for the new soccer pitch, which was being built over a septic field.

Hedwig clutched me by the shoulder while Nat stood there with his
oversized mitt stroking an overgrown gray and brown beard.

"This is where juw h'are! We were looking h'all over for juw."

At first, I thought it was good news.

"I'm trying to begin my Summit application early."

Unlike the other family applications, for Summit we had to
produce papers and a slew of homework stuff that demonstrated a

willingness to be in classes every day in Skinner. The only things left between me and entering Summit – the final family – were doing that complicated application, and a taking on a leadership role, like becoming a dorm head, or being a student support in the next propheet.

"We're going to ask that you pack your bookbag back up. You follow us up to the house."

Nat didn't usually speak directly to any kid who wasn't already in Summit, and I knew something was up the way they observed me so closely as I packed my items: A thick book on John Locke, and my current assignment on Woodrow Wilson and the League of Nations where I was learning about President Wilson's so-called Fourteen Points.

On the way up to the house, neither of them spoke, and I started to get that feeling of anvils falling into my stomach. Something was wrong. I realized that in my backpack, which Hedwig might be searching soon, I kept my love letters to Vera.

Hedwig and Nat said nothing while we removed coats and boots and entered the house. Trouble was in the air. As soon as we got to the dining room, Nat said, "Go sit at that booth. We'll find you a worthy work assignment. You will write a full and complete dirt list. You will write out all of your disclosures. Consider this a full-time. You're on bans from every student until you acknowledge how serious this is. I better see what I need to see on that dirt list, Zack."

Why am I here? What am I supposed to tell them?

No one yet told me why the full-time was prescribed. Since the option of running away was long gone, I went back to my pre-RMA automatic reactions: Retracting inside of myself, allowing the loneliness to consume me and power the internal demonic thinking that had led me to this point.

Rejected. Isolated. Castigated. Dismal. Alone with myself at the booth or digging a drainage ditch the size of the RMA van and about as deep.

The next day, Hedwig came back to me at my booth. She'd read all my writing assignments – all the dirt I could come up with, my lists of all the things I had done that were possibly out of agreement – in the notebook I left on the table when I went out for ditch duty. She was shaking her head at the pages she had ripped out of my notebook.

"I don't believe juw. Juw're holding back on jour dirt list. Juw're not looking deep enough. This was not a full inventory. Juw're holding back on being accountable. I'm not going to do the fucking work for juw. I know it would be easier, but juw'll never get to the Summit by having me do the work. How much are JUW willing to put into this? If juw will trust this process, juw'll get so much out of it."

"Hedwig. If it's not what I already told you when I came back from my home visit – about meeting Vera at the airport, and French kissing, then I don't know. I already copped to my dirt. And besides, you gave me the privilege to write letters with Vera, and write a representation for a dating privilege with her after I get into Summit. I should have told you it was more passionate than I made it sound. Is that it?"

Was it that I had gotten a hard-on?

How would she possibly know about that?

"That's not it. This is about something juw've been holding onto for a while. Maybe even before juw came here. Juw need to keep coming clean. Believe me. I know juw are holding back on jourself. Juw are holding back on the program, and juw're holding back on jour whole life."

What?

"If juw were to die today, would juw be a giver, or a taker?"

Why would she ask me that?

"A taker."

"Thass right. Juw know it baby. Do juw want that?"

"No."

"Juw are going to sit here until juw can get honest and stop sabotaging yourself. What happened to that level of h'awareness juw had after the Brothers? Thass when juw were honest. Thass when juw were real. Thass when juw could be trusted. Thass the Dooger I want to see."

They wanted something else from me, and I wracked my brain for what it was.

What exactly could the school have on me?

Even if they don't turn out to have anything on me, the point is that somehow, I'll deserve it. And the school will get the credit for designing my full-time to help prepare me for Summit.

This felt familiar. The first week of my full-time reminded me of my first week at RMA, right after my dad tricked me into coming, in another act of predetermination. And I remembered returning to RMA in the Sheriff's cruiser, a year and a half ago, to once again cross the River Styx.

A trapped, betrayed pall fell over everything. I ate and breathed hopelessness, just like during my first hours in Idaho. I also felt a tearing within me. Another piece of me was being pried away from the rest of me.

I was accused. Of something. And I was expected to confess. To something.

†

This full-time would be a watershed moment.

Being falsely accused caused me to scrutinize intent, trustworthiness, and forgiveness. It cast doubt on my belief in the staff's infallibility and the tenets of the Summit Workshop. It caused me to examine the shame that seemed to make people tick, and my inability to ever think of myself as a giver or a leader. It caused me to question whether I was worthy to live, or to die.

When my full-time ended, a few weeks later, I believed I was right where I needed to be, for the Summit.

PART FOUR RESOURCES

Factors That Influence Conformity

[Solomon] Asch went on [in the 1950s] to conduct further experiments in order to determine which factor influenced how and when people conform. He found that:

Conformity tends to increase when more people are present, but there is little change once the group size goes beyond four or five people.

Conformity also increases when the task becomes more difficult. In the face of uncertainty, people turn to others for information about how to respond.

Conformity increases when other members of the group are of a higher social status. When people view the others in the group as more powerful, influential, or knowledgeable than themselves, they are more likely to go along with the group.

Conformity tends to decrease, however, when people are able to respond privately or if they have support from at least one other individual in a group.

—https://www.verywell.com/
the-asch-conformity-experiments-2794996

May 11, 1988

Dear [Middle-School Principal, Charlottesville, VA]

Yesterday and today I examined Zachary Bonnie. My diagnoses, in order of present primary urgency, are: 1. adolescent agitated depression, and 2. residual attention deficit – hyperactivity disorder....Zachary should be on medical leave of absence for the primary urgent diagnosis, and until he is adequately treated for his affective illness, no academic stresses, demands, or promotional decisions should be made.

Educational issues must, at this time, take a "back seat," as Zachary's medical situation is clearly what must take precedence now.

[...] Zachary's depression must be treated. All academic considerations must take second place relative to this major medical-psychiatric condition....Zachary [has] a domain of neuropsychological deficiency that is dragging him down in a variety of work-productive situations....

—Martha Bridge Denckla, MD, Director, Developmental Neurobehavior Clinic, Professor of Neurology and Pediatrics, The Johns Hopkins University School of Medicine.

(Dated two months before author's first admission to RMA in July 1988)

†

...[T]he stages people go through as their attitudes are changed by the group environment and the thought-reform process [were] labeled by psychologist Edgar Schein as the stages of "unfreezing, changing, and refreezing."

Unfreezing. In this first stage, your past attitudes and choices – your whole sense of self and notion of how the world works – are destabilized by group lectures, personal counseling, rewards, punishments, and other exchanges in the group.

Changing. You sense that the solutions offered by the group provide a path to follow. You feel that anxiety, uncertainty, and self-doubt can be reduced by adopting the concepts put forth by the group or leader.

Refreezing. In this final phase, the group reinforces you in the desired behavior with social and psychological rewards, and punishes unwanted attitudes and behaviors with harsh criticism, group disapproval, social ostracism, and loss of status.

—Margaret Thaler Singer with Janja Lalich, *Cults in Our Midst: The Hidden Menace in our Everyday Lives*, Jossey-Bass Publishers, 1995, pp 74–77

– END –

Turn the page
for
Coming Attractions...

Zack Bonnie

COMING ATTRACTIONS

In the following pages, you'll see several excerpts, in which Zack completes the program and graduates from RMA.

- More
- The Book of Mom
- Workshops
- The CEDU program
- Graduation Day

You'll also read an important letter sent to Zack by a person who partially inspired the character of Vera Cruces, and a short story Zack wrote soon after graduating from RMA.

- Vera's Apology

- The Carousel (fiction)

Zack Bonnie

320

More

More from the **Dead, Insane, or in Jail** series is underway. Because academic research will be required prior to producing the next installment, the process will likely take more time to complete than the interval that passed between the first two books in this series.

In whatever format the continuation of the **Dead, Insane, or in Jail** series emerges, it has been my goal from the beginning of this project to demystify complex subject matter by demonstrating a few important junctures leading up to the final months of the thirty-month CEDU program.

Already the intention is to add multimedia to the project, to demonstrate the vectors of human perception, the social-evolution and cohesion of humankind, and the cataclysmal history of human interference on these matters.

As kids at the school, we were persuaded to prove our loyalty to a new belief system, to let down personal defenses, and become prepped to form deep attachments with staff. Shame played such an organic, central role in enforcing institutional conformity that it even took hold of kids who had never been sexually active in their lives.

We're also learning all we can about Charles E. Dederich's influence on Mel Wasserman's vision to create the first CEDU campus in 1967; the function of what were meant to be lifetime bonds among the kids in the program, and the bonds made between kids and the staff (essential to understanding CEDU's impact on my life). It was the final six months (and the first six!) that had such an impact on me; the concepts of CEDU's "I & Me" and "Summit Workshop" deserve specialized, overdue attention by means of research.

Staff became more than just the treatment specialists who were allowed to hug and hold and smoosh with us – they became the new parents. To impress them, and receive respect from them, was what I lived for. Those relationships with staff provided essential confirmation about the person I was becoming in their environment. Trusting the staff and trusting the tools of the program went hand in hand.

Just as these first two books take the reader's time to set the pieces in place, so it took a long time in the specific CEDU milieu to appropriately connect. Only after such long preparation could the final workshops be so powerful as to permanently change the way an individual processes information.

To be notified about our research initiatives, speaking events, other special content, and – of course – progress on what might be more than just a book, and our multimedia aspirations, please visit the website at **deadinsaneorinjail.com** and join the Readers Circle.

Follow our news at **facebook.com/deadinsaneorinjail**, and join the conversation with **@ZackDIJ_book** on Twitter.

—ZB

The Book of Mom

Dear Zack:

[Hedwig told Hattie that I can finally show you...] the book I've just finished [writing]. It's called LEAVE OF ABSENCE and, as I hinted, it's about a boy your age and about his parents too. I used a lot of details from our lives (your brother's too) and it's important to me that you understand that this is a work of fiction, even though a lot of the particulars really happened. When I talk about the mother and father's feelings (their anger and worry about their son) I'm writing about FICTIONAL CHARACTERS even though some of the stuff will seem very familiar to you. I do worry that IF the book gets published, some people might think the character of the boy IS YOU, even though he isn't. Mainly, though, I worry about what you will think. As an example, the kid (I named him Douglas Jules Mitchell) is the youngest of four boys and I make a big point over the fact that the mother wanted a girl and not another boy. I think (to myself) if Zack reads that he might wonder if I wanted HIM to be a girl. And the fact is, I didn't. I wanted boys very much (though as you know, with [your sister], I was thrilled to have a daughter). And then when I develop the character of the father, I make him an only child who lost his father in a drowning and this man identifies with the oldest boy, more than the others. The oldest boy is named after the father and grandfather. I worry that when you read that you will think that Daddy identifies with [your brother] more than with you, and that's not true either.

I guess what I'm trying to say is that fiction is fiction even if some of the details (the boy gets very angry and depressed, acts out terribly, uses bad language, has trouble in school) are taken from real life. Anyway the writer friends who've read the book all LOVE the character of Douglas and think he's such a great kid.

Another important thing is that Douglas is killed in a truck accident and when he talks, it's a ghost talking.

[...]

I love you. Why don't you write?

LOVE, Mommy

—Letter from author's mother

Hattie and Prescott had both approved of *The Book of Mom,* and several of the bigwig staff like Nat and Hedwig were beginning to read it. I knew because they'd come up to me and tell me how much they were learning and how talented my mom was. So when I had done all my work crews and chores, the only reading material I was permitted was my mom's "fiction" about a teenage boy who "messed up in eighth grade" and got sent to a school where "kids who are having problems can work them out." Ain't that special? Check it out:

†

In my family it's really important to "experience success." ...

[...] While I usually try not to listen, that word [successful] has a way of tickling my brain. If you must know, it worms its way through the mumbo-jumbo like a damn dagger.

"I'm gonna be all right," I said to cool them down.... "I know I messed up in eighth grade, but I'm gonna do all right when I get to high school."

"Messed up?" Dad said, his voice getting louder. "You call two D's and three F's messing up? You call running away and under-age drinking messing up?"

"You've got the ability," Mom said. "We have no doubt about that."

[...] "There isn't any question you're as smart as your brothers," Mom said, "but you need to focus your attention."

"Shut up," I whispered....[M]y mother had just said the two things I never let her say – and she'd put them both in one sentence. She knew I hated having my brothers mentioned, and even worse I hated hearing about focusing my attention. Ever since sixth grade my parents had been stuck on this "Attention Deficit Disorder" business which is the biggest pile of crap any head shrinker ever dreamed up.

"Don't talk to your mother that way," Dad said. "We're tried to get you to recognize your problems, but you've refused. We can't stand by and let your whole life slip away. That's the reason we're sending you to this school where kids who are having problems can work them out."

—Excerpt from [The Book of Mom] manuscript by author's mother. Reproduced with permission.

Workshops

I = Thinking [self]

ME = Feeling [self]

ME LOVES

ME just counseled with [Ernesto].

 I was young and fighting with my brother and he was holding ME down. He was on top of me and ME couldn't get up.

 —Excerpted from author's workshop notebook

What I tells ME...

I tells me to quit the school;

I tells me he has always fucked up;

I tells me to abuse me by having me hit me;

I tells me that nothing's changed;

I tells me that he can't make it here;

me is a drug addict;

me's burnt;

me is a pervert;

that nobody can love me because me is scum.

Me is shit.

Me is not a leader.

I tells me that we killed me.

That me is warped;

me is a slut;

me is dumb;

that we would be better off dead.

That he's different;

that drugs are great;

to carve on me, to hit the door, to use the phone in the bridge, to stop this assignment because it is getting too hard.

I tells me that he is ugly, his dick is too small, he is gross, he is scared, RMA is a joke

To set it on fire.

I tells me to act, to smile and say 'I'm fine', to spew, to sabotage graduation.

I tells me no sleep until 2:45am.

I tells me not to trust the program, not to love [Darlayne], not to fight for love, that a little dope isn't bad, that me can't be a father, that me is a bad boy and ME is a shitty son.

I don't deserve to make my parents happy.

The world is dismal.

I tells me not to tell anybody I'm not well.

—Excerpted from author's workshop notebook

✝

What Me needs:

ME NEEDS TO FIGHT I.

—Excerpted from author's workshop notebook

✝

My epitaph:

Here lies Zack Bonnie born January 4, 1974, died November 5, 1990

He lived life greedy and a failure. He lived to be the worst he could possibly be he was born alone, he lived alone and died alone. He died starving of malnutrition if you will. A stinky raggedy old corpse. A perambulator and carcass I wouldn't hesitate to say.

327

He spent this time choosing death and fear he chose drugs and eccentric negative behavior as his makeup. Hate was his motto and distrust was his rule-book to his game of life. He existed on scraps of care, the appeal of love here and there. Yes here lies Zack Bonnie. Fuck him.

To my sister don't live as I have done I love you. You should live your life as I wish I lived mine!

To mom and dad I love you. I am sorry I died in guilt of not being a good son. I died a bad person because of what I've done. I'm sorry.

[Kelly and Darlayne...] I'll see you in about 50 years. To all my friends thanks for the treasures they are. Right here by my side but please choose not to live your life by lies. Live deep. [My brother] you are a success better than I. I die

—Author writing assignment from Summit Workshop, RMA November 1990 [29 months in the program, four weeks until graduation]

✝

Dear Mom and Dad, I want my freedom and I forgive you for _____:

I forgive you for telling me I was a bad son.

I forgive you for telling me I was stupid.

I forgive you for putting me on drugs so I would do well in school.

I forgive you for telling me to get a haircut all of the time.

I forgive you for telling me there is a chemical imbal-ance in my brain.

I forgive you for not wanting to touch me.

I forgive you for penmanship lessons.

I forgive you for hitting us.

I forgive you for not liking any of my girlfriends.

I forgive you for telling me to be more polite.

I forgive you for making me go to temple all the time.

I forgive you for making me go to church too.

I forgive you for giving away Spot, my dog.

I forgive you for making me go see grandma right before she died.

I forgive you for not liking my friends.

I forgive you for making me take psych tests.

I forgive you for putting me on pills and telling me that was the only way I would feel better about myself.

I forgive you for telling me to be more like dad and [my brother].

I forgive you for fighting when I was young and it scared me so much.

I forgive you for not telling me [grandfather] was dead.

I forgive you for washing my mouth out with soap.

I forgive you.

I forgive you for making I.

I forgive you for saying I could not see friends anymore.

I forgive you for making me go to Survival.

I forgive you for not being cool like I said other parents were.

"I am a forgiving and trusting man" Zack

—RMA writing assignment completed by author, shortly before graduation from RMA, December 1990

https://www.youtube.com/watch?v=xEkEHgCHs_8

(Music video of Melanie Safka's *What Have They Done to My Song*; still photo with lyrics)

The CEDU Program

I had taken over Me. Me was corrupted, but it was going to have to be a secret. Zack had made it through the Summit because I had taken over Me. Me had fought. Me had fought very hard, but I was bigger. I was stronger. Zack used to be sure of what was right and fair, but I corrupted that. Sometimes Zack wants Me to not be a jelly child mass, but he can't help it.

Me knows.

I thinks.

Me's parents were coming. . . . I say Me can't tell time on his own. He's so fucking dumb he doesn't even know what day it is. He *needs* I to tell him – Me. I scolds.

Nat waved his magic marker in front of the easel and the words "I am responsible for all that I see" appeared.

The captain holstered the marker and then folded his hands on top of his head. "What do you think this means?" he wondered aloud at us. Micah, as usual, was the first to respond.

"It's like we make a choice every day, you know, to be in the situation or not be in a situation like because whatever we chose got us into that situation to begin with. Like with me."

Nat raised his hand to cut him off. "And what if something happens to you?"

†

I have the worst "stretch" possible. I got sooo screwed – King Authur, gallant knight of the round table. Host of the party. For God's sakes that was my Challenge Night!!! Anyway, I got sooo resistant. I thought I was going to get thrown out. Needless to say I went last for about 20 minutes.

My contract is absolutely fanstastic though.

The game was lame.

The life-boat thingy was HORRIBLE. I was so resistant. I refused to do it.

Then I refused to give [the You Die] death votes.
Then I refused to cast you LIFE [You LIve] votes [to the
passengers in the Workshop]. Finally I turned to the
fascilitator Ok [Nat] You live. It was kind of funny. The
whole thing was like the Brothers [Keeper propheet.]
I learned a lot, but wouldn't want to do it again.

—Excerpted from author journal entries and
unsent letters

Graduation Day
December 8, 1990

Wanting to make sure of a good fit, Dad had brought three sizes. Trying on the suits my dad brought into Warrior headquarters used up the time we had alone together. Next, the proceedings would begin. I could hear other parents fussing at members of my PG. This time, we were experiencing things the same. We'd rehearsed the procession twice yesterday, and graduation rituals were old hat to the veteran staff. Darlayne Hammer always dressed in that flowered dress with white stockings down to blue clogs, and Prescott Freshwater always sported his flashiest bow tie and suspenders. My staff presenter would lead me down to the stonework of the pit, to join my peer group for commencement ceremonies. After that, I'd have to leave the campus. None of us would be allowed to contact staff or older younger brothers and sisters, or to be in touch with the program for six months after we left.

"Zack, stop shifting around and stand up straight. That haircut is good. A good trim, as my father would say. Richard, the shoes. Put them on, Honey."

Mom breathed in my ear. I basked in the attention now. I wanted – no, needed – people manhandling me and standing practically on my shoulders, especially Mother. After I put the dirty bucks on my feet, she wrapped the tie around my neck. I could smell home, not that I'd ever be going back there.

"This is such a special day. It reminds me of the day I graduated from college. Don't forget that I was the first of the Irish side of our family to go to college. Oh, I'm so proud of you! Now. We could decide what you're going to do next, for the next chapter. We hear that there is a postgraduate seminar for CEDU graduates in Los Angeles next year – I think it's in March – anyway, your father and I were even thinking about going. Maybe scout if there could be a job for you after boarding school – Now! I know that that isn't your first preference but Daddy and I think this is the best academic decision."

In the house, I stood on the center stone, dressed in the suit.

Zack am standing pretty in the pit. When a lot of weak little people don't fear I, respect I, know I am in control, I will let Me take over some control. Now Zack talk and make smile big. Make act Zack. No! Fight. No, think. Feel?

"Thanks, This is. Wow. Um, firstly there's some people I need to thank. Nat, Hedwig, well —

LOOK! FEEL!

— all the people that work here: I just want to first say how much I LOVE this PLACE! But glad to FINALLY BE LEAVING! WOO HOO!"

Raise fist, dumb Zack, I judge. Me make tears to act for everybody's dumb Me. I am in control. I think. Feel Me! Make tears. This is what happy feels, I let you.

"...And my sister, can you join me in the pit here? Thank you. To have this opportunity to share with you how special it is that you could be here. With me. Now you can see the real Me."

DUMB!

"Take this rose and know that within it and within its seed lies the rose of TOTAL PERFECTION."

Me can't make I. I can make Me. We make Zack.

Suck on this memory, Bitch!

The Summit: you are a TAKER. A No-LIVE vote. Drowning. Dying. Drama. Delivery. Rebirth. A perambulating carcass on the way. Never will be what I once thought with Me together. New Me. New voice. Never has been; never can be. Only love you will never have. Real only I. Life hates Zack. I have Zack. Our choice to use our tools. I am responsible for how you feel. I USE US! I USE US!

The graduation ring glistened on my finger.

Tomorrow, Idaho will be left behind.

[Vera's] Apology

Dear Zack

Shit; you wanna talk about making some amends lets talk about what an incredible bitch I am. To be blunt I am selfish for hurting you and then treating it like it was all you (as if I ever was innocent – even before I met you I was a lying bitch) I lied to hurt you and any one who thought they could get close to me. If I decide to send this letter you'll be either crapping bricks or laughing hysterically. Cant blame you for anything.

Number one I feel bad that when [we saw each other] I really fucked up by messing around with you. I mean that was just so anti-[CEDU]. My first big step towards moving away from my [I & Me and Summit Workshops]. Plus – shit – the whole concept of having to see someone (probably) every day that <u>knew</u> what I <u>knew</u>. And by the time I lied and said you had raped me (I think that's what I said – lies are confusing) I was so far out of touch with my contract it did not bug me that I would hurt you. Actually I looked at it (the lie) as a good way to ensure that I would not have to look someone in the face who had a contract, too. I wanted to stay the fuck away from you. All in all I was being a selfish lying deceiving "friend" who wanted to create havoc in everyone elses life. I am sorry that I did those things. I am truly sorry.

I don't know what you are doing now a days or if you have anything to do with your contract anymore. Let me tell you about me…I go to <u>A</u>dult <u>C</u>hildren of <u>A</u>lcoholics twelve-step meetings where my main issues are lying and my contract (living with it and actually using it for a change) But anyway…

How about if when I get home you and I pick things up – start over – use our Brothers Keeper and attempt to have an honest (on my part) relationship. I need someone like you (strong and honest) to help me through my program. (The first step of ACA is "we admitted we were powerless over ourselves and that our lives have become unmanageable" in thought it's easy to accept but doing the work that goes with it just sucks ;~) I need a shoulder to cry on (once in a Blue Moon) and someone to indict me when I need to hear it (even when I don't want to) and I need it from someone who can see through my lies. Lies are my drugs. They have been all my life.

And I want it to end right now. So if you can ever find it in your heart to forgive me please please write me back. [...]

I would give you a phone number but hey no such luck. No phone.

(Right now I am listening to that one group that you used to (a year or so ago) really like) the Doors – Soft Parade.

Gotta go

[Vera Cruces]

...PS if you thought RMA was bad at least you didn't go to this hell-hole. Here they teach us not to deal with our feelings. They want us to just stuff 'em down, and as long as we look good who cares how we feel. I am really glad I got involved with ACA or I'd be dead here.

—Entire letter from [Vera Cruces] to author, received a few months after Zack graduated from RMA

The Carousel (fiction)

by Zack Bonnie

The one she leads us to looks like an old stage-coach. Two white mares tug at the plastic reins. She sits down close to me and pulls a metal bar down over our heads with a clank, locking us in. People flood around us, taking their places on the other objects: orange turtles and bright green crickets; one boy makes himself at home in a black jack-o-lantern. He looks like a fox finding a new den.

Finally, chains are put across the entrance to prevent escapees, or trespassers like those hiding behind the little biplane and the chipped race car.

Everyone looks around to catch a glimpse of another face, to know what that other person is thinking, even for a moment. I look at my companion. She does look beautiful. Wind softly blows her bouncy, curly hair. Her golden locks breeze around her shoulders. I have no idea what she is thinking.

The ride starts to spin. It seems as if one of the mares at the front of the coach turns her head to me and gives me a knowing wink. Stupidly staring at the plastic horse fanny in front, I blink my eyes several times in confusion.

During a now light-speed rotation, I focus on the faces of the next victims in line for the carousel. The hand on my arm begins to rub up and down, demanding attention.

"Everything is so wonderful with this new perception!"

Yes, my perception has definitely changed. Now that I notice the music and how it makes me nauseous, I can feel grains of sugar between my teeth from the blue, toxic cancer-causing cotton candy that shrank on my tongue, before I got volunteered for this experiment on the results of centripetal torment. No longer do I see two magnificent pieces of plastic workmanship, but rather, two black beasts carrying me to my own funeral. The little boy who had earlier reminded me of that mammal famous for being witty, now looks like a fiery demon in his carved out, black vegetable.

Other passengers look to me like ogres, drool splattering and dripping out of their mouths, as they open them to scream. It seems like their eyes are screaming, too. They all seem so happy, and the artificial crickets, elephants, and baskets that contain all of the bellowing monsters spin madly about, as if mocking me.

"Isn't it wonderful how happy everyone looks!" The female voice chirps in my ear.

A large man, missing his shirt and sporting faded tattoos of skulls on his shoulder – he also reminds me of my bus driver from school – decides that we have had enough fun. He unhooks the chains and slows down the revolving torture chamber from a little box that apparently controls the speed of the merry-go-hell.

I stand up and am dizzy. I plow into a grinning oversized housefly. Some of the paint has been scraped off one of the eyes, and someone gouged their initials into a wing. Regaining my balance, my hand finds a pipe near the steel steps down. Someone has taken pleasure in leaving their gum on that pipe. I can feel my fingers dig into it and smoosh through as I topple down the last step. The feeling of the earth under my feet gives me relief and reminds me that I am still alive.

The girl follows me off of the funky spaceship. She has bright, glowing eyes, a purple lollipop dangling out of her hand. The mouth attached to the body with the lollipop has the gall to suggest:

"How fun this is. Let's go ride the faster one on the other side!"

337

She points to some dingy oversized record player that looks like it is spinning at Mach 2. Without waiting for my reply she snatches my hand and leads me at a ferocious rate through puddles of spilled root beer and one too many mean-looking clowns.

We arrive at a line and stop.

I can feel her hand, sweating, slip into my own, as I turn to look at the frowning roundabout that I've just endured. I can't help but notice the way the characters of the ride resemble sharp, jagged teeth, silhouetted in the lights of the carousel.

—Short story by author, written in March 1991 at Christchurch School, a boarding school in Virginia, three months after graduating from RMA.

That's it for now! More is underway.

To stay current with our progress, news on activism, advocacy, and academic research, as well as creative arts and collaborative multimedia projects, please visit **deadinsaneorinjail.com**.

Follow us at **facebook.com/deadinsaneorinjail**, and join the conversation with **@ZackDIJ_book** on Twitter.